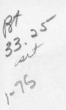

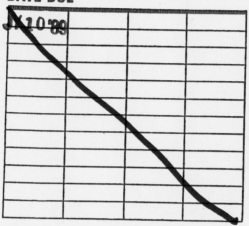

BURT FRANKLIN: RESEARCH & SOURCE WORKS SERIES 887
American Classics in History and Social Science 223

THE HISTORY OF

THE SUPREME COURT

OF THE

UNITED STATES

John Jay——

THE HISTORY OF
THE SUPREME COURT

OF THE

UNITED STATES

WITH

BIOGRAPHIES

OF ALL

THE CHIEF AND ASSOCIATE JUSTICES

BY

HAMPTON L. CARSON

A. D. 1790—1902.

MAGNIFICENTLY ILLUSTRATED

WITH PORTRAITS OF THE 58 JUDGES
ENGRAVED BY MAX AND ALBERT ROSENTHAL.

VOLUME I.

BURT FRANKLIN
New York, N. Y.

"*What, Sir, is the Supreme Court of the United States? It is the august representative of the wisdom and justice and conscience of this whole people, in the exposition of their constitution and laws. It is the peaceful and venerable arbitrator between the citizens in all questions touching the extent and sway of Constitutional power. It is the great moral substitute for force in controversies between the People, the States and the Union.*" —HORACE BINNEY.

Published by LENOX HILL Pub. & Dist. Co. (Burt Franklin)
235 East 44th St., New York, N.Y. 10017
Originally Published: 1902
Reprinted: 1971
Printed in the U.S.A.

S.B.N.: 8337-45069
Library of Congress Card Catalog No.: 77-172197
Burt Franklin: Research and Source Works Series 887
American Classics in History and Social Science 223

Reprinted from the original edition in the Princeton University
Library.

TO

THE CHIEF JUSTICE AND ASSOCIATE JUSTICES

OF

THE SUPREME COURT OF THE UNITED STATES

THESE VOLUMES

ARE

RESPECTFULLY DEDICATED.

PREFACE.

OWING to the continued demand for this work the publishers have issued this new Edition in which the biographical sketches of the Justices, and references to leading and notable cases are brought down to the present time, inclusive of the Tariff Insular Cases.

The official reports of the Supreme Court of the United States, in many volumes, covering thousands of pages, embrace cases upon questions of exceeding interest and importance. The reader will find these mentioned in the text and will observe that the citation of them has been brought down to date, and that biographical sketches of all the Justices appear in their proper places, prepared from authentic data, accompanied by their portraits, etched from paintings or photographs, copies of each of which, the author, with much effort, obtained.

The portraits have been etched by the well-known artists of Philadelphia, Max Rosenthal and Albert Rosenthal, who suggested the idea of illustrating the text, and whose knowledge, judgment, taste and skill in the execution of portraits of distinguished Americans are familiar to all collectors and historical students.

The subject has been treated chronologically. Topics and doctrines illustrative of different phases of our national growth are presented in the exact order of their occurrence and in natural sequence, displaying each epoch in contrast with those which precede and follow it, thus affording convenient opportunities of introducing at intervals, and not in mass, biographical sketches of the Judges. Spirit, movement and variety are thus sought to be imparted to the narrative, and the activity of the Court as a powerful agent in promoting our development as a nation portrayed.

It was found necessary in dealing with fifty-eight distinct subjects of biography, to guard, on the one hand, against constant repetition of matter arising from the fact that many judges participated as colleagues in the determination of leading cases, and, on the other, against the arrangement common to biographical dictionaries, which, if observed, would have brought all the pictures together in the middle of the book. It was found that any discussion of the cases based upon the order of subjects as presented by the Constitution of the United States would result in a treatise upon Constitutional Law, for which there was no room, the field being already occupied by the Commentaries of Mr. Justice Story, Professor Pomeroy's "Constitutional Law," Judge Cooley's work on "Constitutional Limitations," and other well-known and valuable text-books. The aim of the writer has been to present a History of the Court, and not a scientific treatise. By first tracing the sources of the jurisdiction conferred by the Constitution upon the highest court in the nation, and examining into the meaning of the Third Article as interpreted by the words and publications of the framers, as well those of their friends as of their critics ; by following this with a perusal of the account of the organization of the Court, and the sketches of the men appointed to its bench, and then proceeding to a discussion of their work divided chronologically into natural epochs of development, the reader is enabled to glide down the stream of time, viewing men and their achievements in the exact order of their introduction to the scene, and thus enjoy a panoramic display of the growth of our Federal jurisprudence.

The writer desires to express his grateful acknowledgments to the Chief Justice and the Associate Justices of the Court for their active interest and sympathy, and for the contribution of important and authentic matter, as well as for permission to use the seal of the Court as a device upon the covers of the book.

The work, in two volumes of convenient size, contains an unbroken history of the Court from its origin to the present, and is presented in a form, which it is believed will make it serviceable to the law student as well as to the practitioner.

Philadelphia, 1902.   H. L. C.

CONTENTS.

CHAPTER I.

PART I.

SOURCES OF THE JURISDICTION OF THE SUPREME COURT OF THE UNITED STATES—1680-1774.

CHAPTER II.

Special Fitness of the Framers of the Constitution for their Work: Classification of Sources of Jurisdiction: Admiralty Cases: Colonial Vice-Admiralty Courts: Jurisdiction: Acts of Trade: Colonial Judges: Extension of Jurisdiction: Revenue Cases: Colonial Opposition: Remonstrance of First Continental Congress.

CHAPTER III.

Steps toward a Federal Jurisdiction: Washington's Letters: Establishment of State Admiralty Courts: Appeals to Congress Regulated: Methods of Procedure.

CHAPTER IV.

Special Committees: Standing Committee of Appeals: Growth of Federal Power: Case of Sloop "Active."

CONTENTS.

CHAPTER V.

CHAPTER VI.

CHAPTER VII.

PART II.

THE ESTABLISHMENT OF THE SUPREME COURT.

CHAPTER VIII

CHAPTER IX.

CHAPTER X.

PART III.

THE SUPREME COURT OF THE UNITED STATES.

CHAPTER XI.

CHAPTER XII.

CHAPTER XIII.

CHAPTER XIV.

CHAPTER XV.

ILLUSTRATIONS.

A HISTORY

OF THE

SUPREME COURT OF THE UNITED STATES.

CHAPTER I.

GENERAL INTRODUCTORY VIEW.

A HISTORY of the Supreme Court of the United States, although chiefly of interest to the legal profession, cannot fail to contain much matter that will prove attractive to the general reader. It relates to one of the three great Departments of the National Government. It will involve not only an account of the establishment and organization of the tribunal itself, the development of its authority, and the manner in which its great powers have been exercised, but also an exploration of the sources of its jurisdiction to the earliest period of our national life. The former can be drawn from the inexhaustible mines of wealth to be found in the public records; the latter can be traced to the judicial powers exercised by the Continental Congress through the agency of Committees, and finally through the first Federal Court of Appeals, established January 15th, 1780, known as The Court of Appeals in Cases of Capture.[1]

---

[1] The records referred to consist of the Debates in the Federal and State Conventions which preceded and followed the Framing of the Constitution of the United States, generally known as Elliott's Debates on the Federal Constitution (4 vols.) and

1

Such a history will involve also a consideration of many of the phases of our social and political existence. Just as the student of English Constitutional History finds in the trials of Raleigh, Strafford, Sydney, Russell, the Seven Bishops and other martyrs and patriots, the most striking examples of civil and religious polity, so the student of our history will discover, in the State Trials of the United States and in decisions upon fundamental Constitutional questions, the most faithful pictures and the most authentic memorials of the temper, the manners, the politics and the sentiments of the age. In the almost-forgotten case of the Sloop *Active* we can trace the successive features of a notable struggle for federal supremacy, through a period of thirty years, marked by the most dramatic incidents; exhibiting in its inception the political imbecility of the Continental Congress when brought into conflict with the power of a State, and in its final issue the complete and triumphant vindication of National authority. In the prosecutions brought under the Alien and Sedition Laws; in the trial of Henfield for illegally enlisting in a French privateer; or of Callender, indicted for a libel upon President Adams; in the trials of the Western Insurgents for insurrection against the excise laws; in the case of Robbins, on a claim for delivery to the British Government on a charge of murder; of Aaron Burr for high treason; of Mr. Justice

Supplement, containing the Madison Papers; Pennsylvania and the Federal Constitution; Maclay's Debates in the First Senate of the United States; Benton's Abridgment of Debates of Congress; Revised Statutes of the United States; Statutes at Large; Records of the Supreme Court of the United States; Reports of the Decisions of the Supreme Court of the United States; Journals of the Continental Congress; Articles of Confederation; Secret Journals of Congress; MS. Papers of the Continental Congress in the Library of the State Department; MSS. in the Office of the Clerk of the Supreme Court of the United States; Colonial Records and early State papers.

Chase, impeached for misconduct as a Judge; in the famous case of Marbury *v.* Madison; in the Dartmouth College case; in Gibbons *v.* Ogden; in the Dred Scott decision, in the Slaughter House cases, and in the Legal Tender cases, we find abundant material from which important facts of history can be drawn. These cases lie at the foundation of our jurisprudence and are destined to guide and control the most distant posterity.

Such a work will mingle the features of biography with a narrative of momentous events, portraying the character of famous judges and advocates, displaying the talents and learning of the sages of the law, while describing the scenes in which they were conspicuous actors. It will exhibit the birth, growth and decay of customs, the abolition of ancient institutions and the extension of maxims of free government to all the affairs of citizenship. It will delineate, on the one hand, the attitude of States in moments of defiance to National authority, or in the hour of their final resignation and defeat; and, on the other, will describe the limits of their independent and uncontrollable sovereignty. It will illustrate the conduct of individuals under an infinite variety of .circumstances, while depicting the common phases of litigation.

In fact, the Court stands in such close relationship to the political and private rights of individuals in defending them from assault, and plays such an important part in defining our national obligations, and in determining the lawful bounds of State and Congressional authority under the Constitution of the United States, that no careful student of our institutions, who desires to comprehend the exact nature of his status as a citizen of our Federal Republic, will rest content with an examination of the debates in Congress or the administrative acts of the Presidents. For fullness and completeness of knowledge, for breadth of view and accuracy of information, for the true construction and interpretation of our Great Charter, he must turn to the decisions of the Judiciary which illuminate with steady and effulgent rays the history of the nation. The law embodies the story of a nation's development, and this truth has been recently dwelt upon by an eminent teacher of legal science, who declares: "The student of law in our times has come to recognize the fact that law is, in a sense, a branch of history, and is to be studied in a historic spirit and by a historic method; and as the student of law now recognizes the relation which exists between law and history, so also has the student of history come to recognize that a certain relation subsists between history and law."[1]

If we divide our Constitutional history into periods marked by the War of the Revolution, the chaos and dismay that preceded the Framing of the Constitution, the Organization of the Government, the early Presidential administrations, the War of 1812, the term of Marshall's judicial service, the subsequent ascendency of State Rights, the agitation upon slavery, the Civil War, and the days succeeding those of Reconstruction, we will find subjects furnished for judicial action which stamp with characteristic variety the periods themselves. We may expect, therefore, to discover in the decisions of the Federal Court of last resort not only the result, but an account of the many processes of our national development. We may gaze upon a panoramic view of our Constitutional jurisprudence, unfolding itself in executive acts

[1] Professor Henry Wade Rogers in his "Introduction to a Course of Lectures before the Political Science Association of the University of Michigan, upon The Constitutional History of the United States as seen in the Development of American Law."

and legislative policies, affecting both our foreign and domestic relations, revealing the extended domain of the law, and displaying, as on a chart, as did the Pillars of Hercules in ancient times, the ultimate limits of national jurisdiction. Within these are the coast lines and harbors and rich possessions of individual right.

Much material will be found full of fascination for the student of mankind. The contentions and conduct of men, whether springing from avarice or enterprise, whether stained with blood or stamped with the features of commercial competition, present a picture of society full of life and color, varying with the habits of thought and action of the age in which they occur, and dramatic in their grouping and character. The mighty contests of the forum deal with principles of universal application and facts of thrilling interest; they elicit the most astonishing displays of eloquence, logic and learning, and are followed by decisions of profound significance pronounced by jurists of incorruptible integrity, and of abilities which have commanded the respect of the world. They exhibit theatres of human action which, like many famous fields of battle, are memorable for the triumph of truth over error, for hard-won victories of justice over wrong. Amid the din of conflict between personal interests, and above the deep-mouthed thunder of the combat between contending sovereignties, the calm tones of our great tribunal have been distinctly heard, commanding States as well as citizens to submit without the spilling of blood to a legal settlement of differences. In this respect the Court is the Conservator of the Peace of the Nation, and her voice is the Harmony of the Union.

The manner, too, in which the Court is constituted is worthy of the closest attention. It was one of the sagacious utterances of Edmund Burke that, "Whatever is supreme in a State ought to have, as much as possible, its judicial authority so constituted, as not only to depend upon it, but in some sort to balance it. It ought to give security to its justice against its power. It ought to make its jurisdiction as it were something exterior to the State." It may be safely asserted that this has been accomplished, in a great measure, in the judicial system of the United States. The dream of the philosopher has been realized. A separation almost complete has been effected between the judicial and the legislative and executive departments of our government. The wisdom of such a separation, first definitely expressed by Montesquieu, has been finally vindicated. In the making of laws the Judiciary has no share, nor has it any part in executive power. The happy manner in which the Framers of our Federal Constitution secured the independence of the Judiciary,—by the mode of appointment of the Judges, by making their tenure of office dependent upon good behavior, by the provision that the compensation of the Judges shall not be diminished during their continuance in office, thus emancipating them from the control of the Legislature, and from the temptation of making their decrees a matter of barter,—has excited the admiration of all philosophical students of our institutions.[1]

The establishment of the Supreme Court of the United States was the crowning marvel of the wonders wrought by the statesmanship of America. In truth the creation of the Supreme Court with its appellate powers was the greatest conception of the Constitution. It embodied the loftiest ideas,

---

[1] Francis Lieber, "Civil Liberty and Self-Government," Woolsey's Edition, p. 203. Story's "Commentaries on the Constitution," Vol. III, § 1571 et seq.

of moral and legal power, and although its prototype existed in the Superior Courts established in the various States, yet the majestic proportions to which the structure was carried became sublime. No product of government, either here or elsewhere, has ever approached it in grandeur. Within its appropriate sphere it is absolute in authority. From its mandates there is no appeal. Its decree is law. In dignity and moral influence it outranks all other judicial tribunals of the world. No court of either ancient or modern times was ever invested with such high prerogatives. Its jurisdiction extends over Sovereign States as well as over the humblest individual. It is armed with the right as well as the power to annul in effect the statutes of a State whenever they are directed against the civil rights, the contracts, the currency or the intercourse of the people. It restricts Congressional action to Constitutional bounds. Secure in the tenure of its Judges from the influences of politics, and the violence of prejudice and passion, it presents an example of judicial independence unattainable in any of the States and far beyond that of the highest Court in England.[1] Yet its powers are limited and strictly defined. Its decrees are not arbitrary, tyrannical, or capricious, but are governed by the most scrupulous regard for the sanctity of law. It cannot encroach upon the reserved

---

[1] This is admitted by Professor Bryce, who, in writing of the Supreme Court, says: "The justices are nominated by the President and confirmed by the Senate. They hold office during good behavior, *i. e.*, they are removed only by impeachment. They have thus a tenure even more secure than that of English Judges, for the latter may be removed by the Crown on an address from both Houses of Parliament. Moreover, the English Statutes secure the permanence only of the Judges of the Supreme Court of Judicature, not also of Judges of County or other local Courts, while the provisions of the American Constitution are held to apply to the inferior as well as the superior Federal judges." (James Bryce, "The American Commonwealth," Vol. I, p. 226.)

rights of the States or abridge the sacred privileges of local self-government. Its power is never exercised for the purpose of giving effect to the will of the judge, but always for the purpose of giving effect to the will of the legislature, or, in other words, to the will of the law.[1] Its administration is a practical expression of the workings of our system of liberty according to law. Its Judges are the sworn ministers of the Constitution, and are the High Priests of Justice. Acknowledging no superior, and responsible to their consciences alone, they owe allegiance to the Constitution and to their own exalted sense of duty. Instructed and upheld by a highly educated bar, their judgments are the ripest fruits of judicial wisdom. Amenable to public opinion, they can be reached, in case of necessity, by impeachment by the Senate of the United States. No institution of purely human contrivance presents so many features calculated to inspire both veneration and awe.

The peculiar nature of the jurisdiction of the Court requires the Judges to be statesmen as well as jurists, and in most instances, tested by the results, wisely and well have they acted. Their decisions are not confined to mere questions of commercial law or narrow municipal regulations, but may involve the discussion and settlement of principles which affect the policy and welfare of the nation. The Court cannot consider abstract problems, however important, nor can it frame a fictitious issue for argument to satisfy a speculative interest in the result. It cannot anticipate by an hour the solution of a practical difficulty. It deals with the present and the past; it cannot put the remedy in force before the right accrues; but given a question, fairly presented by

---

[1] C. J. Marshall, in Osborn *v.* Bank of the U. S., 9 Wheaton, 866 (1824).

the pleadings in a cause, then, however humble the parties to the suit, or however trifling the amount involved, the decision may sweep beyond the petty bounds of local customs or sectional statutes into the broad domain of international law, or rise into the loftiest regions of Constitutional jurisprudence. The Court has always upheld the National character of our Government and vindicated the National honor. At the same time it has carefully guarded the reserved rights of the States. The most comprehensive and statesmanlike views have in the main happily prevailed.

A few illustrations will confirm this assertion. A British creditor sued a citizen of the United States upon a debt sequestered by the State of Virginia during the Revolutionary War, and the argument taxed to the utmost the powers of the ablest advocates, while the decision expanded from a statement of the contractual liability of an individual to an assertion that the treaty obligations of the nation were paramount to the laws of individual States.[1] A citizen of South Carolina sued the State of Georgia, and although the storm of indignation that followed the decision upholding the suit led to an amendment of the Constitution of the United States, yet it was fortunate for the independence and moral influence of the Court that the Judges refused to bend before the popular fury.[2] A justice of the peace of the District of Columbia applied for a mandamus addressed to the Secretary of State, to enforce his right to a commission, and the decision sustained and vindicated the power of the Court to declare void an Act of Congress, as being repugnant to the Constitution, subjecting, once and forever, all executive and ministerial officers as well as Congress itself to the control of the Court

[1] Ware *v.* Hylton, 3 Dallas, 199 (1796). [2] Chisholm Exr. *v.* Georgia, 2 Dallas, 419 (1793).

in expounding the fundamental law.[1]   An individual holding lands under a patent granted by a State brought suit against a trespasser, upon the covenants in his deed, and a statute of the State which had been passed in violation of his private rights was hewn to the ground.[2]   An humble institution of learning resisted the attempt of a Legislature to amend its charter without its consent, and the decision placed all charters within the protection of the Constitutional clause which forbids States to impair the obligation of contracts.[3]   A local branch of the Bank of the United States objected to State taxation, and the power of a State to destroy an agency of the general Government was denied in an "opinion" which has proved to be a veritable bulwark of national authority.[4]   The State of New York claimed the exclusive right to the navigation of the Hudson, and sought to confine it to her licensees, as a reward for the invention of propelling boats by steam.   The decision destroyed the monopoly and emancipated the commerce of the nation from sectional control.[5]   A State arrogated to itself the right to prohibit the transportation of merchandise from other States except on payment of toll or tribute, and the decision declared that inter-state commerce should be free.[6]   Again a State endeavored to enforce a like prohibition with reference to the passage of citizens of the United States, from one part of the country to the other, through that State, and the decision upheld the personal right of unchallenged locomotion.[7]   On numerous occasions the

---

[1] Marbury *v.* Madison, 1 Cranch, 158 (1803).

[2] Fletcher *v.* Peck, 6 Cranch, 87 (1810).

[3] Dartmouth College Case, 4 Wheaton, 518 (1819).

[4] McCulloch *v.* State of Maryland, 4 Wheaton, 316 (1819).

[5] Gibbons *v.* Ogden, 9 Wheaton, 1 (1824).

[6] Almy *v.* The State of California 24 Howard, 169 (1860).   Welton *v.* State of Missouri, 91 U. S. 275. (1875).

[7] Crandall *v.* State of Nevada, 6 Wallace, 35 (1867).

States have endeavored to compel the payment of a tax before a citizen of another State should be at liberty to buy or sell within their borders. In every instance the decision has sustained the national character of our Union. Had the decisions been the reverse of what they were, and affirmed the pretensions of the States, which had been uniformly sustained by their own highest tribunals, the character and condition of our country would have been transformed into a scene of conflict between vexatious restrictions upon interstate commerce, and the States themselves would have been converted into prison cells, from which none could escape except upon payment of gate-money to the gaoler. A quarrel as to tolls arose between two bridge companies in Massachusetts, and the decision rescued the States from every effort to suppress those progressive improvements by which the earth has been subdued to the dominion of man, while at the same time proper and necessary restrictions were imposed upon the claims of exclusive right set up under color of legislative grant.[1] A negro in Missouri brought an action to assert the title of himself and family to freedom, and the decision led indirectly to the emancipation of a race.[2] A federal army officer refused to recognize a writ of Habeas Corpus issued from the Supreme Court, and the sword was snatched from the breast of the citizen by the hand of the civil power. The principle was established that where the Courts are open, and in the proper exercise of their jurisdiction, the right of a citizen to a trial by jury cannot be denied or abridged—a decision of such importance as to be clothed "with the heritage of immortality."[3] A debtor attempted to discharge him-

---

[1] Charles River Bridge *v.* Warren Bridge, 11th Peters, 420 (1837).
[2] Dred Scott *v.* Sanford, 19 Howard, 393 (1857).
[3] Ex parte Milligan, 4 Wallace, 2 (1866).

self by the tender of government paper, and the war powers and the general sovereignty of the National government, and of its right to maintain itself, were stated and sustained.[1] A grant of a State was assailed on the plea of monopoly, and the decision saved the sovereignty of the State from annihilation, and put a just interpretation upon Federal power.[2]

These are but a few of the many instances of faithful service by the Court to the interests of the Nation, and although some of them were subjected at the time to fierce criticism, and may be still questioned by many, yet, viewed as a whole, they cannot fail to enlarge our sense of obligation to the Court. Few laymen appreciate, and many lawyers forget, the extent of their debt; but those who have studied the matter most profoundly are the most outspoken in their expressions of gratitude and praise. Besides these, which were public in character and far-reaching in their effect, arising under the Constitution, the laws of the United States or treaties made under their authority, or out of controversies to which the United States was a party, or out of controversies between States, or between a State and the citizens of another State,— the Court has performed a vast amount of silent and unseen work in the broad and fruitful field of commercial law, enlarging the bounds of the science of jurisprudence, and refining and strengthening the professional apprehension of the rights, duties and obligations of men in our complex state of society. Cases affecting Ambassadors or other public ministers and consuls; cases involving the rights, duties and liabilities of shipowners, shipmasters, mariners and material

---

[1] Hepburn *v.* Griswold, 8 Wallace, 603 (1870) ; Legal Tender Cases, 12 Wallace, 457 (1871 ; Juillard *v.* Greenman, 110 U. S. 421 (1883).

[2] Slaughter House Cases, 16 Wallace, 36 (1873).

men; questions of prize, the conflicting rights of captors and claimants, of neutrals and belligerents, trading under licenses, or privateering under letters of marque and reprisal; cases of admiralty and maritime jurisdiction; controversies between citizens or corporations of different States; questions of negotiable paper, insurance, partnership and personal relations in endless variety, have tested the energies of the Court. The business of the Supreme Court springs from that of a continent. It arises out of many systems of laws differing from each other in important particulars. It includes the most diverse cases tried in the lower courts in many different modes of procedure; some under the practice of the Common Law; some under the Chancery of England; some borrowed from French or Spanish law; some under special laws framed for the execution of Treaties entered into by the United States; and many more so anomalous as to be incapable of accurate classification. Yet the stability and uniformity of the course of decision are remarkable, and are due in a great measure to the length of time that the Judges have held office under the tenure of good behavior, but chiefly, as has been remarked by one of their number, because it is one of the favors which the providence of God has bestowed on our happy country, that for the period of sixty-three years, from the days of John Adams as President to those of Abraham Lincoln, the great office of Chief Justice was filled by only two persons, each of whom retained to extreme old age his great and useful qualities and powers.[1]

It will not be inappropriate to quote a few of the opinions of our most distinguished statesmen and jurists as to

---

[1] Remarks of B. R. Curtis upon the death of Chief Justice Taney, at a meeting of the Boston Bar, held Oct. 15, 1864.

the place occupied by the Court in our national economy, and to these may be added the views of accomplished foreign writers who have made our institutions the subject of close study. Washington, with sagacious insight into the true character of our government, then just established, declared, "Considering the judicial system as the chief pillar upon which our national government must rest, I have thought it my duty to nominate for the high offices in that department, such men as I conceived would give dignity and lustre to our national character."[1] Henry Clay pronounced the Supreme Court to be one of the few great conservative elements of the government. Pinkney called it "a more than Amphictyonic Council;" Webster spoke of it "as the great practical expounder of the powers of the government," and with awful solemnity declared, "No conviction is deeper in my mind than that the maintenance of the Judicial power is essential and indispensable to the very being of this government. The Constitution, without it, would be no Constitution —the Government, no Government. I am deeply sensible, too, and, as I think, every man must be whose eyes have been open to what has passed around him for the last twenty years, that the Judicial power is the protecting power of the government. Its position is upon the outer wall. From the very nature of things, and the frame of the Constitution, it forms the point at which our different systems of government meet in collision, when collision unhappily exists. By the absolute necessity of the case the members of the Supreme Court become Judges of the extent of Constitutional

---

[1] Letter of Washington to James Wilson, enclosing his Commission as an Associate Justice of the Supreme Court of the United States, dated Sept. 30, 1789. Original in possession of Miss Hollingsworth, of Philadelphia.

powers. They are, if I may so call them, the great arbitrators between contending sovereignties."[1] Horace Binney declared that "It is the august representative of the wisdom and justice and conscience of the whole people. It is the peaceful and venerable arbitrator between the citizens in all questions touching the extent and sway of Constitutional power. It is the great moral substitute for force in controversies between the people, the States and the Union." Sir Henry Maine speaks of it as a "unique creation of the founders of the Constitution." Bryce, paraphrasing an expression of the Civil law, calls it "the living voice of the Constitution;" De Tocqueville says that "a more imposing judicial power was never constituted by any people;" Lord Brougham does not hesitate to pronounce that "the power of the Judiciary to prevent either the State Legislatures or Congress from overstepping the limits of the Constitution, is the very greatest refinement in social polity to which any state of circumstances has ever given rise, or to which any age has ever given birth;" while Von Holst, in his elaborate "Constitutional History," treats the decisions of the Court with the profoundest respect.

The title of the Court to public veneration and esteem does not rest alone on the peculiar character of its jurisdiction, or its powers, or the wisdom with which they have been exercised, but largely upon the reputation of its Judges for purity and ability. The earliest members of the Court were those who had been conspicuous actors in the great drama of the Revolution, and who had played no unimportant part in the work of framing the Constitution. The first Chief Jus-

[1] Speech of Daniel Webster in the House of Representatives of the United States, Jan. 25, 1826.

tice, though not a profoundly learned lawyer, was a man whose character was "a brilliant jewel in the sacred treasures of national reputation," and "when the spotless ermine of the judicial robe fell on John Jay, it touched nothing not as spotless as itself." Beside him sat William Cushing, for many years the learned Chief of the Judiciary of Massachusetts; James Wilson, of Pennsylvania, whose transcendent merits as one of the most sagacious and eloquent logicians of the age, and one of the profoundest of our early statesmen, are looming into larger and still larger proportions as years go by; John Blair, of Virginia, with Wilson, a distinguished member of the Federal Convention, and a Judge of much experience in the Courts of his State. A few years later came John Rutledge, the most renowned of the sons of South Carolina, this time summoned to preside over the Court, after having declined to act as an Associate Justice, whose brilliant faculties sustained a sudden and sad eclipse, in part the cause and in part the effect of his rejection by the Senate; James Iredell, of North Carolina, the study of whose works cannot fail to awaken admiration of his qualities as a judge and his virtues as a man; and Thomas Johnson, of Maryland, formerly a member of the Continental Congress, and a lawyer of admitted power. Still later appeared Oliver Ellsworth, of Connecticut, a giant in the law, and the acknowledged author of our judiciary system; William Paterson, of New Jersey, the author and able advocate of the State Rights Plan in the Federal Convention, and Samuel Chase, of Maryland, a Signer of the Declaration of Independence, rough, impetuous and overbearing in manner as a judge, though fearless and honest, subsequently impeached for misconduct, but honorably acquitted. A younger generation succeeded, and the Court rose steadily, with John Marshall as Chief Justice, and

Bushrod Washington, Alfred Moore, William Johnson, Brockholst Livingston, Thomas Todd, Joseph Story and Gabriel Duvall as Associate Justices, until it touched the highest pinnacle of glory and power. This was the Golden Age of the Supreme Court. Of Marshall, the mighty Chief of peerless reputation, by whose hand the Constitution was moulded into its final and permanent form, it would be impossible to write in terms of praise that would be deemed extravagant. Statesmen of all parties and jurists of all nations unite in pronouncing him to have been the greatest judge that America has produced, a man whose character is the "most exquisite picture in all the receding light of the early days of the republic." Washington was to Marshall what Sir Francis Buller was to Lord Mansfield, while Story, by his education, scholarship and extraordinary gifts as a writer, has won imperishable fame both at home and abroad. The remaining judges, with the exception of Moore, whom ill health forced to an early retirement, sat by the side of Marshall for many years, contributing to the growing strength of the Court and sharing in its renown. Not less useful, though far less known, were the labors of Smith Thompson, of New York, the associate of Kent; Robert Trimble, of Kentucky— too early snatched away, but leaving a judicial reputation earned by but few after so short a period of service,—John McLean, of Ohio, Henry Baldwin, of Pennsylvania, and James M. Wayne, of Georgia, whose vigorous minds and ample learning gave solidity to the structure which their predecessors had reared. The Court then entered on a new career; its former Constitutional doctrines were modified, and the influences to which it was subjected were shaken by the stormy passions that agitated the political sea. Although Chief Justice Taney has suffered much in reputation from the consequences of the Dred Scott

2

decision, yet few men, who will take the pains to study temperately the work of his long and conspicuously able judicial career will be unwilling to admit that his mind was of the highest order, that he steadily and firmly upheld and administered the great powers entrusted to the Court by the Constitution and laws of his country, as he understood them, and that his character was pure beyond reproach. As an upright and able magistrate, as a learned jurist, he was for twenty-eight years the most conspicuous figure upon a bench adorned by such men as Philip P. Barbour, of Virginia, formerly Speaker of the House; John Catron, of Tennessee, of acute and vigorous mind, with great power of juridical analysis and a marvellous capacity for labor; John McKinley, of Alabama, for some years a member of Congress, of high rank at the bar, and deficient neither in learning nor ability; Peter V. Daniel, of Virginia, the dissenting judge; Samuel Nelson, of New York, prominent in his knowledge of patent law; Levi Woodbury, of New Hampshire, the cotemporary of Webster, Clay and Hayne in the Senate; Robert C. Grier, a jurist of capacity; John A. Campbell, of Alabama, of vast learning, of active, penetrating mind, and of illustrious reputation in after years as a practitioner before the Court, wherein he once sat as an Associate, and Benjamin R. Curtis, of Massachusetts, perhaps the greatest jurist New England ever produced, certainly without a peer since the days of Jeremiah Mason and Theophilus Parsons. The next generation of Justices, although with one exception removed by death, can be recalled as familiar and venerated objects of popular regard. Nathan Clifford, learned and venerable; Noah H. Swayne, acute and logical; David Davis, who preferred the curule chair of a Senator to the robes of a Judge; Chief Justice Chase, the famous author of our national banking system; William Strong, whose name indicates his hardy qualities of mind; Ward Hunt, sensible and discreet; Chief Justice Waite, self-possessed, modest, but sturdy and alert; William B. Woods, Stanley Matthews, brilliant but erratic; and Samuel F. Miller, second only to Marshall as an interpreter of the Constitution, together constituted a Court which could be safely relied on for sound law and incorruptible judgments. To write of the living might savor of indelicacy, but nothing can be hazarded in the statement that the Court at the present time contains Judges whose profound and accurate learning, more massive and compact than that of former days, has left but little for future generations to regret.

Although at times shadows have rested upon its reputation and authority, which it will be the duty of the historian to notice, the Court enjoys the esteem of the Bar and the confidence of the People. No heavier responsibility rests upon the President of the United States than that of making fit appointments when vacancies occur. To sustain the lofty standard of the Court should be his highest aim. No motives of personal friendship or of political gratitude should tempt him to lower the tone of this great tribunal. The most commanding professional abilities, and the most unsullied private and public character should be demanded of every man who aspires to such high place. Wisdom, learning, integrity, independence and firmness have become the adamantine foundations of the Court. The politician, the trickster, the demagogue, the disloyalist, the narrow-minded practitioner, wise in his own conceit, but unknown beyond a petty locality, should have no entrance there. Men of strength, of unspotted lives, whom power cannot corrupt, or influence intimidate, or affection swerve; men of exalted ideas of duty and honor, ready to dedicate themselves as the highest servants of Heaven to the noblest mission on earth, are alone fit to be entrusted with the awful power of sitting in final judgment upon the rights of States and the liberties of individuals in the great Court of last resort under the Constitution of the United States.

A history of the Court would be incomplete if it failed to touch upon the Bar. The character of the Bench is largely a reflection of the character of the Bar. The Judges are drawn from its members. Besides this, an able bar can never tolerate a feeble bench, while an able bench will always elevate and educate a bar. They act and re-act on each other. No puerile argument or deceitful statement of facts can hope to prevail as long as the judges maintain the purity of the moral atmosphere that surrounds them. The rectitude of the bench means the rectitude of the bar. They are corollaries of each other. Viewed as a body, the members of the bar of the Supreme Court of the United States, with but few exceptions, have been intelligent, astute, laborious, well trained and well informed; manly in conduct, fearless in their defence of freedom and right, upright in principle, just and patriotic, cherishing a high and delicate sense of individual honor, displaying a proper regard for the dignity of their profession, and ever ready to acquiesce with profound respect in the decisions of the Court when once pronounced; while some of them have exhibited abilities of such transcendent character as to dazzle and astonish the nation. Among the forty distinguished men who have filled the office of Attorney-General—the official head of the profession—occur the names of Edmund Randolph, a legal flash-light; Theophilus Parsons, a profound lawyer, though not a brilliant one; William Wirt, who combined the skill of the literary artist with the knowledge of a jurist; William Pinkney, the glory of his generation, of whom Judge Story wrote,

"He possesses, beyond any man I ever saw, the power of elegant and illustrative amplification;" Henry D. Gilpin, an accomplished classical scholar; Benjamin F. Butler, a model advocate; Hugh S. Legarè, as much a master of Demosthenes and Cicero in the original, as of Vattel, Burlamaqui, Grotius and Wheaton; Reverdy Johnson, the acknowledged head of a bar once led by Luther Martin and Robert Goodloe Harper; Caleb Cushing, a man omnipresent in all departments of learning, and Jeremiah S. Black, whose argument in defence of the right to trial by Jury will live as long as our institutions last. Besides these were men who owed none of their influence to official station, who have brought, from all parts of the country, to the discussion of great questions, powers of the highest order. They have furnished to the Court the material of which the majestic temple of our jurisprudence has been built. It is true, as has been recently remarked by Mr. Justice Bradley, that the system of railroads and the consequent ease of communication, have had the effect of lessening the elevated and eclectic character of the arguments made before the Court. But there are times still when in a great cause the highest professional abilities are taxed to their utmost, and arguments are made which in splendor of eloquence and wealth of learning will vie with any of the olden times.

In truth it is impossible to estimate the intellectual and moral energies of the American Bar, its brain power, its vigor of reform, its prudent conservatism, its thrilling traditions, its beauties of principle, its glories of achievement, its mighty potencies to mould the destinies of States. The world of thought belongs to jurisprudence; the domain of every science and every field of literature acknowledge her title. The labors of the philosopher, however gigantic his scale of thinking, are not too lofty for her contemplation, nor dalliance with the Muses too frivolous to be despised. The universe has been swept in pursuit of knowledge; the treasuries of learning have been sacked; the vaults, where the wisdom of every age and clime is hidden, and the practical experience of centuries embalmed, have been opened and examined. The Institutes of Gaius, and the Pandects of Justinian; the Laws of Alfred, and the Magna Charta of King John; the Ordinances of the Sea; the pages of Coke and Hale; the decrees of Hardwicke, and the judgments of Stowell; the blood-bought experiences of the human race, and the lessons taught by the centuries that have gone, the precious principles bequeathed to us by the Fathers of the Republic have been stated, reasoned upon, expounded, illustrated and enforced by the mightiest intellects of Bench and Bar. It is not enough to point to the gilded dome, the fretted roof, the sculptured architrave, the ornate column or the richly decorated frieze, to impress upon the mind the wondrous character of the building. Attention should be called to the hidden arches, the mighty vaults, the base-stones far beneath the surface of the ground. There is the secret of its strength. The decisions of the Supreme Court of the United States, and the principles which they embody, constitute the foundations of our institutions—foundations which neither the earthquake of revolution can shake, nor the eruptive fires of civil war destroy. The House may become corrupt, the Senate may yield in time to wealth or ambition, but so long as the Supreme Court maintains its lofty teachings, so long as its maxims of interpretation and the principles which underlie its work are understood and cherished by the loyal people of the land, so long will a pledge exist that the liberties of America will prove immortal.

PART I.

SOURCES OF THE JURISDICTION OF THE SUPREME COURT
OF THE UNITED STATES.
1680–1774.

CHAPTER II

INTRODUCTION : SPECIAL FITNESS OF THE FRAMERS OF THE CONSTITUTION FOR
THEIR WORK : CLASSIFICATION OF SOURCES OF JURISDICTION : ADMIRALTY
CASES : COLONIAL VICE ADMIRALTY COURTS : JURISDICTION : ACTS OF TRADE :
COLONIAL JUDGES : EXTENSION OF JURISDICTION : REVENUE CASES : COLONIAL
OPPOSITION : REMONSTRANCE OF FIRST CONTINENTAL CONGRESS.

THE Third Article of our Federal Constitution delineates in striking outlines the jurisdiction of the Federal Courts, and embodies in three brief sections the pregnant matter out of which has been developed the most remarkable judicial establishment the world has seen.

The first section vests the judicial power of the United States in one Supreme Court, and in such inferior Courts as Congress may, from time to time, ordain and establish : it regulates the tenure of office of all Federal Judges, prescribing that of good behavior, and guards their compensation against diminution.

The second section defines the extent of the judicial power, declaring that it shall extend to all cases in law and equity arising under the Constitution, the laws of the United States, and treaties made under their authority; to all cases affecting ambassadors, other public ministers and consuls; to all cases of admiralty and maritime jurisdiction; to controversies to which the United States shall be a party; to controversies between two or more States; between a State and citizens of another State; between citizens of different States; between citizens of one State claiming land under grants of different States, and between a State, or the citizens thereof, and foreign States, citizens, or subjects.

The original jurisdiction of the Supreme Court is expressly limited to all cases affecting ambassadors, other public ministers and consuls, and those in which a State shall be a party; while in all the other cases mentioned, the jurisdiction is appellate, both as to law and fact, with such exceptions, and under such regulations as Congress shall make.

Trial by Jury is provided for all crimes, except in cases of impeachment, and such trial is to be held in the State where the crime shall have been committed, or, when not committed within any State, at such place or places as Congress may by law have directed.

The third section defines the crime of treason against the United States. The testimony of two witnesses to the same overt act, or confession in open court, is necessary to a conviction: Congress is empowered to declare the punishment, but no corruption of blood, or forfeiture, except during the life of the person attainted, shall be wrought by an attainder.

Such is the language of the Article creating and defining the judicial power of the United States. It is the voice of the whole American people, solemnly declared, in establishing one great department of that government, which was, in many respects, national, and in all supreme. It must be patent to all who are familiar with the fact that our Constitution was not a creation but a growth, that these results were not reached *a priori*. The truth is that this Article is an epitome of past judicial and legislative experience lighted up by a sagacious forecast. of the future.

Its authors combined a very rare union of the best talents, information, patriotism, probity, and public influence which the country afforded. Of the members of the Federal Convention, thirty-nine had seen active service in the Continental Congress; seven were signers of the Declaration of Independence; thirty-one were lawyers by profession, of whom four had studied in the Inner Temple, and one at Oxford under Blackstone; ten had served as Judges in their own States, of whom four were still upon the Bench; one had been a Judge of the old Federal Court of Appeals in Cases of Capture; seven had been chosen to serve as Judges in Courts specially constituted to determine controversies between the States as to territory and boundary, under the power conferred on Congress by the Ninth Article of the Confederation; eight had assisted in framing the Constitutions of their respective States; three had aided in the codification or revision of their own State laws; eight had served as Governors of States; five had been present at the Annapolis Convention; and three were universally recognized as oracles upon questions of local government as well as public or international law. All of them—whether lawyers or civilians—had witnessed the practical operation of our judicial institutions under the Crown of England and the Articles of Confederation, and had enjoyed the best opportunities of observing the merits and defects of both systems.

The profound intellects of James Madison and Alexander Hamilton, who ranked as jurisconsults, met in high debate such practical jurists as Oliver Ellsworth, George Wythe, David Brearley, John Blair, and George Read, and such forensic disputants as James Wilson, Jared Ingersoll, Abraham Baldwin, and Luther Martin. Their discussions were illuminated by the brilliancy of Gouverneur Morris, John Dickinson, Edmund Randolph, and John Rutledge, and were tempered by the ripened wisdom of Franklin, and the marvellous sagacity of Washington. Not less useful, though of a subordinate degree of excellence, were the labors of George Mason, Rufus King, William Samuel Johnson, William Paterson, and Roger Sherman; while the criticisms of such experienced merchants as Robert Morris, Elbridge Gerry, and Thomas Fitzsimmons, and such respectable lawyers as Richard Bassett, Gunning Bedford, Jr., and Caleb Strong, contributed no small share to the general result of the deliberations of such an assemblage of statesmen.

While abundantly provided with a theoretical knowledge of the requirements of their task, it may be safely asserted that in arranging the judicial power they intended chiefly to enforce what experience had shown to be salutary in preserving harmony among the States and with foreign nations, and what wisdom dictated as essential to secure obedience to the authorities vested in the different departments of the Government. Hence, it will be found that a large portion of the judicial power bestowed by the Constitution of the United States closely resembles that exercised by the Continental Congress, although the greater part of the system, as we now view it, has grown out of the establishment of a General Government expressly designed to affect the concerns of a nation embracing a continent.

In analyzing the Article of the Constitution relating to the Judiciary, with a view of tracing the sources of the jurisdiction of the Supreme Court, and of measuring accurately the extent and value of the lessons of the past, it is proper to scan the acts of the Continental Congress to ascertain what steps were taken towards the erection of a Judiciary to determine controversies arising out of the War for Independence.

Prior to the outbreak of hostilities the Colonies had their own separate judicial systems which constituted an important part of the framework of local government, but these were manifestly without authority to deal with interests not exclusively local. Several important classes of controversy soon arose, which in time led to a Federal jurisdiction; such were admiralty causes, affecting questions of prize; piracies and felonies committed on the high seas; controversies between the States, affecting rights of soil and boundary; disputes between individuals claiming under grants from different States; suits against a State in the courts of another State, and matters relating to the post-offices of the United States.

ADMIRALTY CAUSES.

Of these the Admiralty causes, by far the most frequent and important, first claim attention.

During the war between France and England, which terminated in the Peace of Ryswick in December, 1697, the colonists had taken advantage of the opportunities afforded them to carry on a direct commercial intercourse with Scotland and Ireland. The complaints of English merchants that New York would not respect the Acts of Trade, that Pennsylvania and the Carolinas were nests of pirates and rogues, and that the mariners of New England distributed the products of the tropics throughout the world, led to the establishment of the Board of Trade and Plantations, a permanent commission, consisting of a President and seven members, known as "Lords of Trade," who were invested with a jurisdiction similar to that previously exercised by plantation committees of the Privy

Council. The statutes for carrying the Acts of Trade into effect were consolidated; all direct trade with Ireland and the Colonies, except the export of horses, servants, and provisions, was prohibited, and, until the Union, Scotland was included, on the plea that if any imports were allowed they would be made a cover for smuggling. The appointment of the Colonial Governors was subjected to Royal approval, and an oath was imposed to enforce the Acts of Trade. All colonial statutes or usages conflicting with Acts of Parliament, were declared void, and, as a further security to British interests, Courts of Vice-Admiralty were established throughout the Colonies, in some instances by virtue of a right reserved in their charters, and in others without such right, with power to try admiralty and revenue cases without a jury. A strenuous resistance was made, especially in the chartered colonies, but after long and solemn argument, the doctrine was maintained by the Privy Council that the King had power to establish an admiralty jurisdiction in every domain of the crown, whether chartered or not. The right of Appeal from the Colonial Courts to the King in Council was also sustained in accordance with early practice in appeals from sentences in the English Court of Admiralty, and thus an extensive judicial control over the Colonies was obtained.[1]

After 1708 all appeals from the vice-admiralty courts were, in questions of prize, referred to certain Commissioners, constituting a standing committee of the Privy Council, provided appeals were made within fourteen days after sentence, and security was given that the appeals would be prosecuted

---

[1] Bancroft's "History of the United States." The Author's last Revision, Vol. II, pp. 79–80; Hildreth's "History of the United States." Revised Ed., Vol. II, pp. 196–199.

with effect:[1] and in instance and revenue cases an appeal lay to the High Court of Admiralty in England and thence to the Delegates.[2]

It was again asserted that an appeal lay to the King in Council but this opinion seems to have been subsequently relinquished.[3] In England cognizance of revenue cases was never claimed by the Court of Admiralty; that field being appropriated by the Common law to the Court of Exchequer, but in the colonies, the Vice-Admiralty Courts obtained a novel and extensive jurisdiction under the provisions of the celebrated Navigation Act of 12 Chas. II. c. 2 and the Revenue Act of 7 & 8 William III. c. 22, some features of which were intended for the more effectual suppression of piracy. The point was contested on the ground that revenue cases were not in their nature causes civil or maritime, but in 1754 it was fully and finally settled in favor of the jurisdiction in the case of the Vrow Dorothea, which was carried on appeal from the Vice Admiralty of South Carolina to the High Court of Admiralty, and thence to the Delegates in England.[4]

COLONIAL VICE-ADMIRALTY COURTS.

In some of the colonies the power of the Crown to establish Vice-Admiralty Courts was beyond dispute. In Mas-

[1] J. Franklin Jameson, "Essays in the Constitutional History of the United States."—"The Predecessor of the Supreme Court," pp. 13-14. 2 Browne's "Civil and Admiralty Law," p. 454. Blackstone's "Commentaries," Book III, *69-70. Sergeant's "Constitutional Law," pp. 14-15.

[2] Note to "The Samuel" 1 Wheaton, 19 (1816); 2 Browne's "Civil & Admiralty Law," 493.

[3] 2 Browne's "Civil and Admiralty Law," 493.

[4] Vrow Dorothea, 2 Rob. 246 (1754). 2 Browne's "Civil & Admiralty Law," 493, note. Note of Mr. Wheaton to the case of the Sarah, 8 Wheaton, 396 (1823). Sergeant's "Constitutional Law," p. 5. Chalmer's "Colonial Opinions," pp. 193-512.

sachusetts there was a plain reservation in the Charter, but the power was exercised even where no such reservation existed, and where, by express grant, the prerogative had been conferred upon the Proprietary. Thus in Pennsylvania the Charter conferred upon William Penn the sole right of appointing and establishing Judges, and by a subsequent provision he was made personally liable to see to the enforcement of the Navigation Acts and all the complicated requirements of the British colonial trading system, and was further bound to see that fines and duties in accordance with these regulations were duly imposed, and that when levied they found their way into the hands of the proper authorities.[1]

These functions were at first discharged by the Executive Council, for we find that, as early as July 12, 1684, upon information by the Sheriff of New Castle County that he had seized a ship which was an unfree bottom, it was ordered that the President, Thomas Lloyd, might empower such as he saw fit to be a Court of Admiralty for the determination of the case, and that on all other like occasions the President and present members might in the absence of the Council proceed to act according to the necessity of the case. Within two months a ship called the "Harp" of London was regularly proceeded against before the Council and condemned as a French bottom, in no way made free to trade or import goods into his Majesty's plantations in America, and, under the forfeiture clauses expressed in the Acts of Navigation, was sold.[2]   But in 1693 William Penn incurred the displeasure of the Court and was for a time deposed from his government, and Benjamin Fletcher was duly commissioned Vice-

---

[1] Charter to Wm. Penn, Sections V, XIV.
[2] Penna. Col. Records, I. pp. 68–69.

Admiral of New York, the Jerseys and New Castle with its dependencies, and invested with all proper power to create Vice-Admiralty Courts within these limits.[1] Shortly after this a Vice-Admiralty Court for Pennsylvania and its territories was regularly constituted by royal and not proprietary authority, and a commission issued under the seal of the High Court of Admiralty of England to Colonel Robert Quarry to act as Judge.[2] ✗ By this time Courts of Vice-Admiralty were in full operation in all of the colonies. Anthony Stokes, his Majesty's Chief Justice in Georgia, says that all the commissions issued were alike, and in terms declared that the jurisdiction extended "throughout all and every the seashores, public streams, ports, fresh water rivers, creeks or arms, as well of the sea as of the rivers, and coasts whatsoever of our said provinces."[3] All causes, civil and maritime, embracing char-

---

[1] Historical Notes to the Duke of Yorke's Book of Laws, pp. 539 et seq.

[2] Minutes of Penna. Provincial Council, Feb. 12, 1697–8. 1 Col. Records, 500.

[3] Anthony Stokes, "A View of the State of the British Colonies in North America and the West Indies," pp. 150–168. For form of Commission see Stokes, p. 166. Benedict's Admiralty, §§. 142, 160. Duponceau on Jurisdiction, p. 158. Sergeant's "Constitutional Law," p. 4, note.

It has been a question learnedly discussed by those who have examined the matter whether the language quoted in the text conferred a different or more extensive jurisdiction than that allowed in England from the interpretation given by the Common Law Courts to the restraining statutes of 13 and 15 Rich. II. ch. 3, 2 Henry IV. ch. 11, and 27 Elizabeth ch. 11, and whether in point of fact the colonies were familiar with a larger jurisdiction than that prevailing in the mother county. The weight of authority, however, is in favor of the assertion that the admiralty jurisdiction actually exercised in the colonies transcended the narrow bounds prescribed by the jealousy of the Common law, and closely approached that now exercised by the Courts of the United States. Upon this side of the controversy appear the names of Story, Wayne and Nelson, sustained by those of Washington, Catron, McLean, and the overshadowing authority of Marshall and Taney; and on the other appear those of Woodbury, Baldwin and Daniel, whose dissent is powerfully expressed in opinions as remarkable for their learning and ingenuity as those of the majority of the Court. See De Lovio *v.* Boit, 2

ter parties, bills of lading, policies of marine insurance, accounts and debts, exchanges, agreements, complaints, offences, and all matters relating to freight, maritime loans, bottomry bonds, seamen's wages, and many of the crimes, trespasses and injuries committed on the high seas or on tidewaters were included within their jurisdiction. They also took cognizance of all cases of penalties and forfeitures under the Act of 7 & 8 William III., and exercised a general authority to apprehend and commit to prison persons accused or suspected of piracy.[1]

An examination of the records of the Vice-Admiralty Court in Pennsylvania from 1735 to 1746, the only portion now known to exist, discloses the fact that its business, though inconsiderable in amount, consisted of proceedings by the Collector of Customs by information against vessels and goods for breaches of the Acts of Parliament relating to the revenue; libels for seamen's wages; orders for the surveys of damaged vessels and goods and of wrecks, appraisements, with power to the Commissioner appointed to adjust the salvage in cases of wreck; records of protests, and, towards the end of the time, registers of letters of marque and reprisal granted by the governors, and prize proceedings against vessels captured from the French and Spaniards.

Gallison, 398 (1815).   Waring *v.* Clark, 5 Howard, 459 (1847); New Jersey Steam Navigation Co. *v.* The Merchants' Bank, 6 Howard, 344 (1848); Wilmer *v.* The Smilax 2 Pet. Ad. Dec. 295 (1804); Davis *v.* the Brig Seneca, 18 American Jurist, 486 (1838); The Sloop Mary, 1 Paine, 673 (1824); Bains *v.* The Schooner James and Catherine, 1 Baldwin, 544 (1832); The Huntress, Davies R. 104, note; Peyroux *v.* Howard, 7 Peters, 324 (1833); U. S. *v.* Coombs, 12 Peters, 72 (1838); The Schooner Tilton, 5 Mason 465 (1830).

[1] Benedict's Admiralty, §. 161. Duponceau on Jurisdiction, pp. 137–140. Lawrence Lewis, "The Courts of Pennsylvania, in the 17th Century" in "Penna. Magazine of History and Biography," Vol. V. pp. 177–178.

COLONIAL VICE-ADMIRALTY JUDGES.

From the names and characters, both official and private, of the Judges who discharged the duties of the vice admiralty, we catch glimpses of the fluctuating politics of the times both here and abroad. In New York in 1682, under the authority of James, Duke of York, Thomas Dongan acted as Vice-Admiral. Six years later Governor Edmund Andros was commissioned by James II, but his term of service was as brief as that of his royal master, for so severe and rapacious was his rule, that he was seized, imprisoned and sent to England for trial, and the next year William and Mary bestowed the office upon Henry Slaughter. In 1692, Governor Benjamin Fletcher acted under a commission which embraced "ye province of New Yorke, Colonyes of East and West Jersey, province of Pennsilvania, et Countries of New Castle and its dependencies." In 1698 we find the popular and highly accomplished Earl of Bellamont acting in New York, Massachusetts Bay, New Hampshire and its dependencies; his wise and equitable administration being in striking contrast with that of his successor, Edward Hyde, Lord Cornbury, the odious persecutor of the Quakers, Governor of New York, Connecticut, East and West Jersey, who was commissioned by William III. in 1701, the monarch expressly reserving the right of appeal to the High Court of Admiralty in England. Two years later the well-known Roger Mompesson exercised his sway from the Piscataqua to the Capes of the Delaware, for his commission ran into Massachusetts Bay, New Hampshire, Connecticut, Rhode Island, New York, East and West Jersey, Pennsylvania, New Castle and its dependencies,[1] but in

---

[1] Street's "New York Council of Revision," 75. 1 Logan Papers, 200.

3

some way Col. Quarry again secured a commission for Pennsylvania and West Jersey, which superseded that of Mompesson to that extent.[1] In 1704 John Moore was deputy Judge of the Vice-Admiralty for Col. Seymour, Governor of Maryland, and Vice-Admiral of Maryland, Pennsylvania and New Jersey; while in 1721, under George I., Mompesson was displaced in New York by Francis Harrison, and once more, in Pennsylvania, by William Assheton, a cousin of William Penn, to whom a commission was issued by Governor Keith. In 1735 the "Hon. Charles Read, Esq.," is called on the "Docquets" "the Comissary of the Court of Vice-Admiralty of the Province of Pennsylvania," and on the Minutes of his Court is styled "Sole Judge."[2] In 1737 the High Court of Admiralty in England bestowed the office in Pennsylvania upon Andrew Hamilton, the most renowned colonial lawyer of his day, who ten years before had won worldwide celebrity by his bold and eloquent defence of John Peter Zenger, anticipating by fifty years the contention of Erskine that in cases of criminal libel the jury were the judges of the law as well as of the facts. His successor, in 1741, was Thomas Hopkinson, "the ingenious Friend," to whom Franklin acknowledged himself indebted for a communication of "the power of points to throw off the electrical fire," and who yielded the place after ten years of service to Edward Shippen, afterwards Chief Justice of Pennsylvania, who made the position one of importance and great pecuniary value, until, in 1768, the appointment of Jared Ingersoll, the elder, of Connecticut, as Commissioner of Appeals in Admiralty for

---

[1] 1 Logan papers, 281, Nov., 1703. Penna. Col. Records, Vol. I, p. 575.

[2] Martin's "Bench and Bar of Philadelphia," p. 5. Records of the Vice-Admiralty Court in Pennsylvania, in the Office of the Clerk of the District Court of the United States for the Eastern District of Pennsylvania.

New York, New Jersey, Pennsylvania, Maryland and Virginia, drew much business away from the regular Vice-Admiralty Courts. Shippen held the place, however, until the outbreak of the Revolution, when he lost all the offices he had held under the crown. In New York, about 1740, Lewis Morris had succeeded Francis Harrison, and was himself succeeded, after age and infirmities had disabled him, in 1762 by his son, the Hon. Richard Morris, who was in time displaced by Jared Ingersoll, the father of the member of the Federal Convention of the same name.[1]

Public events were now so shaping themselves as to render it of little consequence who held the office, except to make the incumbent an object of suspicion and dislike. The skies were overcast, and the storm-clouds of the coming revolution were soon to emit the lurid lightnings of war.

COLONIAL GRIEVANCES.

In 1768, in the spirit of aggression which had animated the Stamp Act, an Act of Parliament was passed to establish the Courts of Vice-Admiralty in all the colonies on a new model, expressly for the purpose of more effectually recovering the penalties and forfeitures imposed by the Acts framed for the purpose of raising a revenue in America. Their juris-

[1] The materials of the foregoing account are to be found in Stokes' "View of the Colonies;" Benedict's "Admiralty," §§ 142–145 ; Penna. Col. Records, Vol. III., p. 172, Vol. IV., p. 250; Lewis' "Courts of Pennsylvania in 17th Century." Penna. Mag. of History and Biography, Vol. V., p. 141 ; Sergeant's "Constitutional Law," note to p. 4 ; Keith's "Provincial Councillors of Pennsylvania," pp. 56–265; 2 Proud's "History of Pennsylvania," p. 291 ; Pennsylvania Magazine of History and Biography, Vol. VII., p. 23 ; Martin's "Bench and Bar of Philadelphia,"—the work of a painstaking and accurate antiquary ; The Records from 1735 to 1746 of the Colonial Vice-Admiralty Court in Pennsylvania.

diction was extended far beyond the ancient limits, and the obnoxious statutes were stretched, not only to the collection of duties, but to the trial of causes arising merely within the body of a county *infra corpus comitatus*, and but remotely connected with admiralty or revenue affairs.[1]

These measures were met with angry remonstrances on the part of the colonists, which soon ripened into open opposition. The powers given to the Admiralty Courts to dispense with juries were denounced "as instances of grievous oppression, and scarce better than downright tyranny." In the words of John Adams, when announcing the declaration of the town of Braintree: "The most grievous innovation of all is the extension of the power of courts of admiralty, in which one judge presided alone, and, without juries, decided the law and the fact, holding his office during the pleasure of the King, and establishing that most mischievous of all customs, the taking of commissions on all condemnations." This language was echoed by Conway, in the House of Commons; the Act, he said, breathed oppression; it annihilated juries and gave vast power to the Admiralty Courts.[2] Another vicious feature was that the Judges of the Admiralty derived their emoluments exclusively from the forfeitures which they themselves had full power to declare.[3]

For nine years the contest was fiercely waged, and finally in the Address to the People of Great Britain, a paper drawn by John Jay, and adopted by the First Continental Congress, on the 21st of October, 1774, it was made the burden of bit-

---

[1] 4 Geo. III. c. 15–c. 34.   5 Geo. III. c. 25.   6 Geo. III. c. 52.   7 Geo. III. c. 41, c. 46.   8 Geo. III. c. 3.   22.

[2] Bancroft's "History of the United States," Author's Last Revision, Vol. III. pp. 147–205.

[3] Journals of Congress, Vol. I. pp. 21, 33, 47.

ter complaint that it had been ordained by Parliament that whenever offences should be committed in the colonies against particular acts imposing duties and restrictions upon trade, the prosecutor might bring his action for the penalties in the Courts of Admiralty, by which means the subject lost the advantage of being tried by a jury of the vicinage, and was subjected to the sad necessity of being judged by a single man, a creature of the crown, and according to the course of a law which exempted the prosecutor from the trouble of proving his accusation, and obliged the defendant either to evince his innocence or to suffer.[1] In the Address to the Inhabitants of the Colonies it was boldly charged that the judges of the Vice-Admiralty Courts, appointed by the crown and dependent upon it for support, were empowered to receive their salaries and fees from the effects to be condemned by themselves.[2] The same grievance was dwelt upon in the Petition to the King.[3] On the 24th of October, 1775, Congress entered into the celebrated Articles of Association,[4] and declared that the English Crown had extended the powers of the Admiralty Courts beyond their ancient limits, depriving the American subject of a trial by Jury, and authorizing the Judges' certificate to indemnify the prosecutor from damages; that oppressive security was required from a claimant of ships and goods before he could be allowed to defend his property. It was also stated that a Court had been established in Rhode Island for the purpose of taking colonists to England to be tried, subject to all the disadvantages that result in a

[1] Journals of Congress, Philadelphia, 1777, Vol. I. p. 41.
[2] *Ibid.*, pp. 49–51.
[3] *Ibid.*, pp. 68–71.
[4] *Ibid.*, p. 36.

foreign land "from want of friends, want of witnesses, and want of money."

Thus it appears that in every important State paper of the period the abuses of the admiralty powers were denounced in angry terms as substantial violations of the rights of freemen.

CHAPTER III.

EFFORTS TO SECURE REDRESS.

FOR almost a year the energies of Congress were chiefly directed to a publication of the wrongs of the colonies, and in futile efforts at reconciliation. Further Addresses were issued to the inhabitants of Quebec and Canada, to the Assembly of Jamaica and to the people of Ireland, by which it was endeavored to enlist their sympathies in behalf of their suffering fellow-subjects. Non-importation, non-exportation and non-consumption agreements were entered into. After the war had actually begun, the military and naval forces were put upon a Continental basis, officers were commissioned, a Commander-in-chief was appointed, and rules and regulations for the army and navy were adopted. The questions of stores and supplies, the manufacture of powder and arms, the furnishing of troops, the appointment of Continental treasurers, the establishment of a general hospital and general post-office, the fixing the quota of troops and money for each colony, the emission of bills of credit, the consideration of military movements in the North, the siege of Boston, the operations in the neighborhood of Crown Point and Ticonderoga, and correspondence with the agents of the colonies in England in settling their accounts, occupied, almost exclusively, the attention of Congress. As time went on, however, and outrages upon American commerce were committed by British ships of

war, attention was called to the necessity of some effective
method of redress by placing the authority of law behind
the force of arms. The first step was taken in Massachusetts.
Elbridge Gerry, a young merchant of Marblehead, and a
member of the Second Provincial Congress during its session
of June, 1775, proposed the appointment of a committee to
prepare a law to encourage the fitting out of armed vessels,
and to establish a Court for the trial and condemnation of
prizes. Although opposed on account of its apparent inconsistency with the provincial character of Massachusetts, the
law as reported was passed on the 10th of November, 1775, and
is "the first actual avowal of offensive hostilities against the
mother country to be found in the annals of the Revolution."[1]

The preamble is a curious effort to reconcile the theory of
obedience and the fact of resistance; to maintain nominal allegiance with actual rebellion. It was ingeniously grounded on
the royal charter of the Province which authorized the levying
of war against the common enemy of both countries, and declared that Great Britain had become such an enemy with her
ships of war and armies employed against the common interest,
and that accordingly, as loyal subjects, the men of Massachusetts were bound to employ all the power given by the Charter
to capture and destroy them.[2] John Adams termed this one of
the "boldest, most dangerous and most important measures
and epochas in the history of the new world—the commence-
ment of an independent national establishment of a new maritime and naval power."

---

[1] Austin's "Life of Gerry," Vol. I. p. 94.

[2] The Act and its Preamble were printed in the London Magazines of the day as
a political curiosity. The Act itself is printed in its entirety in Austin's "Life of
Gerry," Vol. I., Appendix A. It is also printed in the *Boston Gazette* of Nov.
13, 1775.

STEPS TOWARDS A FEDERAL JURISDICTION.

In the Autumn of 1775 there were two classes of armed vessels cruising in the waters of Massachusetts, one sailing under the authority of the Continental Congress and the other under the authority of the Massachusetts Assembly. Captures were made by each, and conflicting questions of prize arose before any proper provision had been made by Congress for the regular condemnation of captured vessels. General Washington, then conducting the operations of siege against the town of Boston, found himself both embarrassed and annoyed by constant references for the determination of these questions. In a letter addressed to the President of Congress, dated the 11th of November, 1775, he enclosed a copy of the Massachusetts law, and declared that as the armed vessels fitted out at the Continental expense did not come under its terms, he would suggest that Congress should point out a summary way of proceeding. He then pertinently asks: "Should not a Court be established by authority of Congress to take cognizance of prizes made by the Continental vessels? Whatever the mode is which they are pleased to adopt, there is an absolute necessity of its being speedily determined on; for I cannot spare time from military affairs to give proper attention to these matters." [1]

Not hearing of the resolves of Congress, in a letter of December 4, 1775, he again declared that it was some time since he had suggested a Court for the trial of prizes made by the Continental armed vessels, which he would "again take the liberty of urging in the most pressing manner." [2]

---

[1] Sparks' "Life and Letters of Washington," Vol. III., pp. 154–155.
[2] *Ibid.* Vol. III., p. 184.

On the 26th of the same month, he wrote to Richard Henry Lee, "I must beg of you, my dear Sir, to use your influence in having a Court of Admiralty or some power appointed to hear and determine all matters relative to captures; you cannot conceive how I am plagued on this head, and how impossible it is for me to hear and determine upon matters of this sort, when the facts, perhaps, are only to be ascertained at points 40, 50 or more miles from Boston, without bringing the parties here at great trouble and expense. At any rate, my time will not allow me to be a competent judge of this business." [1]

Although Washington appears to have been in ignorance of the action of Congress, they were not inattentive to the subject-matter of his communications. In fact, they acted with remarkable promptitude. His first letter, received six days after its date, was immediately referred to a special committee consisting of George Wythe, Edward Rutledge, John Adams, William Livingston, Benjamin Franklin, James Wilson and Thomas Johnson.[2] On the 25th of November, 1775, they recommended that armed vessels and ships of force should be fitted out; that all war vessels which should fall into the hands of the colonists should be seized and forfeited, and that all transports containing naval or military stores for the use of the British army or navy should be seized and their cargoes confiscated. In order to give these resolutions effect and subject prizes to judicial condemnation, Congress suggested to the several legislatures to erect Courts of justice, or give jurisdiction to Courts then in being, for the purposes of determining all cases of capture, and to provide that all

[1] Sparks' "Life and Letters of Washington," Vol. III. p. 270.
[2] Journals of Congress, Vol. I. p. 183.

trials be had by a jury under such qualifications as should seem meet. It was ordered that all prosecutions should be commenced in the Court of that colony in which captures should be made; if no such court be at that time erected, or if the capture be made upon the open sea, then in the court which the captor should find the most convenient; but no captor was to be permitted to remove his prize from any colony competent to determine concerning the seizure after he had carried his prize within any harbor of the same. The important provision was made that in all cases an appeal should be allowed to Congress, or such person or persons as they should appoint, for the trial of the appeals; appeals were to be demanded within five days after definitive sentence, and lodged with the Secretary of Congress within forty days afterwards, and security was to be entered.[1]

Provision was also made for the proper distribution of prize-money.

This act was the first step towards the establishment of a national judiciary. But, though in the right direction, it did not reach its end. It created no tribunal, it provided no method of procedure, and no means of enforcing decrees. It was silent as to original jurisdiction, and left the extent of the appellate power in doubt; so much so, indeed, that collision occurred subsequently at several points between the States and Congress. It engrafted trial by jury upon admiralty proceedings, a novelty of uncertain value, as the event proved. It assumed authority which it did not undertake to define, and must be regarded as a crude and imperfect piece of legislation. Although moulded into more regular shape by various amendments, it is still interesting as the source of

---

[1] Journals of Congress, Vol. I. p. 184.

the admiralty jurisdiction exercised by Congress during the entire Revolutionary period.

Some of its defects did not escape the penetration of Washington, who wrote, "The resolves relative to captures made by Continental armed vessels only want a Court established for trial to make them complete." It was not until five years later that this thought was acted on.[1]

STATE ADMIRALTY COURTS.

In the meantime the colonies, except Massachusetts, whose action had preceded that of Congress, adopted with more or less promptitude the suggestion that they should erect Admiralty Courts, or clothe existing tribunals with the requisite authority.

Pennsylvania, as was to be expected from her close contact with Congress, led the way by the action of her Council of Safety, on the 3d of February, 1776, in approving the resolves of Congress as to the distribution of prize-money,[2] and on the 26th of March her House of Representatives resolved that there should be erected a Court of Admiralty, with an "able and discreet" person as a Judge, to take cognizance of and try the justice of captures, with power to summon a jury. A Marshal was appointed and the forms

---

[1] Professor Jameson has shown in an interesting and learned manner that the preference of Congress for trial by committee was mainly due to the presence of a doubt whether the powers of the Federal Government extended to the creation of a court, and also to the fact that the colonists had been accustomed to see prize cases carried on appeal from the Colonial Vice-Admiralty Courts to the standing commissioners of appeal of the Privy Council. "Essays in the Constitutional History of the United States," pp. 13–15.

[2] Minutes of Council of Safety, 10 Penna. Col. Records, 476.

of the libel and other process and proceedings were regulated. In all cases an appeal was to be allowed to Congress, and provision was made for taking testimony by depositions, or *ex parte* upon notice, *de bene esse.*[1] Rhode Island in January, South Carolina in April, Connecticut and Maryland in May, New Hampshire in July, New Jersey and Virginia in October, Georgia in November, Delaware, and North Carolina in December of 1776, instituted similar Courts under various titles. New York did not act until March of 1778, and then restricted the jurisdiction by re-enacting in substance the provisions of 15 Ric. II. c. 3, which forbade the cognizance of any matters not occurring strictly upon the sea.[2] In most of the colonies trial by jury was provided for. Maryland left it to the option of the parties, Connecticut and Georgia gave it to special County Courts, Pennsylvania, New Hampshire and Massachusetts made it obligatory. In some of the States the Judge of the Admiralty was appointed by a simple commission without a statutory specification of his powers, or any expression in his commission as to their extent; in others the

---

[1] Votes of the Pennsylvania Assembly, Vol. 6, p. 698. This resolve was supplied by the Act of 9th September, 1778, recorded in Law Book I, p. 212, which provided that "The finding of said jury shall establish the facts without re-examination or appeal," and was in time supplanted by that of 8th March, 1780, which abolished trial by jury in Admiralty causes and restored the practice of the Civil law. McKean's Edition of Laws of Pennsylvania, p. 308. Prof. Jameson states that the Pennsylvania Court was established before the middle of January, 1776, and cites a letter of Thomas Lynch to Washington, dated January 16th, of that year, published in the "Correspondence of the Revolution," edited by Sparks, Vol. I., p. 125, but an examination of the letter leads me to believe that the writer referred to the Resolves of Congress of the preceding November. This is confirmed by the record evidence above cited, as well as by the fact that the Pennsylvania House of Representatives had adjourned from Nov. 25, 1775, until Feb. 12, 1776.

[2] 1 Greenleaf's "Laws of New York," 11, 18, 150, 152, 338. Benedict's "Admiralty," § 166.

courts were established with powers regulated by statute. The right of an appeal to Congress was variously provided for; the concession, as in Pennsylvania, South Carolina and Virginia, being liberally extended to all cases, while in others, as in New Hampshire and Massachusetts, it was restricted jealously to cases of capture by vessels fitted out at the charge of the United States, but in all other cases an appeal was to lie to the Supreme Court of the State. Thus it will be seen that in the different States the constitution of the Admiralty Courts and the limits of their jurisdiction departed widely from each other.[1] Changes of sentiment towards the Federal Government are distinctly visible from time to time. A reactionary feeling displayed itself in parts of New England. Rhode Island, by Act of November, 1780, reciting that as some States disallowed an appeal, and that those who do and those who do not are therefore on an unequal footing, declared that if any citizen of a State which disallowed an appeal to Congress was dissatisfied with the judgment of the Admiralty Court of Rhode Island, he might have an appeal to the Supreme Court of the State. New Hampshire, who had previously confined the jurisdiction of her own appellate Court to cases of capture made by vessels fitted out by her own citizens, now extended it to captures effected by Continental ves-

---

[1] The foregoing account is drawn from Benedict's "Admiralty," § 166; Jameson's "Essays in the Constitutional History of the United States," pp. 11-12; J. C. Bancroft Davis, "The Committees of the Continental Congress chosen to hear and determine appeals from Courts of Admiralty and the Court of Appeals in Cases of Capture," 131 U. S. Reports, Appendix XIX.; Doane v. Penhallow, 1 Dallas, 218 (1780); Penhallow v. Doane, 3 Dallas 57 (1795); United States v. Peters, 5 Cranch, 115 (1809); and the Laws, Schedules and Constitutions of the various States, as contained in the magnificent and unrivaled Tower Collection of Colonial Laws, in the Library of the Historical Society of Pennsylvania.

sels and vessels of New Hampshire jointly, endeavoring thereby to curtail the powers of Congress.[1] At the same time Pennsylvania abolished trial by jury in admiralty causes, and provided that in all cases of prize, capture or recapture, the facts should be determined by the law of nations and the acts and ordinances of Congress, before the Judge of Admiralty, by witnesses, according to the course of the Civil law, and that in all cases an appeal should lie from the final decree of the State judge to such judges or court as Congress should appoint to determine such appeals.[2] Virginia, too, provided that her judges of admiralty should be governed in their proceedings and decisions by the regulations of Congress as well as by the Acts of her Assembly; by the laws of Oleron and the Rhodian and Imperial laws, and by the laws of nature and nations, thus creating a wide and beneficent jurisdiction, far more liberal than that dictated by the policy of sister States, or contained within the narrow limits observed by the English Admiralty at the time.[3] A little later New York again curtailed her maritime jurisdiction, and declared that her Court of Admiralty should not meddle with anything done upon the waters of the State within the limits of a county.[4]

---

[1] Rhode Island Schedules, Penhallow *v.* Doane, 3 Dallas, 54 (1795).

[2] Act of March 8, 1780, McKean's Edition of Pennsylvania Laws, 308. This act was due no doubt to the danger of maintaining the controversy which arose out of the famous case of Gideon Olmstead, hereafter noticed in the text, which produced a serious collision between Pennsylvania and Congress, and led to conferences between Committees of Congress and of the State Legislature.

[3] Laws of Virginia, 1779, Chap. 26; (Nicolson's Laws, p. 104.)

[4] Laws of New York, 14th Feb., 1787. Chap. 24 (Vol. II. p. 394.)

CHAPTER IV.

CONGRESSIONAL COMMITTEES OF APPEAL: SPECIAL COMMITTEES: STANDING COM-
MITTEE OF APPEAL: GROWTH OF FEDERAL POWER: CASE OF SLOOP "ACTIVE."

FROM this brief view of the State establishments we turn to the action of Congress. The purpose of that body to take only appellate jurisdiction was misunderstood at the outset. The first application was for the exercise of its original jurisdiction, made on the 31st of January, 1776, by Mr. Barbarie, owner of a sloop and cargo said to have been taken by the enemy and retaken by one of the Continental vessels of war; but he was informed that he ought to prosecute his claim before the Court to be appointed in the colony to which the prize had been carried.[1] A similar application was made in the case of the *Nancy*, but it was resolved that "the cause pertaineth to the judicature established in the colony of Connecticut for hearing and determining matters of the kind."[2] On the 4th of April, however, Congress was tempted, upon the memorial of an interested party, to regulate the sale of a prize-vessel, which had been run ashore, and the disposition of the proceeds; but as it afterwards appeared that the prize-master had acted contrary to the mode prescribed, and without the authority of Congress, the previous resolution was repealed.[3]

---

[1] Journals of Congress, Vol. II, p. 46.   Judge Davis's Pamphlet on Federal Court of Appeals in Cases of Capture, p. 4 ; 131 United States Reports, Appendix XIX.

[2] *Ibid.* p. 74.

[3] *Ibid.* pp. 116–174.   Davis's Pamphlet, p. 5.

The first appeal came up on the 5th of August, 1776, in the case of the *Thistle* which had been tried in the previous June before Judge George Ross and a jury in the Admiralty Court of Pennsylvania, upon the libel of the commander of the *Congress*, a private sloop-of-war, which had captured the schooner in the Gulf of Florida while bound on a voyage to Jamaica, with a cargo of supplies intended, as was alleged, for the British army. The case was heard upon libel, answer and proofs, after due notice in the public prints of the day, and was conducted by the well-known Joseph Reed and the celebrated William Lewis, then on the threshold of his distinguished professional career. The jury found, contrary to the overwhelming weight of the testimony, that a part of the vessel and cargo belonged to inhabitants of Great Britain, and that the residue belonged to persons who were also enemies, and thereupon the Judge entered a decree of condemnation as prize and directed a public sale.[1] From this verdict and sentence the owner appealed. At first there was a disposition on the part of Congress to hear the case as a body, but after various postponements it was referred to a special committee consisting of Messrs. Stockton, Huntington, Paine, Wilson and Stone, whose report, reversing the decree, was received and approved on the 25th of September.[2]

A few days later the gallant exploits of John Manly, Daniel Waters and John Ayres, commanders of the three armed vessels, *Hancock*, *Lee* and *Lynch*, who did so much to create a reputation for the American navy, were reviewed in an appeal by the captors of the *Elizabeth* against[i]

[1] See original papers in the case of the *Thistle* in the Office of the Clerk of the Supreme Court of the United States. Also Supplement to *Pennsylvania Evening Post*, June 15, 1776, No. 219, p. 301.

[2] Journals of Congress, Vol. II, pp. 280, 289, 307, 328, 390.

4

a decree of Judge Joshua Brackett, of the Court Maritime of New Hampshire, discharging the vessel and cargo. Messrs. Paine, Huntington and Stone again acted as a special committee, with Messrs. Wythe and Smith, when after full argument by counsel, and a most elaborate review of the facts drawn up by the future Chancellor of Virginia, the report of the committee, reversing the decree, was, after a slight modification, adopted, and the cause was remitted to the State Court with directions to proceed and carry out the judgment of the appellate court.[1]

The practice of referring appeals as they were presented to special committees, the members of which were styled "Commissioners," was adhered to in several cases;[2] but in the mean time, it was determined, with a view of securing some uniformity of action, that a special committee of four should be appointed to review such of the resolutions of Congress as related to the capture and condemnation of prizes, and report what alterations or additions should be made.[3] This duty was assigned to George Wythe, John Rutledge,

---

[1] See case of the *Elizabeth.* Papers on file in the Office of the Clerk of the Supreme Court of the United States. Journals of Congress, Vol. II, pp. 369, 370, 387, 389, 393.

[2] The *Charming Peggy*, referred, October 17, 1776, to Messrs. Huntington, Paine, Wythe, Smith and Wilson. Journals of Congress, Vol. II. p. 420. The sloop *Betsy*, referred, November 7, 1776, to Messrs. Wythe, Paine, Wilson, Hooper and Rutledge. *Ibid.* p. 449. The sloop *Vulcan*, referred, November 27, 1776, to Messrs. Wythe, Paine, Wilson, Hooper and Chase. *Ibid.* p. 482. Libel of Esek Hopkins *v.* Richard Derby, ordered December 31, 1778, to be prosecuted before the Committee of Appeals (none named as members). *Ibid.* p. 320. The brig *Richmond*, referred, January 4, 1777, to the committee appointed on November 27th last, Mr. J. D. Sergeant and Mr. William Ellery being named in place of Mr. Wythe and Mr. Paine. Journals of Congress, Vol. III, p. 6. The brig *Phœnix*, referred, January 11, 1777, to the same committee. *Ibid.* pp. 16, 195.

[3] Journals of Congress, Vol. II. p. 420, 17th October, 1776.

Robert Treat Paine and Samuel Huntington, and as the result of their conference it was resolved, on the 30th of January, 1777, that a Standing Committee, consisting of five members, should be appointed to hear and determine upon all appeals brought against sentences passed on libels in the Courts of Admiralty in the respective States, agreeable to the resolutions of Congress, and that the several appeals, when lodged with the Secretary, be by him delivered to them for their final determination.[1] The members chosen were James Wilson, of Pennsylvania, Jonathan Dickinson Sergeant, of New Jersey, William Ellery, of Rhode Island, Samuel Chase, of Maryland, and Roger Sherman, of Connecticut. To these were added, in the following March, John Adams, of Massachusetts, George Read, of Delaware, and Thomas Burke, of North Carolina. The composition of this committee was favorable to an intelligent and dispassionate performance of its duties, as its members were among the most experienced lawyers in the public service, but in less than two months it was found to be too numerous for efficient work, and it was again reduced to five, any three of whom were empowered to hear and determine upon any appeal. Messrs. Wilson, Adams, Sergeant and Burke were retained, and James Duane, of New York, was added, with authority to appoint a register.[2] The conviction was gaining ground, however, as the lessons of experience multiplied, that the only method of avoiding the

---

[1] Journals of Congress, Vol. III, p. 43.

[2] *Ibid.* pp. 84-174. Changes took place from time to time in the composition of this committee, until January 15, 1780, when Congress established a Court of Appeals. Those who are interested in tracing these changes will be spared the labor of hunting through the Journals of Congress by consulting the Pamphlet of Judge J. C. Bancroft Davis, on the Federal Court of Appeals, in Cases of Captures, pp. 5-6-7. 131 United States Reports, Appendix XIX.

evils of frequent changes in a body entrusted with judicial powers, was to adopt the original suggestion of Washington; and on August 5, 1777, a day was assigned to take into consideration the propriety of establishing a Court of Appeals.[1]

The subject, though discussed from time to time, was not finally acted on until the 15th of January, 1780. It is important to observe that the necessity of vesting in Congress the power to establish judicial tribunals, consisting of Judges who should be independent of that body, had been fully discussed and amply provided for in the final draft of the Ninth Article of Confederation. Though not agreed upon until November 15, 1777, or finally ratified by all the States until March, 1781, yet there was displayed in its various stages of development the rapid growth of the idea that the United States in Congress assembled should have the sole and exclusive right of establishing rules for deciding, in all cases, what captures on land or water should be legal, and in what manner prizes taken by land or naval forces in the service of the United States should be divided or appropriated. To these were added the power of granting letters of marque and reprisal in time of peace, appointing Courts for the trial of piracies and felonies committed on the high seas, and establishing Courts for receiving and determining finally appeals in all cases of capture, with the proviso that no member of Congress should be appointed a judge of any of said Courts, and further, that the judicial power to be established by Congress should be the last resort on appeal in all disputes between two or more States concerning boundary or jurisdiction, as well as in all controversies concerning the

---

[1] Journals of Congress, Vol. III, p. 312.

private right of soil claimed under different grants of two or more States.[1]

Herein lay the germ of our National judiciary—the seminal principle which subsequently unfolded itself in the Constitution of the United States. The public mind was now ready to receive it, the soil had been prepared, and it required but time and favorable circumstances to quicken it.

A case was now presented to Congress which made a profound and permanent impression, and did more to expose the weakness of the system under which the States were operating than any other event to be found in the judicial annals of the period.

In September, 1778, Gideon Olmstcad, of Connecticut, and three associates were captured by the British and carried to Jamaica, where they were put on board the sloop *Active*, bound for New York with a cargo of supplies, and forced to assist in the navigation of the vessel. They rose upon the master and crew, took possession of the sloop, and steered for Little Egg Harbor. When in sight of land they were forcibly taken by the armed brig *Convention*, belonging to Pennsylvania, and carried to Philadelphia, where the *Active* was libeled as prize. A claim was also made by the captain of a privateer cruising in concert with the *Convention*. The case was tried in the State Admiralty Court before Judge Ross and a jury, under an act which provided that the find-

---

[1] Compare the projected Articles of Confederation presented by Dr. Franklin on the 21st of July, 1775, with those in the handwriting of John Dickinson, on the 12th of July, 1776, and those reported in the new draft of 20th of August, 1776, by the Committee of the Whole, and the proceedings subsequent to the 8th of April, 1777, when the matter was taken up and debated, and the final form determined on November 15, 1777. Secret Journals of Congress, Vol. III, p. 502. Tit. History of the Confederation, published at Boston, 1820. Also Preston's "Documents Illustrative of American History," pp. 223, 224.

ing of facts by the jury should be final, without re-examination or appeal. The Connecticut captors were awarded but a fourth of the prize, the residue being divided between the State of Pennsylvania and the officers and crew of the *Convention* and the privateer. An appeal was taken to Congress, and referred to the Standing Committee of Appeals, and, after a full argument, the action of the State Court was reversed. Judge Ross refused to recognize the authority of Congress, insisting that the verdict was conclusive, and, in defiance of a writ in the nature of an injunction, issued by the Congressional Committee, ordered the sloop and cargo to be sold and the proceeds to be brought into Court. Thereupon the Committee declared that they were unwilling to resort to any summary proceedings lest consequences might ensue dangerous to the peace of the United States, but firmly declined to hear any other appeals until their authority as a Court of last resort should be so settled as to give full effect to their decrees. The matter was taken up by Congress and a spirited declaration entered upon its Journals in support of its authority, based upon the argument that a control by appeal was necessary to secure a just and uniform execution of the law of nations, and that it would be an absurdity to trust such matters to the accidental verdicts of juries in the State Courts. Conferences were held between Congressional and Legislative Committees with little effect, and so far as the rights of Olmstead were concerned, the decree in his favor remained a *brutum fulmen* until, many years afterwards, he secured the powerful interposition of the Supreme Court of the United States.[1]

---

[1] United States *v.* Judge Peters, 5 Cranch, 115 (1809) See *post.*, pp. 213–214. Also Papers in the case of the sloop *Active*, in the Office of the Clerk of the Supreme Court of the United States; The Whole Proceedings in the case of Olmstead *v.* Rittenhouse, by Richard Peters, Jr., Philadelphia, 1809.

CHAPTER V.

ESTABLISHMENT OF THE COURT OF APPEALS IN CASES OF CAPTURE: JUDGES: CASE OF THE BRIG "SUSANNAH": DECAY OF THE COURT: ANALYSIS OF ITS WORK.

THE Continental Congress had declared that the absolute control by appeal was vested in them "over all jurisdictions for deciding the legality of captures on the high seas." But although powerless to enforce their decree, the members were so deeply impressed by the necessity for some definite action that on the 15th of January, 1780, they resolved "that a Court be established for the trial of all appeals from the Courts of Admiralty in these United States, in cases of capture, to consist of three Judges, appointed and commissioned by Congress, either two of whom, in the absence of the other, were to hold the said Court for the despatch of business."[1] The Court was to appoint its own register: trials were to be had therein according to the usage of nations and not by jury. The Judges were to hold their first session at Philadelphia, and afterwards at such times and places as they should deem most conducive to the public good, not further eastward than Hartford, Connecticut, or southward than Williamsburg, Virginia: the salaries were to be fixed, and in the mean time twelve thousand dollars were to be advanced to each. A few days later Congress proceeded to the election of Judges, and selected George Wythe, of Virginia, William Paca, of Maryland, and Titus

---

[1] Journals of Congress, Vol. VI, p. 10.

Hosmer, of Connecticut. The former declined, and Cyrus Griffin, of Virginia, was chosen in his stead. Commissions were issued;[1] the Court was styled "The Court of Appeals in Cases of Capture;" suitable oaths were prescribed; the method of conducting an appeal was stated, and all appeals then depending before Congress or the Commissioners of Appeals were referred to the newly erected tribunal, and all papers relating thereto were transferred from the Secretary of Congress to the register of the Court.[2] The resolution as adopted, though far in advance of anything that had been accomplished up to this time, lacked several important provisions which had been inserted in the first draft. Clauses providing that the Judges should have the powers of a court of record in fining and imprisoning for contempt and disobedience; that the State Admiralty Courts should execute their decrees, and that a Marshal should be appointed, were stricken out.[3] Thus a tribunal of which much was expected was shorn of necessary and proper powers, on the ground that it would not be wise to confer too high authority upon the Court or assume too extensive a jurisdiction for Congress, so difficult was it to overcome the prejudices of statesmen, even in the light of current events, against liberal grants to the Federal Government. The tenure of the Judges was uncertain, and on June 25, 1781, an ordinance providing that they should "hold their commissions during good behavior" was lost.[4] The Court occasionally required aid from legislative action.

---

[1] For form of Commission see Journals of Congress, Vol. VI, p. 15.

[2] *Ibid.* p. 52.

[3] Papers of the Old Congress in the State Department at Washington, 29, 375. "Ordinance for Establishing," &c., endorsed "December 5, 1779;" a vote of four States for it and four against, is noted upon it.

[4] Journals of Congress, Vol. VII, p. 107.

In the case of the *Holker* an appeal had been entered, but owing to the indisposition and death of the register the necessary stipulations had not been entered into within due time. The Court refused to receive the bonds offered, being "by strictness of law incapable to interpose." Congress, by resolution, instructed the Court to receive and hear the appeal upon notice to the opposing parties and the entry of proper security.[1] An effort was also made to bring in an ordinance for the regulation of the proceedings of the Admiralty Courts in the States, and to revise and collect into one body the resolutions of Congress; to establish convenient rules of decision, and to call on the several legislatures to aid the powers reserved to Congress by the Articles of Confederation, but it bore no fruit.[2]

The work of the Court was performed during the first two years by Messrs. Paca and Griffin, Judge Hosmer having died in office early in August, 1780. Their decisions, though few in number, met with the approbation of foreign governments and jurists, and drew from the Count de Vergennes, at that time Prime Minister of France, an expression of admiration, which he directed the Chevalier de la Luzerne, the envoy of that nation, to communicate to Mr. Paca.[3] In November, 1782, Paca became Governor of Maryland, and resigned his judgeship; and, on December 5th, George Read, of Delaware, and John Lowell, of Massachusetts, were chosen to serve with Mr. Griffin, the presidency being given by lot to Mr. Read.[4]

It appears from the record that Congress had not resigned

---

[1] Journals of Congress, Vol. VII, p. 141.
[2] Journals of Congress, Vol. VII, p. 120.
[3] Sanderson's "Lives of the Signers," Vol. IV, p. 122.
[4] Journals of Congress, Vol. VIII, p. 21.

all control over the actions of the Court, for on the 8th of January, 1784, upon the memorial of one of the agents of the Prussian ship *Minerva*, concerning a decree of the Court of Appeals, it was resolved that the memorial, with the papers accompanying it, be referred to the judges to report to Congress, as speedily as may be, the proceedings, proofs and judgment in the case. It is not known, however, what became of this instruction.[1]

In the same month the case of the brig *Susannah* was brought before Congress, upon the representation of the legislature of New Hampshire, touching the extent of the right of appeal to Congress in cases of capture under their Act of Assembly, and it was ordered that all proceedings upon the sentence of the Court of Appeals ought to be stayed.[2] The matter involved an examination of the powers of Congress, substantially the same as that in the Olmstead case; but though reported on at great length, and leading to a somewhat acrimonious debate, in the course of which a motion that it was improper for Congress in any manner to reverse or control the decisions, judgments, or decrees of the Court of Appeals was lost, the question was not finally settled until brought before the Supreme Court of the United States, in the shape of the case of Penhallow *v.* Doane, which finally determined the controversy in favor of the action of the Court in support of Federal power.[3] The business of the Court soon dwindled, and in a letter of December 23, 1784, the judges informed Congress that all the cases which had been brought before them had been determined. The Com-

---

[1] Journals of Congress, Vol. IX, p. 16.
[2] *Ibid.* Vol. IX, pp. 17, 27, 33, 68.
[3] Journals of Congress, Vol. IX, p. 69. Penhallow *v.* Doane, 3 Dallas, 54 (1795).

mittee to which the matter was referred reported that in their opinion the Judges were still in commission, and that it would still be necessary for the Court to remain upon its present establishment, except with respect to salaries, which should cease, and that in lieu thereof they should receive a per diem allowance during the time they should be in active service, including the time spent in necessary traveling. This led to a remonstrance from Mr. Griffin, but on the 9th of February, 1786, Congress resolved that though fully impressed with a sense of the ability, fidelity, and attention of the Judges of the Court of Appeals, yet, as the war was at an end, and the business of the Court in a great measure done away, attention to the interests of their constituents made it necessary that the salaries of the Judges should cease.[1]

About the same time the State Courts began to assume jurisdiction over appeals, while in Pennsylvania the High Court of Errors and Appeals was expressly constituted by the Act of February 28, 1780, to hear appeals from the Supreme Court, the Register's Court, and the Court of Admiralty, and the Act was conformed to in several cases which did not reach the Federal Court.[2] The labors of the Court of Appeals in Cases of Capture, however, were not yet at an end. On the 27th June, 1786, on the report of a committee to whom were referred several memorials and petitions from persons claiming vessels in the Admiralty Courts of some of the

---

[1] Journals of Congress, Vol. IX, p. 304.

[2] Montgomery *v.* Henry, 1 Dallas, 49, April, 1780. Talbot *v.* The owners of Three Brigs, *Ibid.* 95, September, 1784. In this case it was contended that an appeal properly lay to the Federal Court of Appeals, but the decision of John Dickinson, then a Judge of the High Court of Errors and Appeals, sustained the State jurisdiction. Purviance *v.* Angus, *Ibid.* 180, September, 1786. All of these were appeals from the Admiralty Court in Pennsylvania, and proceeded no further.

States, praying for hearings and re-hearings before the Court of Appeals, it was resolved by Congress that the judges be directed, in every case, to sustain appeals and grant re-hearings or new trials wherever justice and right might require it. It was also ordered that the Court assemble in the following November, at the City of New York, for the despatch of such business as might come before it.[1] The last entry in the Journals of Congress relating to the Court was on the 24th of July, 1786, empowering it to hear an appeal against a decree in the Court of Admiralty of South Carolina, condemning the sloop *Chester*, in which Alexander Hamilton appeared for the appellants. The judges met again, however, in New York, during May, 1787, as appears by several reported cases, and by opinions and decrees delivered at that time.[2] They then proceeded to Philadelphia, where, on the 16th of May they held their last session, and adjourned without day, and the Court, which has been characterized by Professor Jameson, not simply as the predecessor, but as one of the origins of the Supreme Court of the United States, passed into history at the very moment when the Federal Convention was engaged in the lofty task of erecting a far more comprehensive and effective judiciary as a part of the system adopted by the people of the United States in order to form a more perfect union, establish justice, insure domestic tranquillity, provide for the common defence, promote the general welfare and secure the blessings of liberty to themselves and their posterity.

[1] Journals of Congress, Vol. IX, p. 201.
[2] Lake *v.* Hulbert and Chester *v.* Experiment, 2 Dallas, pp. 40–41 (1787).

ANALYSIS OF THE WORK OF THE COURT.

An analysis of the papers, records and proceedings of the Court of Appeals, which were deposited in the Office of the Clerk of the Supreme Court of the United States, under the Act of Congress of May 8, 1792, shows that there were one hundred and ten prize cases decided by special committees, the Standing Committee of Appeals in the Continental Congress, and the Court of Appeals, exclusive of the eight reported by Dallas.[1] In forty-five of these the judgments of the State Courts were reversed; in thirty-nine the judgments were affirmed; twelve were dismissed, the parties not appearing; jurisdiction was declined in two; four were settled by the parties; while the final action in eight is not known, as the decrees are missing; one was stricken off because the appeal came too late, and in one the action is doubtful. Twelve cases came from Pennsylvania, in eight of which the judgments were affirmed, and in three reversed, the remaining case being settled. Three cases came from New Hampshire, in all of which the judgments were reversed. Twenty-seven cases came from Massachusetts, of which fifteen were affirmances, seven reversals, two were settlements, two were dismissals, and in one the result is unknown. Two came from Virginia, both being reversed. Rhode Island furnished ten, in two of which the judgments were affirmed, in seven reversed, and one case was dismissed. Georgia supplied but two, one being affirmed, and in the other the result is unknown. Maryland had one affirmance to three reversals.

---

[1] See list given by Hon. J. C. Bancroft Davis in Pamphlet already quoted, verified by an examination of the papers in the Office of the Clerk of the Supreme Court of the United States, and 2 Dallas' Reports, 1 to 42.

North Carolina four affirmances and five reversals and two dismissals. South Carolina, like Georgia, presents one affirmance and one unknown result. Connecticut out of fifteen cases counts one affirmance, ten reversals, four dismissals and one unknown result. New Jersey met with better fortune, the affirmances numbering six, the reversals four, the dismissals two and the unknown results three. Delaware furnished one affirmance and two settlements. New York does not appear in the list, owing to the fact that during the greater part of the war the British were in actual occupation of her only sea-port.

An examination of the records in each case, consisting of certified copies of the proceedings in the Courts below, and of depositions and proofs, leads to a general concurrence with the results reached by the appellate body. It is clear that the very large number of reversals is almost exclusively due to the mistaken views taken by the juries of the facts. In almost every case the verdict was swayed by local considerations and sectional prejudices. Each claimant of a prize naturally sought the Courts of his native State and there secured the favorable action of his fellow-citizens in the face of sometimes overwhelming adverse proof. Captures were made of friendly vessels, bound on innocent errands, as in the case of the *Thistle*, while in that of the *Elizabeth*, the Wardens of the Old North Meeting-House, in Boston, claimed that they had been despoiled of one iron spindle, two large iron clamps and three pounds of sheet-lead intended for the weather-vane. In another case the redoubtable General Putnam bitterly complains of the loss of a barrel of oysters, and in another several spinsters of Providence charged that the enterprising Captain Manly had seized as his prize a lot of household articles belonging to them. Conflicts, too, arose out of joint captures made by vessels fitted out at the expense of two or more individual States, or of a State vessel and one cruising under Continental authority. The action of the Appellate Court seems in most instances to have been guided by sound sense, impartial justice, skill and experience in applying the rules of evidence and by a competent knowledge of prize law. Reversals upon pure questions of law were very rare, and it is a high tribute to the judicial knowledge, impartial conduct and correct judgment of Judge Francis Hopkinson, of the Admiralty Court of Pennsylvania, that out of forty-nine cases, in which he has reported his decrees, and the reasons upon which they were based, but nine appeals were taken, and in eight of these he was sustained.[1] A similar meed of praise is due to Timothy Pickering, Jr., Judge of the Maritime Court of Massachusetts, and to John Foster, Judge in Rhode Island of the Court erected for the Control of Prize Causes. The valor, enterprise and brilliant successes of the American Navy are imperishably preserved in the records of the Court whose career we have traced during a period which constitutes one of the most dramatic chapters in the history of the nation.

It has been well observed by a recent writer that it cannot be doubted that the Court of Appeals in Cases of Capture, though, as remarked by counsel in the case of Jennings *v.* Carson,[2] "unpopular in those States which were attached to trial by jury," had an educative influence in bringing the people of the United States to consent to a successor. It could hardly be that one hundred and eighteen

---

[1] The Works of Francis Hopkinson, Vol. III. "Judgments in the Admiralty of Pennsylvania," Philadelphia, 1792. Bee's Admiralty Cases, South Carolina (339–440).

[2] Jennings *v.* Carson, 4 Cranch, 9 (1807).

cases, though all in one restricted branch of judicature, should be brought by appeal from State Courts to a Federal tribunal without familiarizing the mind with the complete idea of a superior judicature, in Federal matters, exercised by Federal Courts.[1]

---

[1] Professor J. Franklin Jameson, "Essays in the Constitutional History of the United States," p. 44, to whose admirable paper, as well as to that of Hon. J. C. Bancroft Davis, I am deeply indebted, although in every instance I have consulted the original authorities and reached my own results.

CHAPTER VI.

OTHER FEDERAL COURTS: COURTS FOR THE TRIAL OF FELONIES AND PIRACIES: COURTS FOR THE DETERMINATION OF CONTROVERSIES BETWEEN THE STATES AS TO BOUNDARY, TERRITORY AND JURISDICTION: CONTROVERSIES BETWEEN INDIVIDUALS CLAIMING LANDS UNDER GRANTS OF TWO OR MORE STATES: SUIT BY AN INDIVIDUAL AGAINST A STATE.

COURTS FOR THE TRIAL OF FELONIES AND PIRACIES.

CLOSELY allied to the Admiralty jurisdiction which we have just reviewed was the grant to Congress by the Ninth Article of the Confederation of the sole and exclusive right and power of appointing Courts for the trial of piracies and felonies committed on the high seas. This power was exercised upon the 5th of April, 1781, by the passage of an Ordinance which, after reciting that it was expedient that such Courts should be speedily created and offenders brought to trial, ordained that every person who should commit any piracy or felony upon the high seas, or should be charged as accessory to the same, either before or after the fact, should be proceeded against by grand and petit juries, according to the course of the Common law. No separate Court was established, but the justices of the Supreme or Superior Court of judicature, and the judge of the Court of Admiralty of the several and respective States, or any two or more of them, were designated as being constituted and appointed judges for hearing and trying such offenders.[1] In States where there

---

[1] Journals of Congress, Vol. VII, p. 65.

were several Judges of the Admiralty, the Governors were directed to commission one of them exclusively to join in performing these duties. Process was regulated; the pains of death, forfeiture of lands, goods and chattels were prescribed as punishments, and the benefit of clergy was denied whenever the same was taken away for like offences committed upon land. The ordinance was subsequently amended on March 4th, 1783, but merely in minor particulars.[1]

COURTS FOR THE TRIAL OF CONTROVERSIES BETWEEN STATES.

The second important class of cases in which the Continental Congress was called upon to exercise judicial powers, or, what was in effect the same thing, delegate judicial authority by erecting courts, was in controversies between the States as to territory and boundaries, or between individuals claiming lands under grants from different States. These naturally attracted much attention because of the questions of sovereignty involved, which had raged with such fierceness as in some instances to lead to bloodshed, and to conditions of civil disturbance which threatened to impair the harmony of the Union. Of such grave importance had the matter become, and so apparent was the necessity for National control, that in the Ninth Article of Confederation, adopted by Congress on the 15th of November, 1777, which contained a specific enumeration of Federal powers, it was provided that the United States in Congress assembled should be the last resort on appeal in all disputes and differences then subsisting, or that might arise thereafter, between two or more States con-

[1] Journals of Congress, Vol. VIII, p. 109.

cerning boundary, jurisdiction or any other cause whatsoever. A mode of establishing a Court in each case was specifically prescribed, and all controversies concerning the private right of soil claimed under different grants of two or more States were to be settled, as near as might be, in the same manner. It is interesting to observe that in the draft of the Articles of Confederation presented by Dr. Franklin on the 21st of July, 1775, the matter is but lightly touched, the only provision being that the power and duty of Congress should extend in this particular to "the settling all disputes and differences between colony and colony about limits, or any other cause, if such should arise."[1] It was not until the draft by John Dickinson appeared on the 12th of July, 1776, that the matter began to assume the definite form in which it was finally adopted.[2]

The change is due to the fact that in October, 1775, the controversy between Connecticut and Pennsylvania as to the territory known as Wyoming had proceeded to such extremities as to attract widespread attention. At that time the delegates of the smaller State informed Congress that they had met those from Pennsylvania, but had been unable to adjust the disputes between the people of the two colonies on the waters of the Susquehanna, which had led to actual war, and asked for a special committee to consider the matter and report.[3] John Rutledge, Samuel Chase, Thomas Jefferson, James Kinsey and Stephen Hopkins were formally appointed, and, in December, Congress, by resolution, recommended that

[1] Franklin's Draft, Article V. History of the Confederation. Secret Journals of Congress, Vol. I, p. 26, par. 9.

[2] Compare Franklin's Draft, Article V, with Dickinson's Article XVIII, and the Final Article IX, as adopted. Secret Journals, pp. 268, 269, 281, 340.

[3] Journals of Congress, Vol. I, pp. 220, 221.

the contending parties cease hostilities and every appearance of force, until the dispute could be legally determined; that all property taken should be restored to the original owners, that there should be no interruption to freedom of travel, and that all prisoners on either side should be permitted to return to their homes; that as far as possible the former status should be re-established, and that nothing in these recommendations should prejudice the claims of either party.[1] The territory in dispute embraced one degree of latitude and five degrees of longitude; it contained more than five million acres of land, rich in hidden and unknown treasures of coal, iron and oil; sheltering in its bosom that fair and fertile valley made desolate by Indian massacre, and immortalized in the verse of one of the most gifted of English poets; a region fascinating to the artist as well as to the historian, beautiful in scenery, romantic in traditions, a royal heritage, which Connecticut pioneers, under the terms of a charter, both boundless and indefinite, had begun to colonize as early as 1753. In 1768 they came into conflict with settlers under the Penns, who had obtained the Indian title, and who claimed that they were within the bounds prescribed by the Charter of Charles II. Then ensued a contest for control, the erection of stockades, the building of forts, sieges in mid-winter, storming parties, taking of prisoners, stratagems, ruses and surprises, until, in 1771, the Connecticut men were left in quiet possession. They established a government, laid out townships, formed settlements, levied and collected taxes, passed laws for the direction of civil suits and for the punishment of crimes, and maintained themselves in peace and prosperity, until taken under the law and protection of the

---

[1] Journals of Congress, Vol. I, p. 299.

"ancient and high-standing" colony of Connecticut, by the action of her General Assembly, in erecting all the territory from the River Delaware to a line fifteen miles west of the Susquehanna into a town, with all the corporate power of other towns of the colony, to be called Westmoreland, attaching it to the county of Litchfield. It was this effort on the part of Connecticut as a State to assert and exercise her sovereignty over this region that was resisted by Pennsylvania. Under the orders of the Government, Colonel Plunkett, with a force of about five hundred men, and a train of boats and stores of ammunition, moved up the North Branch of the Susquehanna to drive off the Connecticut settlers from the Wyoming country. About three hundred of these met him at Nanticoke, and repulsed him, with some loss of life on both sides. It was at this point that Congress intervened in the manner stated, and recommended to Connecticut that she should not introduce any new settlers to the disputed lands until the further order of Congress. Peace once more reigned, but the Articles of Confederation having been finally ratified by all the States, and entered upon the Journals in March, 1781, by which Congress was invested with full authority and jurisdiction over controversies of this nature, Pennsylvania, through her Supreme Executive Council, presented in the following November a petition respecting the dispute and prayed a hearing. Congress assigned the fourth Monday in June following for the appearance of the States, and directed notice to be given. On the day appointed the States appeared by their agents. An effort was made by Connecticut to postpone the proceedings until "after the termination of the present war," without success, and, after further objections on her part, which were overruled, the agents of the two States were directed "to appoint, by joint consent, commissioners or judges, to constitute a Court for hearing and determining the matter in question." On the 12th of August, 1782, Congress was informed that they had agreed upon the Hon. William Whipple, of New Hampshire, Major-General Nathaniel Greene, of Rhode Island, Hon. David Brearley and William Churchill Houston, Esq., of New Jersey, Hon. Cyrus Griffin and Joseph Jones, Esq., of Virginia, and Hon. John Rutledge, of South Carolina, any five or more of whom should constitute the Court. Subsequently, Mr. Thomas Nelson, of Virginia, and Mr. Welcome Arnold, of Rhode Island, were substituted for General Greene and Mr. Rutledge. It was agreed that the Court should sit at Trenton, in the following November. On the 18th of that month, a quorum then being present, the Court was organized and entered upon its work, with Messrs. Whipple, Arnold, Brearley, Houston and Griffin as its members. The judges were sworn before the Hon. Isaac Smith, one of the justices of the Supreme Court of New Jersey, and John Neilson, Esq., was appointed Clerk. The Court was in session for forty-two days. The combat began by a motion on the part of Connecticut that notice be given to the tenants in possession of the disputed lands to appear and defend. It was ruled that this would be outside of the proper construction of the Ninth Article of Confederation and the terms and design of the commissions issued to the judges. Other dilatory motions were then made, all of which were resisted by Pennsylvania, and then evidence both oral and documentary was offered. Fifteen days were devoted to the arguments, the chief one in behalf of Pennsylvania being made by James Wilson, consuming four days, and in behalf of Connecticut, by William Samuel Johnson, who spoke for three days. The titles on both sides were regularly deduced, by which it appeared that Connecticut claimed that the northern bounds and limits of the Grant to William Penn interfered with and overran a portion of the western lands, granted to Connecticut, for the space of one degree of latitude throughout the whole breadth of Penn's Grant, and that Penn had notice of the fact at the time of taking out his patent. Both parties claimed to have extinguished the Indian titles, and Connecticut showed that her settlers had located and improved their lands, and were in a condition to extend their settlements, and had done so under the sanction of her legislature. Pennsylvania claimed that the Connecticut settlers were intruders, who had violently thrust themselves within the undoubted boundaries of Penn's Grant, and that they had been aided and abetted by their State in defiance of law and justice; besides this, Connecticut had been silent for a century as to her rights before asserting them, and was equitably estopped; the terms of Penn's charter were distinct and clear, while those of the adverse grant were indistinct and indefinite. On December 30, 1782, the Court pronounced the following judgment: "We are unanimously of opinion that the State of Connecticut has no right to the lands in controversy. We are also unanimously of opinion that the jurisdiction and pre-emption of all the territory lying within the charter boundary of Pennsylvania, and now claimed by the State of Connecticut, do of right belong to the State of Pennsylvania." [1]

---

[1] The mass of literature relating to the "Connecticut Claims" is very great, but the result is admirably stated in a paper by the Hon. Henry M. Hoyt, Ex-Governor of Pennsylvania, read before the Historical Society of Pennsylvania, November 10, 1879, entitled "Brief of a Title in the Seventeen Townships in the County of Luzerne: A Syllabus of the Controversy between Connecticut and Pennsylvania." I have traced the matter through the Journals of Congress, Vol. VIII, p. 44, *et seq.* and the "History of Wyoming," by Charles Miner, Esq., Philadel-

Fourteen years later it was discovered, from a letter written by the Hon. Cyrus Griffin, a member of the Court, and then a Federal Judge in the District of Virginia, that it had been agreed by all the Commissioners before determining the controversy, that the reasons for the determination should never be given, and that the minority should concede to the determination as the unanimous opinion of the Court.[1] The decision, which was the only one rendered in controversies between States, under the Articles of Confederation, was acquiesced in by Connecticut, and is pointed to exultingly by Bancroft as a shining example of the beneficence of the authority of the Union in quelling the wild strife between contending sovereignties. The judgment was approved by Congress, and constitutes the first settlement of a controversy between States by the decree of a Court established by the United States.

The owners of the private right of soil under Connecticut felt that they were not concluded by the decision, even though they did not know at that time that such was the view of the Court. On the 23d of January, 1784, upon the report of a Committee, consisting of Thomas Jefferson, Richard Henry Lee and Hugh Williamson, to whom the petition of Colonel Zebulon Butler and others had been referred, Congress resolved to institute a court for the trial of Butler's title, who claimed under Connecticut, and who asserted that he was

---

phia, 1845, a work of profound original research. See also Alexander Johnston's "History of Connecticut," American Commonwealth Series, pp. 275, 284. See also 131 United States Reports, Appendix xix, by Hon. J. C. Bancroft Davis.

[1] The letter was first produced upon the trial of Vanhorne's Lessee *v.* Dorrance, 2 Dallas, p. 304 (1795), tried before Paterson, Judge of the Supreme Court of the United States, sitting with Peters, Judge, in April, 1795. The letter is printed in full by Governor Hoyt, "Brief of a Title, &c.," p. 46.

disturbed by others claiming under Pennsylvania,[1] but proceedings were subsequently suspended until the claimants should particularize their claims and show affirmatively that they were entitled to a court, for, as was pointed out, the trial of private right of soil could only be claimed by those who made it clear that there was a conflict between grantees of two or more States.[2] In September the resolution instituting the Court was repealed, as Colonel Butler could not describe with sufficient certainty the tract claimed, nor name with particularity the private adverse claims under grants from Pennsylvania.[3] "The Pennamite and Yankee War" then began. The militia of Pennsylvania was mustered to enforce the writs of Pennsylvania Courts, the property of the Connecticut men was destroyed, their boundary lines were obliterated and their rights generally ignored, when crowding into the distracted region, under the leadership of Ethan Allen, flushed with his success as the founder of Vermont, came many Green Mountain Boys, in the hope of establishing a new State, which they would force Congress and Pennsylvania to recognize. Affairs soon reached a crisis, in which Colonel John Franklin was arrested for high treason, upon a warrant issued by Chief Justice McKean, and the celebrated Timothy Pickering, once Judge of the Admiralty in Massachusetts, Quartermaster-General of the Continental Army, and afterwards Secretary of State of the United States, was kidnapped to secure his release. But Pennsylvania dissipated the clouds of civil war by a series of Acts dictated by a spirit of justice and toleration, by which the lands of actual settlers were

[1] Journals of Congress, Vol. IX, pp. 30, 31.
[2] Journals of Congress, *Ibid.* p. 57.
[3] Journals of Congress, Vol. IX, Appendix.

confirmed to them, and the district was erected into the County of Luzerne.

Other "controversies" arose, which reached various stages of development, although none of them arrived at a formal decree, but were happily settled by the contending States.

Pennsylvania and Virginia differed as to the famous line " commonly called Mason and Dixon's line," and the matter was brought before Congress on the 27th of December, 1779. That body recommended peace and amity, and in the spirit of that recommendation the subject was withdrawn from the passionate debates of statesmen and the learned opinions of judges, and was consigned to the tender care of the reverend clergy in Virginia and learned college professors in Pennsylvania, aided by laymen who knew little of the exciting frays of politics. After some correspondence, which grew out of an agreement entered into at Baltimore, the Rev. James Madison, the Rev. Robert Andrews, Mr. John Page and Mr. Thomas Lewis, on the one side, and Dr. John Ewing, David Rittenhouse, John Lukens and Thomas Hutchins, on the other, were appointed Commissioners, and on the 23d of August, 1784, reported that the line had been established and that the Ohio River had been reached.[1]

New Jersey and Virginia also had their differences respecting a tract of land called Indiana in the territory Northwest of the Ohio, but the affair was settled by the deed of cession presented to Congress by Virginia on the 1st of March, 1784, and accepted by that body. No Court was ever convened, and a motion to commit a petition presented by Colonel George Morgan, agent for New Jersey, praying for a hearing, was lost.[2]

---

[1] 131 United States Reports, Appendix, liii, liv.
[2] Journals of Congress, Vol. IX, p. 45.

Massachusetts and New York appeared at the bar of Congress upon the 3d of June, 1784, upon a petition presented by the legislature of the first-named State praying for the appointment of a Federal Court to adjudicate a claim made by the latter to land lying between the rivers Merrimac and Charles.[1] A day was fixed and notice given. Massachusetts appeared by John Lowell and James Sullivan; New York by James Duane, John Jay, Robert R. Livingston, Egbert Benson and Walter Livingston, all of whom presented their credentials.[2] They were directed by Congress to appoint by joint consent commissioners or judges, and after some delay they agreed upon Robert Hanson Harrison and Thomas Johnson, of Maryland; John Rutledge, of South Carolina; George Wythe, William Grayson and James Monroe, of Virginia; George Read, of Delaware, and Isaac Smith and William Paterson, of New Jersey, any five of whom were to constitute a quorum, and Congress was empowered to fill all vacancies in case of refusals to serve. Harrison, Rutledge and Grayson declined, and their places were taken by John Sitgreaves and Samuel Johnson, both of North Carolina, and William Fleming, of Virginia. The City of Williamsburg was designated as the place for the meeting of the Court. Months rolled away without action, and finally Congress was petitioned to require the attendance of a quorum and to fix a day certain. But by a belated entry on the 8th of October, 1787, it appeared that the controversy had been settled by the action of the States themselves as far back as the previous December, whereupon the commissions of the Judges were revoked and all proceedings stayed.[3]

---

[1] Journals of Congress, Vol. IX, p. 221. [2] *Ibid.* Vol. X, pp. 9-15.
[3] *Ibid.* Vol. X, p. 254; *Ibid.* Vol. XI, p. 58.

South Carolina and Georgia contended as to their jurisdictions upon the upper waters of the Savannah River at the
confluence of the Tugaloo and Keowee, and on the 4th of
September, 1786, John Kean, Charles Pinckney and John Bull
appeared as agents for South Carolina, and William Houstoun,
George Walton and William Few for Georgia. The case is
especially interesting because it presents the only instance of
inability on the part of the State agents to agree upon the
composition of a Court, and a consequent reference to Congress to strike a Court in the manner provided for in the
Ninth Article of Confederation.[1] Three persons were named
by Congress from each of the thirteen States, and from this
list the agents of each party alternately struck one, until the
number was reduced to thirteen; nine were then drawn by lot
from a box in the presence of Congress. Alexander Contee
Hanson, James Madison, Robert Goldsborough, James Duane,
Philemon Dickinson, John Dickinson, Thomas McKean, Egbert
Benson and William Pynchon were chosen. New York City
was selected as the place of meeting, but no record exists to
show that the Court ever convened. The States settled their
differences by a compact signed on the 28th of April, 1787,
several articles of which were subsequently brought before the
Supreme Court of the United States.[2]

A triangular contest was waged between New Hampshire
and Vermont, New York and Vermont, and Massachusetts
and Vermont, for the control of the region lying between
Lake Champlain and the Connecticut River, which had
been conveyed by Wentworth, the only royal governor in
New England, under the seal of New Hampshire, and be-

---

[1] Journals of Congress, Vol. XI, pp. 157-159.
[2] South Carolina *v.* Georgia, 93 U. S. Rep. pp. 5-6 (1876).

came known as the New Hampshire Grants. French, Dutch and English titles conflicted. In 1750 France, who had control of the Lake, sought to establish herself in the Green Mountains; New York pushed her pretensions to the banks of the Great River, under the proclamation of Cadwallader Colden, then acting as Governor, and appealed to the great crown lawyers of England for support; while the grantees under New Hampshire obtained a royal mandate that the governor of New York "do not, upon pain of His Majesty's highest displeasure, presume to make any grants whatsoever of any part of the land described, until His Majesty's further pleasure shall be known concerning the same."[1]

No attention, however, was paid to this impressive warning. The militia was called on to support Colden's authority: new grants were made and actions of ejectment continued to be pressed in the Courts at Albany. To these the Green Mountain Boys, under the rugged leadership of the hero of Ticonderoga and Crown Point, gave no heed, but rallied at Bennington and organized a convention. Here they erected a sign expressive of their defiance. On the very borders of the disputed territory, a post twenty-five feet high bore on its top a huge catamount's skin, stuffed, its teeth displayed towards the hated province of New York. On the 15th of January, 1777, the name of Vermont was adopted and independence of New York was declared. A constitution was framed, State officers were chosen, Thomas Chittenden was elected Governor, and the new order of affairs was recognized by New Hampshire. New York, however, was not disposed to relinquish jurisdiction so readily. On the 29th of May, 1779, a letter from

---

[1] Bancroft's "History of the United States," Last Revision, Vol. II, p. 361. W. H. Carpenter and T. S. Arthur, "History of Vermont," p. 32.

Governor George Clinton was presented to Congress, accompanied by other papers touching the controversy, which were considered in Committee of the Whole. Messrs. Ellsworth, Edwards, Witherspoon, Atlee and Root were directed to visit the inhabitants of the district and ascertain the reasons why they refused to continue as citizens of the States which had theretofore exercised jurisdiction, and it was declared that as Congress were in duty bound, on the one hand, to preserve inviolate the rights of New York and New Hampshire, so, on the other, they would always be careful to provide that the justice due to the States did not interfere with the justice which might be due to individuals.[1]   By September it appeared that animosities had proceeded so far as to endanger the internal peace of the United States, and that it was indispensable for Congress to interpose for the restoration of quiet and good order.   As the people of the New Hampshire grants denied all jurisdiction on the part of neighboring States, a doubt arose as to the right of Congress to intervene without additional authority; hence it was resolved and "most earnestly recommended" to the States of New Hampshire, Massachusetts Bay, and New York forthwith to pass laws expressly authorizing Congress to hear and determine all differences between them relative to their respective boundaries, in the mode prescribed by the Articles of Confederation, and that they also refer all disputes with the people of the district, and also authorize the determination of differences between the grantees of the respective States touching the title to lands.   New York responded by the Act of October 21st, 1779, and New

---

[1] Journals of Congress, Vol. V, pp. 177, 181.   Carpenter's "History of Vermont," Chaps. III and V.   E. H. Roberts' "History of New York," Vol. II. pp. 401, 406.

Hampshire by an Act passed in November. Massachusetts, having no real interest in the controversy, took no action. "The people of the district" would not submit, however, but made various efforts to be admitted as a State. Their attitude, which converted the question into a political rather than a judicial matter, was upheld by the secret sympathy of New Jersey, Rhode Island and Maryland, and rendered the organization of a Court impossible.[1] Many futile discussions were held in Congress, which were participated in by the leading statesmen of the day, and at one time the conduct of the "pretended State of Vermont" was severely animadverted upon, and restitution required to be made to persons who had been condemned to banishment and confiscation of property. In 1781 Massachusetts assented to the recognition of Vermont, New Hampshire soon followed, and New York in 1790. On the 18th of February, 1791, she was admitted to the sisterhood of States, and became under the Constitution a member of the Federal Union.

SUIT AGAINST A STATE.

A solitary instance occurs of the suit of a private citizen against a State in the Courts of another State. A foreign attachment was issued against the Commonwealth of Virginia in the Court of Common Pleas of Philadelphia County at the suit of Simon Nathan, and a quantity of clothing, imported from France, belonging to that State, was attached. The delegates in Congress from Virginia, conceiving this a violation of

[1] Journals of Congress, Vol. V, pp. 276, 283; *Ibid.* Vol. VI, pp. 16-128; *Ibid.* Vol. VII, pp. 129, 189, 210, 228, 231, 244, 260; "The Federalist," VII; 131 U. S. Reports, Appendix lii.

the law of nations and an affront to the dignity of a sovereign, applied to the Supreme Executive Council of Pennsylvania, by whom the Sheriff was ordered to surrender the
goods. The counsel for the plaintiff, finding that the writ was
suppressed, obtained a rule nisi that the Sheriff should make
a return. The question was elaborately argued, and after
consideration the rule was discharged, on the ground that
every kind of process against a sovereign was a violation of
the law of nations, and that no ministerial officer could be
compelled to serve or return a void writ.[1]

[1] Simon Nathan *v.* Virginia, 1 Dallas, 77, in *Notes.*

CHAPTER VII.

DEFECTS OF THE OLD JUDICIAL SYSTEM: INSTANCES OF JUDICIAL FEEBLENESS ON THE PART OF CONGRESS.

WE have now passed in review the various fields of controversy over which the Continental Congress, both before and after the adoption of the Articles of Confederation, exercised or attempted to exercise judicial control. They are few in number and limited in extent, presenting features which are but paltry in comparison with that boundless and richly diversified region developed and cultivated with such assiduity during the past century in the domain of Constitutional law. Cases of prize and capture, felonies and piracies on the high seas, controversies between States, and disputes between individuals claiming lands under grants from different States constitute but an insignificant portion of that ample and noble jurisdiction now exercised by the Courts of the United States. But no one can deny the value of the work done in those rugged fields, or over-estimate the importance of the truths gleaned by the statesmen of the Revolution, in whose awakening minds the conviction gained strength that in order to preserve harmony, establish uniformity, and enforce obedience there was a paramount necessity of clothing the central government with complete control of all those questions which the stern logic of events had proved could not be safely left to the capricious and irregular action of the States. Conflicting regulations, the numerous progeny of local prejudices and narrow views, had bred evils

6

which more than once combined to weaken or destroy the union. Fragmentary grants, imperfect delegations of power, timid concessions and illiberal restrictions lay like heavy fetters upon the limbs of the nation, impeding freedom of movement and crippling energies which might have been exercised for the public good. The vital defect in the old Congressional judicial system—if such it could be called when so stunted and misshapen—lay in the fact that it depended entirely upon State officers to enforce the judgment of the Appellate tribunal when it reversed the decree of a State Court. State Courts refused to enforce the rights of property acquired under its decrees, and we have seen how powerless the higher Court was rendered in the cases of the *Susannah* and the sloop *Active*. The necessity for a competent judicial power co-extensive with the legislative authority of the Union must have been sorely felt, and it only requires reference to a few instances, traceable through the Journals of Congress, in order to arrive at the conclusion that in very many particulars Congress, both as to its legislative functions and its judicial authority, lay prostrate at the feet of the States. Although *a priori* it would be supposed that the power of punishing infractions of the law of nations would have been vested exclusively in Congress, yet we find that in August, 1779, it was resolved that the authorities of Pennsylvania be informed that any prosecution which might be directed should be carried on at the expense of the United States in the State Courts.[1] And in Sweer's case, which occurred in 1778,[2] counsel were employed by Congress to prosecute in the State Court one who was indicted for altering a receipt given by the vendor

---

[1] Journals of Congress, Vol. V, p. 367.
[2] 1 Dallas, 41.

of goods with intent to defraud the United States. It was urged before Chief Justice McKean, upon a motion in arrest of judgment, that " at the time of the offense charged the United States were not a body corporate known in law." Although this assertion was disregarded by the Court, which declared that " from the moment of their association the United States necessarily became a body corporate; for there was no superior from whom that character could otherwise be derived," yet it was plain that this mock sovereign was without the power of self-defence except so far as assistance was extended by the friendly hand of a State constituting but a single member of the Union.[1]

In November, 1781, Congress recommended to the Legislatures of the several States that they should pass laws punishing infractions of the law of nations, and speedily erect tribunals, or clothe those already existing with power to decide on what constituted such an offence, and to expressly authorize suits for damages by the parties injured, or for compensation to the United States for damages sustained by them from an injury done to a foreign power by a citizen.[2]

The States do not seem to have responded, but, in 1784, De Longchamp was convicted and sentenced, in the Court of Oyer and Terminer of Pennsylvania, for committing a violation of the law of nations by insulting M. Marbois, the Secretary of the French Legation, and for committing assault and battery upon him, the Court declaring that the law of nations formed a part of the municipal law of Pennsylvania. This they enforced without the aid of a statute.[3] After the

[1] See also Journals of Congress, Vol. IV, p. 494; *Ibid.*, Vol. V, p. 283. Respublica *v.* Teischer, 1 Dallas, 335 (1788).
[2] See Journals of Congress, Vol. VII, p. 181.
[3] Respublica *v.* De Longchamp, 1 Dallas, p. 111 (1784).

arrest of the offender the Supreme Executive Council of Pennsylvania gave information of the fact to Congress in a letter, and requested their attention, but nothing seems to have come of the application, and it was left to the State Court to take the action stated.[1]

Congress also proved incapable of enforcing judicially its interpretation of the crime of treason. Although upon the 24th of June, 1776, after independence had been resolved upon, the terms allegiance and treason had been defined, the latter consisting in "levying war against any of the colonies, or being adherent to the King of Great Britain or enemies of the said colonies, giving to him or them aid or comfort," yet it was found to be necessary to recommend to the legislatures of the colonies that they should pass laws for punishing persons "provably attainted of open deed by people of their condition."

Pennsylvania acted promptly, and under her laws we find several instances of persons convicted in the year 1778.[2]

Although the power to establish and regulate Post-Offices throughout the United States had been vested in Congress by the Articles of Confederation, and an Ordinance of October, 1782, imposed penalties for official misdemeanors, which were made recoverable by action of debt in the name of the Post-master-General in the State where the offence was committed, yet Congress had no power to exact obedience or punish disobedience by pecuniary mulcts or otherwise, but these were solely dependent upon the laws and tribunals of the several States. In fine, whenever it became necessary to secure the interests

---

[1] Journals of Congress, Vol. IX, Committee of the States, p. 2.

[2] Respublica *v.* Molder, *Id. v.* Molin, *Id. v.* Carlisle, *Id. v.* Roberts, 1 Dallas, pp. 33–40.

of the nation, an application to the State Legislatures was inevitable.

Another example occurs in the appeal, in 1782, of Congress to the States to pass laws to empower Commissioners, appointed by Congress, to settle the accounts of the Military Department, to call for witnesses and examine them on oath touching their accounts.[1] It was even necessary to pass a resolution requesting the States to enact laws to enable the United States to recover from individuals debts due and effects belonging to them.[2] And, in July, 1784, the Committee of States, which sat during the recess of Congress, complained that none of the State Legislatures had made the provisions requested, by which the interests of the United States had already suffered. As further loss of time would be injurious, they again earnestly requested the adoption of measures to enable the United States to sue for and recover their debts, effects and property, and such damages as they had sustained.[3]

It is clear, then, that in cases of vital importance to the nation, the State jurisdictions retained or acquired a power utterly at variance with the real interests of the nation, except in disputes between the States, questions arising under grants of land by two or more States, and in cases of prize and capture, and piracies and felonies on the high seas. The State Courts, it is true, exercised no jurisdiction in causes arising from impost or revenue, for none such existed prior to the present Constitution of the United States. State imposts existed, and the State tribunals entertained the causes arising out of them. Nor was there under the Confederation

---

[1] Journals of Congress, Vol. IV, p. 83; *Ibid.*, Vol. V, p. 296; *Ibid*, Vol. VII, p. 298.

[2] Journals of Congress, Vol. VII, p. 298.

[3] Journals of Congress, Vol. IX, Committee of the States, p. 18.

any tribunal vested with the appellate power which, before the Revolution, had been exercised by the King in Council over the decisions of the courts in the respective Colonies. That was a destiny reserved for the Supreme Court of the United States.

We are now to see how the various fountains of authority, which we have traced to their original springs, were directed by the strong hands and wise heads of the Framers of the Constitution of the United States into the channel of Federal jurisdiction, until small and feeble rills broaden into deep and majestic tributaries of that lordly current which sweeps on through the Union, visiting without inundating every corner of the Republic, and whose waters are for the healing of the Nation.

PART II.

THE ESTABLISHMENT OF THE SUPREME COURT.

CHAPTER VIII.

DEFECTS OF THE ARTICLES OF CONFEDERATION: WANT OF A FEDERAL JUDICA-
TURE: VIEWS OF HAMILTON, MADISON AND OTHERS: THE FEDERAL CON-
VENTION: PLANS FOR A NATIONAL JUDICIARY: COURSE OF THE DEBATE:
FINAL FORM OF PLAN ADOPTED.

THE want of a Federal Judicature, having cognizance of all matters of general concern in the last resort, especially those in which foreign nations and their subjects were interested, was pointed out by Alexander Hamilton as early as May, 1783, as a grievous defect in the Articles of Confederation. He predicted the infringement of national treaties, the violation of national faith and the disturbance of public tranquillity, by the interference of the local regulations of particular States militating, directly or indirectly, against the powers vested in the Union.[1] In "The Federalist" he dwelt upon the want of a judiciary power as a circumstance which crowned the defects of the Confederation:

"Laws are a dead letter," said he, "without courts to expound and define their true meaning and operation. The treaties of the United

---

[1] Alexander Hamilton, "Resolutions for a General Convention 1783, The Federalist, The Continentalist and other Papers," edited by John C. Hamilton, p. 4.

States, to have any force at all, must be considered as part of the law of the land. Their true import, as far as it respects individuals must, like all other laws, be ascertained by judicial determination. To produce uniformity in these determinations, they ought to be submitted, in the last resort, to one Supreme Tribunal. And this tribunal ought to be instituted under the same authority which forms the treaties themselves." He adds: "The treaties of the United States, under the present Constitution, are liable to the infractions of thirteen different legislatures, and as many different Courts of final jurisdiction, acting under the authority of those legislatures. The faith, the reputation, the peace of the whole Union, are thus continually at the mercy of the prejudices, the passions and the interests of every member of which these are composed. Is it possible that foreign nations can either respect or confide in such a government? Is it possible that the people of America will longer consent to trust their honor, their happiness, their safety, on so precarious a foundation." [1]

James Madison entertained similar views. In a letter dated the 16th of April, 1787,—a month before the meeting of the Federal Convention,—addressed to Washington, he says:

"The National supremacy ought also to be extended, as I conceive, to the judiciary department. If those who are to expound and apply the laws are connected by their interests and their oaths with the particular States wholly, and not with the Union, the participation of the Union in the making of the laws may be possibly rendered unavailing. It seems, at least, necessary that the oaths of the judges should include a fidelity to the general, as well as local, Constitution; and that an appeal should lie to some national tribunal in all cases to which foreigners, or inhabitants of other States, may be parties. The admiralty jurisdiction seems to fall within the purview of the National Government." [2]

The same thoughts were working in the minds of men

---

[1] The Federalist, XXII.
[2] Madison's "Debates and Correspondence," Vol. II, p. 714.

less renowned. William R. Davie wrote to a friend: "Be so good as to favor me, by the next post, with your opinion how far the introduction of judicial powers, derived from Congress, would be politic or practicable in the States;" and Richard Dobbs Spaight expressed a sentiment which was becoming common:

"There is no man of reflection, who has maturely considered what must and will result from the weakness of our present Federal Government, and the tyrannical and unjust proceedings of most of the State Governments, if longer persevered in, but must sincerely wish for a strong and efficient National Government." [1]

With such views all four of the gentlemen named entered the Federal Convention. The main business of that body was opened on the 29th of May, 1787, by Edmund Randolph, the Governor of Virginia, who had been selected by his colleagues, on account of his high position, distinguished talents and skill as a public speaker, to present a series of fifteen resolutions, embodying in a concrete form, for the convenience of modification and discussion, those leading ideas of reform proposed as the basis of an efficient Constitutional system. These resolutions were the result of a consultation among Washington, George Mason, Randolph, Dr. McClurg, Madison, George Wythe and John Blair, the two latter being then Judges of the Supreme Court of Appeals of Virginia. The clause relating to the judiciary provided:

"That a National judiciary be established; to consist of one or more supreme tribunals, and of inferior tribunals; to be chosen by the National

[1] Letter of Davie to Iredell, and of Spaight to Iredell. McRee's "Life of Iredell," Vol. II, pp. 161–168.

Legislature; to hold their offices during good behavior, and to receive punctually, at stated times, fixed compensation for their services, in which no increase or diminution shall be made so as to affect the persons actually in office at the time of such increase or diminution. That the jurisdiction of the inferior tribunals shall be to hear and determine, in the first instance, and of the supreme tribunal, in the *dernier resort*, all piracies and felonies on the high seas; captures from an enemy; cases in which foreigners, or citizens of other States, applying to such jurisdictions, may be interested; or which respect the collection of the National revenue, impeachment of any National officers, and questions which may involve the National peace and harmony." [1]

The foregoing constituted a part of "the Virginia Plan."

The plan presented by Mr. Paterson, known as "the New Jersey Plan," differed in some important particulars. It provided for but one Court, which was to be Supreme. No inferior tribunals were mentioned. The judges were to be appointed by the Executive, and the Judiciary so established were to have authority to hear and determine, in the first instance, on all impeachments of Federal officers, and by way of appeal, in the *dernier resort*, in all cases touching the rights of ambassadors; in all cases of captures from an enemy; in all cases of piracies and felonies on the high seas; in all cases in which foreigners might be interested; in the construction of any treaty or treaties, or in questions which might arise on any of the acts for the regulation of trade or the collection of the Federal revenue; and it was provided that none of the judiciary should, during the time they remain in office, be capable of receiving or holding any other office or appointment during the term of service, or for   thereafter. [2]

---

[1] The Madison Papers—Supplement to Elliott's Debates, Vol. V, p. 128.
[2] *Ibid.* p. 192.

Both plans adopted the tenure of good behavior, and a fixed and immutable compensation.

With these plans before them, the Convention, composed chiefly of lawyers, with four judges among them, proceeded to discussion and elaboration. The resolution that a national judiciary be established passed unanimously, and a further clause that it should "consist of one supreme tribunal and of one or more inferior tribunals" passed in the affirmative. A few days later the words "one or more" were stricken out. A vigorous debate then ensued upon the method of selecting the judges. Mr. Wilson, of Pennsylvania, opposed their appointment by the national legislature. Experience, he declared, showed the impropriety of such appointments by numerous bodies. Intrigue, partiality and concealment were the necessary consequences. A principal reason for unity in the executive was that officers might be appointed by a single responsible person. To this John Rutledge replied that he was by no means disposed to grant so great a power to any single person. The people would think that we were leaning too much towards monarchy. Madison preferred a middle course. He disliked the election of the judges by the Legislature, and was not satisfied with referring the appointment to the Executive. He hinted that he inclined to a selection by the Senate. For the time being his views were adopted without dissent. Rutledge then moved to expunge the clause relating to inferior tribunals. He was against establishing any national tribunal except a single supreme one, and he argued that the State tribunals might and ought to be left, in all cases, to decide in the first instance, as the right of appeal to the supreme national tribunal was sufficient to secure the national rights and uniformity of judgments; that it was making an unnecessary encroachment on the jurisdiction of the States, and creating unnecessary obstacles to their adoption of the new system. He was sustained by Roger Sherman, who dwelt chiefly on the expensiveness of having a new set of Courts, when the existing State Courts would answer the same purpose. Madison replied with great spirit that,—

"Unless inferior tribunals were dispersed throughout the Republic with final jurisdiction in many cases, appeals would be multiplied to a most oppressive degree; that, besides, an appeal would not in many cases be a remedy. What was to be done after improper verdicts, in State tribunals, obtained under the biased directions of a dependent judge, or the local prejudices of an undirected jury? To remand the cause for a new trial would answer no purpose. To order a new trial at the Supreme Bar would oblige the parties to bring up their witnesses, though ever so distant from the seat of the Court. An effective judiciary establishment, commensurate to the legislative authority, was essential. A government without a proper executive and judiciary would be the mere trunk of a body without arms or legs to act or move."

The same view was taken by Wilson and Dickinson; the motion of Rutledge, however, prevailed. But Dickinson, in a powerful speech, returned to the question, and contended that if there was to be a national legislature, there ought to be a national judiciary, and pointed out that there was a wide distinction between the absolute establishment of inferior tribunals and the giving of a discretion to the legislature to establish or not to establish them. He therefore moved "that the national legislature be empowered to institute inferior tribunals." Pierce Butler hotly exclaimed that the people would not bear such innovations; the States would revolt at such encroachments. Even supposing such establishments to be useful, we must not venture on them. The example of Solon should be followed, who gave the Athenians not the best government he could devise, but the best they would receive. Then for the first time Rufus King threw himself into the debate. He scorned the idea of expense, and supported the views of Madison, Wilson and Dickinson. A great majority was then obtained for Dickinson's motion.[1]

A strenuous effort was then made by Wilson to associate the Judiciary with the Executive in a negative on the acts of the Legislature. Without some such provision, he argued, the latter could at any moment sink the Executive into non-existence. Madison adopted this view. The Executive would stand in need of being controlled as well as supported. An association of the judges in his revisionary function would both double the advantage and diminish the danger. It would also enable the judiciary the better to defend itself against legislative encroachments; the utility of annexing the wisdom and weight of the Judiciary to the Executive seemed incontestable. Gerry and Charles Cotesworth Pinckney earnestly opposed a plan by which the Executive "would be covered by the sanction and seduced by the sophistry of the Judges." It would destroy the independence of the judiciary, which ought to be separate and distinct from the other great departments. The motion was lost by a vote of eight States to three, Connecticut, New York and Virginia sustaining the affirmative.[2]

It was unanimously agreed "that the jurisdiction of the national judiciary shall extend to cases which respect the collection of the national revenue, impeachments of all national officers, and questions which involve the national peace and harmony."[3]

---

[1] Elliott's Debates, Vol. V, pp. 155–160.
[2] *Ibid.* pp. 151, 155, 164, 165–166
[3] *Ibid.* p. 188.

In this shape the matter was reported by Mr. Gorham as Chairman of the Committee of the Whole, with the additional resolution that the national judiciary consist of one supreme tribunal, the judges of which should be appointed by the second branch of the national legislature, to hold their offices during good behavior, and to receive punctually, at stated times, a fixed compensation for their services, in which no increase or diminution shall be made so as to affect incumbents. At this stage Alexander Hamilton came forward, and after a speech of great power, in which he struck a high key in support of national supremacy, read a sketch, the seventh section of which was in these words:

"The supreme judicial authority to be vested in judges, to hold their offices during good behavior, with adequate and permanent salaries. This Court to have original jurisdiction in all causes of capture, and an appellative jurisdiction in all causes in which the revenues of the General Government or the citizens of foreign nations are concerned." [1]

The debate was resumed at a later day upon all the essential features involved. Gorham, Sherman and Gouverneur Morris favored the appointment of the judges by the executive with the advice and consent of the second branch, a mode ratified by the experience of several of the States for one hundred and forty years, which was finally agreed to. Morris contended that the legislature ought to be at liberty to increase salaries as circumstances might require. Madison thought that this would be highly improper. Whenever an increase was wished by the judges, or the matter was agitated in the legislature, an undue complaisance in the former would be felt toward the latter. If at such a crisis there should be in Court suits to which

[1] Elliott's Debates, Vol. V, p. 205.

leading members of the legislature might be parties, the judges would be in a situation which ought not to be suffered if it could be prevented. The words "no increase" were then stricken out. The tenure of good behavior was unanimously assented to. Once more the debate raged upon the question of inferior tribunals. Once more Pierce Butler exclaimed that he could see no necessity for such tribunals; surely the State Courts might do the business. Luther Martin declared that they would create jealousies and opposition in the State tribunals and lead to many conflicts of jurisdiction. Gorham reminded the Convention that a Federal Court already existed in the States with jurisdiction for the trial of captures, piracies, &c., on the seas. No complaints had ever been made by the States, or by the courts of the States. Inferior tribunals were essential to render the authority of the national legislature effectual. Randolph observed that the courts of the States could not be trusted with the administration of the national laws. The very objects of jurisdiction would often place the general and local policy at variance. Sherman and George Mason urged that such a power might become absolutely necessary. A vote was then taken, and the resolution empowering the national legislature to appoint inferior tribunals was agreed to. The trial of impeachments of national officers was taken from the Federal Courts, and then on the motion of Madison the Federal jurisdiction was unanimously made to "extend to all cases arising under the national laws, or involving the national peace and harmony."[1]

Wilson now renewed his motion "that the Supreme national Judiciary should be associated with the Executive in the revisionary power." Though the proposition had once been

---

[1] Elliott's Debates, Vol. V, pp. 331, 332.

defeated, he was so confirmed, by reflection, in the opinion of its utility, that he thought it incumbent upon him to make another effort. The judiciary ought to have an opportunity of remonstrating against projected encroachments on the people as well as on themselves. Although the judges as expositors of the laws would have an opportunity of defending their constitutional rights, yet the power did not go far enough. Laws might be unjust, unwise, dangerous, destructive, and yet not be so unconstitutional as to justify the judges in refusing to give them effect. Let them share in the revisionary power and they would have an opportunity of taking notice of those features of a law, and of counteracting by the weight of their opinion the improper views of the legislature. The motion was seconded by Madison.

An interesting debate followed, in which great ability was displayed. Gorham did not see the advantage of employing the judges in this way. As judges they are not to be presumed to possess any peculiar knowledge of the mere policy of public measures, nor could it be necessary as a security for their constitutional rights. The judges of England had no such protection, and yet their jurisdiction is not invaded. Far better would it be to let the Executive alone be responsible, and, at most, authorize him to call upon the Judges for their opinions. Ellsworth heartily approved of the motion. The aid of the Judiciary would give wisdom and firmness to the Executive. A systematic and accurate knowledge of the laws was necessary, which the Executive could not be expected always to possess. The law of nations, also, would frequently come into question. Of this the judges alone would have competent information. Madison considered the object of the motion as of the utmost importance to the meditated Constitution. It would be useful to the Judiciary as a defence against Legislative encroachments; it would be useful to the Executive by inspiring confidence and firmness; it would be useful to the Legislature by preserving a consistency, conciseness, perspicuity and technical propriety in the laws—qualities shamefully wanting in our republican codes. It would be useful to the community at large, as an additional check against a pursuit of those unwise and unjust measures which constituted so great a portion of our calamities. It would not give too much strength to either the Executive or the Judiciary. The evil most to be apprehended was that, notwithstanding this co-operation of the two departments, the Legislature would still be an overmatch for them. All experience had evinced a powerful tendency in the legislature to absorb all power into its vortex. George Mason said he had always been a friend to this provision. It would give a confidence to the Executive which he would not otherwise have, and without which the revisionary power would be of little avail. Gerry had not expected to see this point, which had undergone full discussion, again revived. The object was to secure to the Executive, by the revisionary power, protection against the Legislature. The Executive, who will best know and be ready to defend his rights, ought alone to have the defence of them. There were strong objections to the motion. It was combining and mixing together the legislative and the other departments. It was establishing an improper coalition between the executive and judiciary departments. It was making statesmen of judges, and setting them up as the guardians of the rights of the people. The representatives of the people could be trusted. It was making legislators of the expositors of the laws, which ought never to be done. A better expedient would be to employ competent persons to draw bills for the legislature. Caleb Strong was of the same

7

opinion. It was a well-established maxim that the power of making ought to be kept distinct from that of expounding the laws. The Judges, in exercising the function of expositors, might be influenced by the part they had taken as legislators. Gouverneur Morris declared that the judges of England had a great share in legislation. They were consulted in difficult and doubtful cases. They might be, and some of them were, members of the legislature or of the privy council. The British Executive was strong in his prerogatives, but with us the interest of our Executive would be so inconsiderable and transitory, that he would require all the support he could obtain in resisting legislative encroachments. Luther Martin considered the association of the Judges with the Executive as a dangerous innovation, from which no advantage could be derived. A knowledge of mankind and of legislative affairs could not be presumed to belong in a higher degree to the Judges than to the Legislature. As to the constitutionality of laws that point would come before the Judges in their official character. Thus they have a most effective negative on the laws. Join them with the Executive in the revision and they would have a double negative. The Judiciary would lose the confidence of the people if they were employed in the task of remonstrating against popular measures of the legislature. Besides, in what mode and proportion were they to vote in the Council of Revision?

Madison, Mason, Wilson and Morris again took the floor to answer the objections which had been urged. Gerry and Gorham replied, the former urging that the Executive and the Judiciary would enter into an offensive and defensive alliance against the Legislature; the latter, that as the Judges would outnumber the Executive, the revisionary check would be thrown entirely out of the Executive hands, and instead of enabling him to defend himself, would enable the Judges to sacrifice him. John Rutledge closed the debate with the sententious declaration that the Judges of all men were most unfit to be concerned in the revisionary Council. They ought never to give an opinion on a law until it came before them for judicial determination. Besides, it was unnecessary. The Executive could consult his cabinet, and avail himself of their information and opinions. The vote was then taken, and the motion was lost; three States voting in the affirmative, four in the negative, two dividing, and one being absent.[1]

The various clauses as voted on were then referred to the Committee of Detail, consisting of Messrs. Rutledge, Randolph, Gorham, Ellsworth and Wilson, by whose able and experienced hands the precious and perdurable material furnished by the joint wisdom of the Convention was gradually fashioned into the bold features and majestic form of the Constitution, which finally received its most expressive lineaments from the skillful touches of Gouverneur Morris, whose genius as a literary and political artist rivalled that of Benvenuto Cellini as a sculptor.

The report of the Committee was received on the 6th of August, three months after the assembling of the Convention. The power of appointing the Judges of the Supreme Court was vested in the Senate alone. Whenever a dispute or controversy arose between two or more States respecting jurisdiction or territory and the matter was presented by memorial to the Senate, the contending States were to be notified to appear by their agents before the Senate upon a day properly assigned. By joint consent of the agents, judges or commis-

[1] Elliott's Debates, Vol. V. pp. 344-349.

sioners were to be appointed to constitute a court for the determination of the matter. In the event of disagreement the Senate was to name three persons from each State, and from this list each party was to alternately strike one until the number was reduced to thirteen, and from that number not less than seven nor more than nine names were to be drawn by lot, any five of whom should be commissioned as the judges to finally hear the controversy. If either party neglected to appear, without sufficient cause, or refused to strike, the Senate was to proceed to nominate three persons from each State, and the Clerk of the Senate was to strike in behalf of the absent or refusing party. If any of the parties refused to submit to the authority of such court, or did not appear to prosecute or defend, the Court was nevertheless to proceed to judgment, which was to be final and conclusive.[1]

Controversies respecting land claims under different grants of two or more States were to be determined in the same manner.[2] These provisions were taken, almost word for word, from the Ninth Article of Confederation. The main features of the report in relation to a national judiciary were as follows:

The Judicial power of the United States was to be vested in one Supreme Court, and in such inferior courts as should, when necessary, from time to time, be constituted by the legislature. The tenure was good behavior, the compensation was not to be diminished during continuance in office. The jurisdiction of the Supreme Court was to extend to all cases arising under laws passed by the legislature of the United States ; to all cases affecting ambassadors, other public ministers and consuls; to the trial of impeachments of officers of

---

[1] Elliott's Debates, Vol. V, pp. 379–380.   [2] *Ibid.*

the United States; to all cases of admiralty and maritime jurisdiction; to controversies between two or more States (except
such as should regard territory or jurisdiction); between a
State and citizens of another State ; between citizens of different States; and between a State, or the citizens thereof, and
foreign States, citizens or subjects. In cases of impeachments,
cases affecting ambassadors, other public ministers and consuls,
and those in which a State should be a party, this jurisdiction was to be original. In all the other cases before mentioned it was to be appellate, with such exceptions, and under
such regulations as the legislature should make. The legislature might assign any part of the jurisdiction above mentioned (except the trial of the President of the United States)
in the manner and under the limitations which it should think
proper, to such inferior courts as it should constitute from
time to time. The trial of all criminal offences (except in
cases of impeachment) was to be in the State where they were
committed, and was to be by jury. Judgment, in cases of
impeachment, was not to extend further than removal from
office and disqualification to hold and enjoy any office of
honor, trust, or profit under the United States. But the party
convicted was to be liable to indictment, trial, judgment and
punishment, according to law. The President was liable to
removal from his office on impeachment by the House of
Representatives and conviction in the Supreme Court, of treason, bribery or corruption. Although he had no share in the
appointment of the Judges of the Supreme Court, who might
be called upon to try him, he had the power to appoint the
judges of the inferior courts, without the concurrence of the
Senate or House.[1]

---

[1] See "Report of the Committee of Detail," Elliott's Debates, Vol. V, pp. 377-381.

The report was silent upon the question of associating the Judges with the Executive in a revisionary negative upon the acts of the Legislature; and although Madison, supported by Wilson, made a third effort to secure it, it was disposed of by a remark of Dickinson, that "the Justiciary of Aragon became by degrees the lawgiver." A proposition of Charles Pinckney that "Each branch of the Legislature, as well as the Supreme Executive, shall have authority to require the opinions of the Supreme Judicial Court upon important questions of law and upon solemn occasions," which was referred to the Committee, was smothered.

The first assault upon the Report of the Committee, as presented, was made by its Chairman, John Rutledge, who moved to strike out the provisions for deciding controversies between the States, or claimants of land under grants from different States, which he declared, though necessary under the Confederation, were rendered useless by the establishment of a national judiciary. William Samuel Johnson, Roger Sherman and Jonathan Dayton concurred. Williamson and Gorham thought that the provision might be good in cases where the judiciary were interested, or too closely connected with the parties. Wilson urged the striking out, which was done by a vote of eight States in the affirmative, two in the negative, with one absent.

Johnson then suggested that the judicial power ought to extend to equity as well as law, and moved to insert the words "both in law and equity," so that the clause should read "The judicial power of the United States both in law and equity, shall be vested in one Supreme Court," etc. Read objected to vesting these powers in the same court; they ought to be kept separate. The motion prevailed.

John Dickinson then made an effort to secure a provision

that the judges might be removed by the Executive on the application of the Senate and House of Representatives. He was supported by Gerry. Gouverneur Morris thought it a contradiction in terms to say that the Judges should hold their offices during good behavior, and yet be removable without a trial. Besides, it was fundamentally wrong to subject judges to so arbitrary an authority. Sherman saw no contradiction or impropriety if this were made a part of the constitutional regulation of the Judiciary department. A like provision was contained in the British statutes. Rutledge replied that if the Supreme Court is to judge between the United States and particular States, this alone was an insuperable objection to the motion. Wilson considered such a provision in the British government as less dangerous than here, the House of Lords and House of Commons being less likely to concur on the same occasions. Chief-Justice Holt had successively offended, by his independent conduct, both Houses of Parliament. Had this happened at the same time, he would have been ousted. The Judges would be in a bad situation if made to depend on any gust of faction which might prevail in the two branches of our government. Randolph opposed the motion as weakening too much the independence of the Judges. Dickinson did not fear the union of two Houses, constructed on different principles, for the purpose of displacing a judge, unless he were guilty of improper conduct. His motion was lost, Connecticut alone voting in the affirmative.[1]

Johnson then moved that the judicial power should extend "to all cases arising under the Constitution," and the motion was unanimously agreed to, it being generally supposed that

[1] Elliott's Debates, Vol. V, p. 481.

the jurisdiction given was constructively limited to cases of a judiciary nature, notwithstanding an expression of Madison that the right of expounding the Constitution in cases not of this nature ought not to be given to that department.[1]

In this way, as Mr. Bancroft has pointed out, Madison's scheme of restraining unconstitutional legislation of the States by securing to the legislature of the Union a veto on every act of State legislation was finally abandoned, and the power of revising and reversing a clause of a State law that conflicted with the Federal Constitution was confided exclusively to the Federal judiciary, but only when a case should be properly brought before the Court.[2]

Rutledge next added that the jurisdiction should extend to treaties made, or to be made, under the authority of the United States; and the proposal was adopted.

The clause, "in cases of impeachment," was postponed, and that duty was subsequently assigned to the Senate.[3]

The method of choosing all the Federal judges was then settled without further debate, and the power of appointment, without discriminating between the Supreme Court and inferior tribunals, was bestowed upon the Executive, to be exercised with the advice and consent of the Senate. Finally, upon the proposition of Luther Martin, it was declared "This Constitution and the Laws of the United States made and which shall be made in pursuance thereof, and all Treaties made or which shall be made under the authority of the United States, shall be the Supreme Law of the Land and the Judges in every State shall be bound thereby, any

[1] Elliott's Debates, Vol. V, p. 483.

[2] George Bancroft's "History of the Formation of the Constitution of the United States of America," Vol. II, p. 198.

[3] Elliott's Debates, Vol. V, p. 483.

thing in the Constitution or Laws of any State to the contrary notwithstanding," [1] a declaration which has been termed "the Bill of Rights of the National Judiciary." [2]

The Article relating to the Judiciary was now complete. The metal had been forged and beaten into shape beneath the repeated blows of vigorous and well-trained minds, and was now delivered to be polished to the Committee on Style, consisting of Johnson, Hamilton, Gouverneur Morris, Madison and King, but the elegance of expression which characterized the final draft is due to the pen of Morris.

On the 17th of September, 1787, the Convention completed its work, and committed to the people of the United States, for their approval, that great Charter of Government now known and honored everywhere as the Constitution of the United States. The act of signing was performed in that doubly sanctified chamber of the old State House, in Philadelphia, in which the immortal Congress of July, 1776, had assembled. But three of the members present refused to add their names to "that consecrated roll." The others followed the example of Franklin and consented to the Constitution because they expected nothing better, and because they were not sure that it was not the best that could be had. The opinions they had of its errors they sacrificed to the public good. In all their deliberations they had kept steadily in view that which appeared to them the greatest interest of every true American, the consolidation of the Union, in which was involved their prosperity, felicity, safety and National existence. This important consideration, seriously and deeply impressed on the minds of the members, led each State in the Convention to be less

---

[1] Constitution of the United States, Article VI.
[2] William Allen Butler, Esq.

rigid in points of inferior magnitude than might have been otherwise expected. And thus the Constitution as presented was the result of amity and of that mutual deference and concession which the peculiarity of the political situation rendered indispensable.[1]

The God of wisdom illuminated the deliberations of that hour. The labors of that day preserved for all time the precious fruits of freedom and self-government. Unique in origin; without a prototype in design; of enduring strength and of phenomenal success, in the history of political philosophy the Constitution will always stand alone. And not the least of the wonders wrought by the statesmanship of America was the establishment of a National Judiciary, with a jurisdiction co-extensive with the limits of the legislative power, and no longer destitute of the energies which such a department ought to possess.

---

[1] See "Letters accompanying the Constitution and addressed to the Congress by the Convention." Elliott's Debates, Vol. V, p. 536.

CHAPTER IX.

OBJECTIONS URGED BY THE STATES: ANSWERS THERETO: VIEWS OF THE STATE JUDICIARIES UPON THE POWER OF THE COURTS TO ANNUL AN ACT OF THE LEGISLATURE: SCOPE AND PURPOSE OF ARTICLE THIRD IN THE CONSTITUTION.

IT was not to be expected that the proposed instrument would meet with the full and entire approbation of every State, and it is an interesting subject of study to mark the various objections which were urged against the Article relating to the Judiciary, and the answers which were made by the publicists and essayists of that time.

An intense struggle took place, the most violent passions were fully aroused, and fears and prejudices were madly appealed to when arguments failed of which logic or sober reason could approve. Many of the most famous names in our history were vehement in their opposition, while many others were either neutral, or gave to the Constitution but a lukewarm support. The common fear, and the usual prediction—that the General Government would subvert the State governments, with a loss of personal freedom—appear in almost all the "Observations," "Examinations," "Addresses," "Letters," "Remarks" and "Objections," which were put forth as anti-federal arguments.

Elbridge Gerry, in stating the reasons which determined him in withholding his signature from the completed Constitution, declared that the rights of citizens were rendered insecure by the general power of the legislature "to establish a tribunal without juries, which will be a Star Chamber as to

civil cases."[1]   In his letter to the President of the Massachusetts Senate, he expressed a fear "that the judicial department will be oppressive,"[2] and in a pamphlet, published under
the title of "Observations on the New Constitution and on
the Federal and State Conventions, by a Columbian Patriot,"[3]
he declared :

"There are no well-defined limits of the Judiciary Powers ; they seem
to be left as a boundless ocean that has broken over the chart of the
Supreme Lawgiver, ' *Thus far thou shalt go and no further,*' and as they
cannot be comprehended by the clearest capacity or the most sagacious
mind, it would be an Herculean labor to attempt to describe the dangers
with which they are replete." [4]

Edmund Randolph, who also refused to affix his name to
the Constitution, in a letter to the Speaker of the House of
Delegates, objected that there was no limitation or definition
of the judicial power.[5]   George Mason, the remaining member
of the Federal Convention who refused to sign, was more specific and less rhetorical than Gerry :

"The judiciary of the United States," said he, "is so constructed
and extended, as to absorb and destroy the judiciaries of the several States ;
thereby rendering law as tedious, intricate and expensive, and justice as
unattainable by a great part of the community as in England ; and
enabling the rich to oppress and ruin the poor. [6]

[1] Elliott's Debates, Vol. V, p. 553.

[2] "Letter containing the Reasons of the Hon. Elbridge Gerry for not signing
the Federal Constitution." Elliott's Debates, Vol. I, p. 493.

[3] Reprint in "Pamphlets on the Constitution of the United States, published
during its discussion by the People, 1787-1788. Edited by Paul Leicester Ford."

[4] Upon this Rufus King wrote to John Alsop: "E. G. has come out as a
Columbian Patriot—a pitiful performance. The author sinks daily in public esteem, and his bantling goes unnoticed."

[5] Randolph's Letter—Elliott's Debates, Vol. I, p. 491.

[6] Mason's Letter—*Ibid.* p. 495.

The most strenuous opposition was made by Richard Henry Lee, who, in "Letters of the Federal Farmer," stated and re-stated his lament that the jury trial of the vicinage had been effectually abolished. Under one General Government alone, he argued, there could be but one judiciary, one supreme and a proper number of inferior Courts. It would be totally impracticable in this case to preserve a due administration of justice, and the real benefits of the jury trial of the vicinage, because there are now Supreme Courts in each State, and a great number of county and other courts subordinate to each Supreme Court, most of which were itinerant and held their sessions every year in different parts of their respective States, counties and districts; notwithstanding this, citizens must travel considerable distances to find the place where justice is administered. Although he was not for bringing justice so near to each man's door as to tempt him to engage in lawsuits, yet he thought it one of the greatest benefits in a good government that each citizen should find a Court within a reasonable distance, perhaps, within a few days' travel of his home; so that without great inconvenience and enormous expense, he might have the advantages of his witnesses and jury. But it would be impracticable to derive these advantages from one judiciary—the one Supreme Court at most could only sit in the centre of the Union, and move once a year into the centre of the Eastern and Southern extremes of it, and, in this case, each citizen, on an average, would travel 150 or 200 miles to find this court; that, although inferior Courts might be properly placed in the different counties and districts of the Union, the appellate jurisdiction would be intolerable and expensive.

How little did he foresee the practice of the future; how little did he dream of the railroad, the steamboat and the telegraph, the employment of resident counsel, or other agencies of our modern life.

Another objection that he urged, was that powers ever kept distinct in well balanced governments were improperly blended in the hands of the same men—"in the judges of the Supreme Court is lodged the law, the equity, and the fact."

As the judicial powers of the Federal courts were extended to all cases in law and equity, therefore the powers to determine on the law, in equity, and as to the fact, would all concentrate in the Supreme Court. The Constitution blended all these in the same hands—the same judges. The wisdom of Great Britain had deposited them in different hands—the Common Law jurisdiction was distinct from that of the Chancellor, and the trial by jury was beyond the reach of the powers of both. It was dangerous indeed to vest in the same judges power to decide on the law, and also give them general powers in equity; for if the law restrain them, they need only step into their shoes of equity and give what judgment their reason or opinions may dictate. In short, he asserted that in the Supreme Court as established by the Constitution he saw not a spark of freedom or a shadow of our own or the British Common Law.

How little did he foresee the fusion of law and equity, the adaptation of common law forms to equitable principles, or the skill with which the same judge could apply without confusion the maxims of both.

Again, he urged as an objection, that the judicial powers respect internal as well as external objects. Powers to lay and collect internal taxes, to make bankrupt laws, and to decide, on appeal, questions arising on the internal laws of the respective States, were of a serious nature, and, taken in connection with others proposed to be lodged in the central Government, comprehended all the essential powers of the community, and left nothing of importance to the States. He objected to the extension of the powers of the Federal judiciary to all cases between a State and the citizens of another State, between citizens of different States, between a State or the citizens thereof and foreign States, citizens or subjects. Actions in all these cases, except against a State government, were then brought and finally determined in the law courts of the States respectively, and as there were no words to exclude these Courts of their jurisdiction in these cases, they would have concurrent jurisdiction with the inferior Federal courts in them. There was no need of opening a new jurisdiction in these causes, a new scene of expensive lawsuits, of suffering foreigners and citizens of different States dragging each other many hundred miles into the Federal Courts. An appeal will lie in all these cases from the State Courts or Federal inferior courts to the Supreme Judicial Court of the Union, and a wild conflict of jurisdiction will ensue.

Little did he foresee the ease and convenience of the system he denounced, and how little fraught with danger was the doctrine of concurrent jurisdiction.

Once more did he object that trial by jury was secured only in those few criminal cases to which the Federal laws would extend, as crimes committed on the high seas, against the law of nations, treason, and counterfeiting the Federal securities and coin; but even in these cases the jury trial of the vicinage was not secured, particularly in the large States; a citizen might be tried for a crime five hundred miles from the place where it was committed. In civil cases trial by jury was not secured at all. It was an important question whether jury trial was not excluded from the Supreme Court. In all cases affecting ambassadors, other public ministers and consuls, and in those cases in which a State shall be a party, the Supreme Court was to have original jurisdiction. In all the other cases mentioned, the Supreme Court was to have appellate jurisdiction both as to *law and fact*, with such exceptions and under such regulations, it was true, as Congress might make. But by the word "Court" is understood a court consisting of judges, and the idea of a jury was excluded. As the Court or the judges were to have jurisdiction on appeals, in all enumerated cases, as to law and fact, it followed that the judges were to decide the law and try the fact, and the trial of the fact being assigned to the judges by the Constitution, a jury for trying the fact was excluded. He saw a gleam of hope, however, in the power of Congress to declare exceptions and make regulations.[1] He did foresee, however, and pointed his warning finger to the shadow cast by the coming decision of *Chisholm's Executors* v. *The State of Georgia* :[2]

"How far it may be proper to admit a foreigner," he wrote, "or the citizens of another State to bring actions against State governments, which have failed in performing so many promises made during the war, is doubtful : How far it may be proper so to humble a State as to oblige it to answer to an individual in a Court of law, is worthy of consideration ; the States are now subject to no such actions ; and this new jurisdiction will subject the States and many defendants to actions and processes which were not in contemplation of the parties when the contract was made ; all engagements existing between citizens of different States, citizens and foreigners, States and foreigners, and States and citizens of other States were made, the parties contemplating the remedies then existing in the laws of the States—and the new remedy proposed to be given in the Federal Courts can be founded on no principle whatever."

[1] R. H. Lee, "Letters of a Federal Farmer," in Paul Leicester Ford's " Pamphlets on the Constitution, published during its Discussion by the People," pp. 277–325.

[2] 2 Dallas, 419 (1793).

[3] Ford's Pamphlets, p. 309.

Substantially the same arguments were urged with tremendous force by Luther Martin, then Attorney-General of Maryland, in his notable Letter on the Federal Convention, in which, with remarkable clearness of statement, he dwelt upon the manner in which trial by jury had been destroyed, and a vast and varied jurisdiction snatched from the State Courts.[1]

Patrick Henry exclaimed:

"The purse is gone; the sword is gone; * * * the independency of the judges is impaired; * * * I see the prostration of all our rights. In what a situation will your judges be, when they are sworn to preserve the Constitution of the State and of the General Government? If there be a concurrent dispute between them, which will prevail? They cannot serve two masters struggling for the same object. The laws of Congress being paramount to those of the States, and to their Constitutions also, whenever they come in competition, the judges must decide in favor of the former. This, instead of relieving or aiding me, deprives me of my only comfort—the independency of the judges. The judiciary are the sole protection against a tyrannical execution of the laws. But if by this system we lose our judiciary, and they cannot help us, we must sit down quietly and be oppressed."[2]

In every State similar fears were expressed, and the same gloomy prophecies were made. The counter-statements were numerous and cogent. In Virginia the venerable Edmund Pendleton, the President of the State Convention, ripe in judicial experience, and a member of the highest State Court whose jurisdiction it was alleged had been invaded and impaired, replied to the impassioned invective of Patrick

---

[1] "The Genuine Information, delivered to the Legislature of the State of Maryland, relative to the Proceedings of the General Convention," Elliott's Debates, Vol. I, p. 344.

[2] Elliott's Debates, Vol. III, p. 539.

8

Henry in words which have the calmness of a judicial utterance:

"If there were any person in this audience who had not read the Constitution, or who had not heard what has been said, and should have been told that the trial by jury was intended to be taken away, he would be surprised to find, on examination, that there was no exclusion of it in civil cases, and that it was expressly provided for in criminal cases."

Of those who objected that there was an unlimited power of appointing inferior Courts, he asked, whether it would have been proper to limit this power? "Could the framers of the instrument have extended their ideas to all the necessities of the United States, and seen every case in which it would be necessary to have an inferior tribunal?" By the regulations of Congress, they may be accommodated to public convenience and utility. It would have been folly to have fixed in the Constitution a number that could not have been increased or diminished save by an amendment. As to jurisdiction, assuming that a judiciary is necessary, the power of that judiciary must be co-extensive with the legislative power, and reach to all parts of society intended to be governed. There must be some Court which shall be the central point of operations; and because all the business cannot be done in that Court, there must be inferior Courts to carry it on. Turning to another topic, he said:

"The impossibility of calling a sovereign State before the jurisdiction of another sovereign State showed the propriety and necessity of vesting this tribunal with the decision of controversies to which a State shall be a party."

As to the jurisdiction given in disputes between citizens of different States, he put this case:

"Suppose a bond given by a citizen of Rhode Island to one of our citizens. The regulations of that State being unfavorable to the claims of the other States, if he is obliged to go to Rhode Island to recover it, he will be compelled to accept payment of one third, or less, of his money. He cannot sue in the Supreme Court, but he may sue in the Federal inferior Court; and on judgment to be paid one for ten, he may get justice by appeal. Is it an eligible situation? Is it just that a man should run the risk of losing nine-tenths of his claim? Ought he not to be able to carry it to that Court where unworthy principles do not prevail?"

Paper money and tender laws, he asserted, may be passed in other States, in opposition to the Federal principle, and in restriction of this Constitution, and there will be need of jurisdiction in the Federal judiciary to stop their pernicious effects.[1]

In the same line of calm, but convincing argument, John Marshall, unconscious of the immortal future before him as the greatest of all judicial interpreters of the Constitution, declared:

"Here are tribunals appointed for the *decision of controversies* which were before either not at all, or improperly, provided for. * * * Gentlemen have gone on the idea that the Federal Courts will not determine the causes which may come before them with the same fairness and impartiality with which other courts decide. What are the reasons for this supposition? Do they draw them from the manner in which the judges are chosen, or the tenure of their office? What is it that makes us trust our judges? Their independence in office and manner of appointment. Are not the judges of the Federal Court chosen with as much wisdom as the judges of the State governments? Are they not equally, if not more independent? If so, shall we not conclude that they will decide with equal impartiality and candor?"[2]

---

[1] Elliott's "Debates in the Virginia Convention," Vol. III, pp. 547–549.
[2] *Ibid.*, 551.

Pursuing the Socratic method of closely questioning those whom he would convince, he asks:

"Is it not necessary that the Federal Courts should have cognizance of cases arising under the Constitution and the laws of the United States? What is the service or purpose of a judiciary but to execute the laws in a peaceable, orderly manner, without shedding blood, or creating a contest, or availing yourselves of force? If this be the case, where can its jurisdiction be more necessary than here? To what quarter will you look for protection from an infringement of the Constitution if you will not give the power to the judiciary?"

Replying to the argument built on the narrow meaning of the word "court," he said:

"The exclusion of trial by jury is urged as the prostration of our rights. Does the word *court* only mean the judges? Does not the determination of a jury necessarily lead to the judgment of a court? Is there anything here which gives the judges exclusive jurisdiction of matters of fact? What is the object of a jury trial? To inform the Court of the facts. When a Court has cognizance of the facts, does it not follow that they can make inquiry by a jury?"[1]

Madison argued that a Supreme Court was necessary to secure uniformity in the exposition of treaties. "The establishment of one revisionary superintending power can alone secure such uniformity." The same principles, he held, applied with respect to cases affecting ambassadors and foreign ministers, and also admiralty and maritime cases. As our intercourse with foreign nations would be affected by decisions of this kind, they ought to be uniform. This could only be done by giving the Federal judiciary exclusive jurisdiction. Controversies affecting the interests of the United States ought to be deter-

---

[1] Elliott's Debates, Vol. III, pp. 551–563.

mined by their own judiciary and not be left to partial, local tribunals.[1]

Similar arguments were pressed by James Wilson in Pennsylvania, and Hamilton and Jay in New York. At the same time numerous pamphlets appeared from the pens of those who were not members of the Federal or the State Conventions. Of these the most remarkable were an "Examination into the Leading Principles of the Federal Constitution," by Noah Webster, afterwards known as the eminent lexicographer, an "Examination of the Constitution of the United States," by Tench Coxe, of Pennsylvania, "Remarks on the Proposed Plan of Federal Government," by Alexander Contee Hanson, of Maryland—an essay of close reasoning and marvellous eloquence of expression, and "Observations on George Mason's Objections to the Federal Constitution," by James Iredell, of North Carolina, who owed his subsequent appointment as an Associate Justice of the Supreme Court of the United States to the ability displayed in this very paper which attracted the attention of Washington.[2]

The insinuation that trials by jury are to be abolished, Webster denounced as groundless and beyond conception wicked. It was the circulation of a barefaced falsehood respecting a privilege dear to freemen, and could only proceed from a depraved heart and the worst intentions. The prediction as a probable event that the Federal courts would absorb the judiciaries of the States, he declared to be a mere suspicion, without the least foundation, and he dismissed as trifling all objections based on declarations that the jurisdiction of

[1] Elliott's Debates, Vol. III, p. 532.

[2] All these papers are reprinted by Paul Leicester Ford, in his "Pamphlets on the Constitution of the United States, Published during its discussion by the People, 1787, 1788."

the Federal courts was not accurately defined or easily understood.

Tench Coxe, who had been a member of the Continental
Congress and the Annapolis Convention, quieted the fears of
those who had been disturbed by the loud outcry that almost
every kind of suit would be brought in the Federal courts to
the utter subversion of the local tribunals, by pointing out
that trials for lands lying in any State between persons residing in such State, for bonds, notes, book debts, contracts,
trespasses, assumptions, and all other matters between two
or more citizens of the same State would be held in the State
Court by juries, and the Federal courts could not interfere in
any manner, except where questions were involved concerning
State laws which infringed the Constitution. He also pointed
out that where the trial was to be had between citizens of
different States, the plaintiff would not be obliged to go into
a Court constituted by the State, with which, or with the
citizens of which, his dispute was, but could appeal to a perfectly disinterested tribunal, from which trial by jury was not
excluded.

Alexander Contee Hanson, the future Chancellor of Maryland, scouted the anti-federal arguments:

"As the rod of Aaron once swallowed up the rods of the Egyptian
magi, so also is it feared that these Federal Courts will, at length,
swallow up the State tribunals. A miracle, in one case, is as necessary
as in the other. But let not the officers of State Courts be overmuch
alarmed !"

James Iredell, then a fast rising lawyer of thirty-five
years of age, addressed himself to the objection made by
Mason, and pertinently asked:

"Are not the State judiciaries left uncontrolled as to the affairs of that State only? In this, as in all other cases where there is a wise distribution, power is commensurate to its object. In no case but where the Union is in some measure concerned are the Federal Courts to have any jurisdiction. The State judiciary will be a satellite waiting upon its proper planet; that of the Union, like the sun, cherishing and preserving a whole planetary system."

In seven successive numbers of "The Federalist," Hamilton examined the constitution of the judicial department, in relation to the tenure of good behavior, the provisions for the support and responsibility of the judges, the extent of their powers and jurisdiction, the distribution of their authority, trial by jury and some miscellaneous questions. On all these he wrote as one having authority. He had sat in the Convention, had taken part in the debates, had listened to the objections lodged against every article, and had a memory stored with the precise information which the task required.

The most brilliant of recent historians has observed that "it is not easy for us to form a notion of the effect these papers had on the men who, for the first time, saw them in the Packets and Gazettes," and adds that "there is no reason whatever to suppose that the followers of Clinton gave any more heed to the writings of Publius than did the followers of Hamilton to the foolery of Brutus and the nonsense of Centinel."[1] Whether this sentiment be just, or whether it depreciates the effect produced by the marvellous ability of the authors of "The Federalist," whose work has been seriously and reverently called the Bible of Republicanism, the fact remains that for comprehensiveness of design, strength, clearness and simplicity, the book has no parallel among the writings of men, not even excepting or overlooking those of

---

[1] McMaster's "History of the People of the United States," Vol. I, p. 484.

Montesquieu and Aristotle. The result was happy, and the triumph of the Constitution was complete.

As a part of the judicial history of the period, and as a forerunner of the doctrine of the Supreme Court of the United States in *Marbury* v. *Madison*, decided in 1803,[1] it is of interest to trace the growth of the principle that a Court can declare an act of the Legislature void because of its repugnance to the Constitution of a State. Various claims have been made to the distinction of priority. Rhode Island claims it, and recently it has been asserted that the honor belongs to an argument of Iredell made in a North Carolina case, argued before, but not decided until after, the Rhode Island case of *Trevett* v. *Weeden*, in 1786, while an admirer of Chief-Justice Brearley, of New Jersey, endeavors to show that the laurels belong to him.[2] The truth is, that the palm must be awarded to Virginia.

In November, 1782, the case of *Commonwealth* v. *Caton et al.* came before the Court of Appeals of that State.[3] John Caton and others had been condemned for treason by the General Court under an Act of 1776, defining the offence, which took from the Executive the power to pardon. The House of Delegates, by resolution of the 18th June, 1782, granted them a pardon; but the Senate refused to concur.

---

[1] 1 Cranch, 158.

[2] See Arnold's "History of Rhode Island," Vol. II, Ch. 24, Trevett *v.* Weeden; Cooley's "Constitutional Limitations," 6th Edit., pp. 193–194, note; Hannis Taylor, "The Origin and Growth of the English Constitution," p. 47; Bayard *v.* Singleton, 1 Martin (N. C.) 42 (1787); Hon. A. M. Waddell's Article on "Judge James Iredell," in the "News and Observer," Aug. 11, 1890; Hon. Austin Scott, "Address before the Historical Society of New Brunswick, N. J., on the Federal Convention." See also a learned and admirable paper entitled, "Relation of the Judiciary to the Constitution," by Wm. M. Meigs, Esq., of Philadelphia, The American Law Review, XIX, 175 (1885).

[3] 4 Call (Va.) 5–21.

When the Attorney-General moved that execution of the judgment be awarded, the pardon was pleaded, and the General Court adjourned the case to the Court of Appeals, where the pardon was held to be invalid. Although there was not a direct conflict between the so-called law and the Constitution, and therefore the remarks of the judges are to be regarded as *obiter dicta*, yet the expressions they used are the first to be found relating to the subject. Judge Wythe earnestly and unequivocally asserted the controlling power of the judiciary. After adverting to the particular circumstances of the case, and declaring that, whenever the proper occasion should occur, he would feel it to be his duty to protect one branch of the Legislature against the usurpations of the other, he concluded by saying:

"Nay, more, if the whole legislature—an event to be deprecated—should attempt to overleap the boundaries prescribed to them by the people, I, in administering the justice of the country, will meet the united powers at my seat in this tribunal, and pointing to the Constitution, will say to them, Here is the limit of your authority; hither shall you go, but no further."

The President of the Court, Mr. Pendleton, expressed no opinion, but contented himself with remarking:

"But how far this Court in whom the judiciary powers may, in some sort, be said to be concentrated, shall have power to declare the nullity of a law passed in its forms by the legislative power, without exercising the power of that branch contrary to the plain terms of the Constitution, is indeed a deep, important, and, I will add, tremendous question, the decision of which might involve consequences to which gentlemen may not have extended their ideas."

Chancellor Blair and the rest of the judges, so says the reporter, were of opinion that the Court had the power to declare any resolution or act of the legislature void if in conflict with the Constitution.[1]

The next case in point of date was that of *Holmes* v. *Walton and others*, arising under the seizure laws. The State of New Jersey had passed an act providing for trials by juries consisting of six men. This law was held by Chief Justice Brearley to be unconstitutional. The date of this decision is uncertain, but that it was prior to 1785 is fixed by a reference of Gouverneur Morris, who, in an "Address to the Assembly of Pennsylvania against the abolition of the Charter of the Bank of North America," made in that year, used this language:

"The boasted omnipotence of legislative authority is but a jingle of words. In the literal meaning, it is impious. And whatever interpretation lawyers may give, freemen must feel it to be absurd and unconstitutional. Absurd, because laws cannot alter the nature of things; unconstitutional, because the Constitution is no more if it can be changed by the legislature. A law was once passed in New Jersey which the judges pronounced to be unconstitutional, and therefore void. Such power in judges is dangerous; but unless it somewhere exists the time employed in framing a Bill of Rights and Form of Government was merely thrown away."

[1] See also Rives' "Life of Madison," Vol. II, pp. 262 *et seq.*

[2] Jared Sparks' "Life of Gouverneur Morris," Vol. III, p. 438. There is also a reference to this decision of Brearley in somewhat indistinct terms in the opinion of Kirkpatrick, C. J., in State *v.* Parkhurst, Appendix to 4 Halstead, p. 444.

For these references I am indebted to Hon. Austin Scott, of New Brunswick, N. J. Professor Rogers, of the Law School of the University of Michigan, states that Brearley announced as the opinion of himself and his associates, that the judiciary had the right to pronounce on the constitutionality of laws, in a case before the Court at a session at Hillsborough, in September, 1780. He does not state his authority. Introduction to "Constitutional History of the United States as seen in the Development of American Law," p. 10. Professor McMaster refers to the New York case of Rutgers *v.* Waddington, argued by Hamilton in the Mayor's Court of New York in 1784, but as the decision turned upon general principles, and not upon

The case of *Trevett* v. *Weeden* came before the Supreme Court of Rhode Island in 1786. An Act of Assembly imposed a heavy penalty on any one who should refuse to receive on the same terms as specie the bills of a bank chartered by the State, or who in any way should discourage their circulation. The penalty was made collectable on summary conviction without jury trial. The Court held the act void on the ground that jury trial was expressly given by the Colonial Charter, which then constituted the Constitution of the State. The Judges were punished by a refusal of the legislature to re-elect them at the end of the year, and were supplanted by more pliant tools by whose assistance the paper money was forced into circulation, and public and private debts extinguished by means of it.[1]

The case of *Bayard* v. *Singleton* came before the Supreme Court of North Carolina in November, 1787. An Act had been passed in 1785 requiring the Court to dismiss on motion suits brought by persons whose property had been confiscated, upon a mere affidavit of the defendants that they were purchasers from the commissioners of confiscated property. The case was argued for the plaintiffs by Iredell, Johnston and W. R. Davie, and for the defendants by Alfred Moore, then the Attorney-General, and subsequently Iredell's successor on the Bench of the Supreme Court of the United States. The Court held the law void, as destructive of trial by jury, and

---

a definite conflict between the Act criticized and a fundamental written law, I have not thought it proper to include it in the text. See McMaster's Hist. People U. S., I, 219–220.

[1] Arnold's "History of Rhode Island," Vol. II, chap. 24, p. 525. Cooley's "Constitutional Limitations," 6th Ed., pp. 193–194, note. Judge Cooley states that this was the first case in which a legislative act was declared void by reason of repugnance to a State Constitution, and in this he is followed by Mr. Hannis Taylor, "The Origin and Growth of the English Constitution," p. 47. They are in error.

twenty-seven similar cases were swept from the docket.[1] The argument of Iredell was a powerful presentation of the question, worked out in an original way, and is one of the most characteristic of his productions. It appears in substance in an address to the public, published in August, 1787, and in a letter addressed to Spaight in the same month.[2] Spaight had complained of the decisions of the judges as a usurpation of authority; that the State, instead of being governed by the representatives in General Assembly, would be subject to the will of three individuals, who united in their own persons the legislative and judiciary powers, which no monarch in Europe enjoyed, and which would be more despotic than the Roman Decemvirate, and equally as insufferable. In reply Iredell confessed that it had ever been his opinion that an act inconsistent with the Constitution was void, and that the judges, consistently with their duties, could not carry it into effect. The Constitution was a fundamental law, limiting the powers of the legislature, and with it every exercise of these powers must, necessarily, be compared.[3]

There was no precedent in ancient or modern judicial history before the cases just reviewed were decided, which warranted a court in asserting such a principle, and as has been observed by a recent writer, it was difficult for men trained under the English system of jurisprudence, to conceive the idea that a mere Court should assume the prerogative of setting aside a law enacted by the legislature and approved by the Executive.[4]

---

[1] 1 Martin (N. C.) 42.

[2] McRee's "Life and Correspondence of James Iredell," Vol. II, pp. 145–168.

[3] In 1792 the Supreme Court of South Carolina held that an Act passed by the Colonial Legislature in 1712 was *ipso facto* void as being in contravention of Magna Charta. Bowman *v.* Middleton. 1. Bay p. 252.

[4] Prof. Rogers, *ut supra.*

Such is the history of the development of the principle, up to the time when the Federal Convention was held. John Francis Mercer, one of the Maryland delegates, expressed in strong terms his disapprobation of the doctrine that the judges, as expositors of the Constitution, had authority to declare a law void, and even such a man as John Dickinson, of Delaware, concurred with him, and said "No such power ought to exist," but the contrary view prevailed with the most able of the members of the Convention and passed without challenge, until Thomas Jefferson, in 1788, in "Observations upon the Constitution drafted for Virginia," while conceding the existence of the doctrine, declared his dislike of it, as it made the judiciary department paramount, in fact, to the legislature, "which was never intended and can never be proper." At the same time Hamilton was maintaining the opposite view in "The Federalist." [1]

In the same year the legislature of Virginia passed an act imposing on the judges of the Court of Appeals the duties of judges of the district courts, which was considered so clearly inconsistent with those provisions of the Constitution intended to secure the independence of the judiciary as to call forth a manifesto from the judges, in which the *quæstio vexata* of the legitimate province of the judicial power was met and firmly and explicitly resolved. The legislature yielded and repealed the act.

We have now traced the history of Article Third of the Constitution of the United States in the light of contemporaneous events, and viewed the successive stages of its composition. Its language is familiar to every lawyer and student of

---

[1] Compare Rives' "Life of Madison," Vol. II, p. 262, note, and "The Federalist," No. LXXVIII.

the Constitution. Its general scope and purpose are best stated by Chief Justice Jay, who wrote as follows :[1]

"It may be asked, what is the precise sense and latitude in which the words 'to establish justice,' as here used, are to be understood? The answer to this question will result from the provisions made in the Constitution on this head. They are specified in the Second Section of the Third Article, where it is ordained that the judicial power of the United States shall extend to ten descriptions of cases, viz. : 1st. To all cases arising under this Constitution; because the meaning, construction and operation of a compact ought always to be ascertained by all the parties, or by authority derived only from one of them. 2d. To all cases arising under the laws of the United States; because as such laws, constitutionally made, are obligatory on each State, the measure of obligation and obedience ought not to be decided and fixed by the party from whom they are due, but by a tribunal deriving authority from both the parties. 3d. To all cases arising under treaties made by their authority; because, as treaties are compacts made by, and obligatory on, the whole nation, their operation ought not to be affected or regulated by the local laws or Courts of a part of the nation. 4th. To all cases affecting Ambassadors or other public Ministers and Consuls; because, as these are officers of foreign nations, whom this nation is bound to protect and treat according to the law of nations, cases affecting them ought only to be cognizable by National authority. 5th. To all cases of Admiralty and Maritime jurisdiction; because, as the seas are the joint property of nations, whose rights and privileges relative thereto are regulated by the law of nations and treaties, such cases necessarily belong to National jurisdiction. 6th. To controversies to which the United States shall be a party; because, in cases in which the whole people are interested, it would not be equal or wise to let any one State decide and measure out the justice due to others. 7th. To controversies between two or more States; because domestic tranquillity requires that the contentions of States should be peaceably terminated by a common judicatory; and, because in a free country justice ought not to depend on the will of either of the litigants. 8th. To controversies between a State

[1] Chisholm's Exrs. *v.* The State of Georgia, 2 Dallas, 419 (1793).

and citizens of another State; because, in case a State (that is, all the citizens of it) has demands against some citizens of another State, it is better that she should prosecute their demands in a National Court than in a Court of the State to which those citizens belong; the danger of irritation and criminations arising from apprehensions and suspicions of partiality being thereby obviated. Because, in cases where some citizens of one State have demands against all the citizens of another State, the cause of liberty and the rights of men forbid that the latter should be the sole judges of the justice due to the latter; and true Republican Government requires that free and equal citizens should have free, fair and equal justice. 9th. To controversies between citizens of the same State claiming lands under grants of different States; because, as the rights of the two States to grant land are drawn into question, neither of the two States ought to decide the controversy. 10th. To controversies between a State, or the citizens thereof, and foreign States, citizens or subjects; because, as every nation is responsible for the conduct of its citizens towards other nations, all questions touching the justice due to foreign nations or people ought to be ascertained by and depend on national authority. Even this cursory view of the judicial powers of the United States leaves the mind strongly impressed with the importance of them to the preservation of the tranquillity, the equal sovereignty and the equal right of the people.''

CHAPTER X.

T HE old Congress of the Confederation, among its last acts had provided that the First Congress under the Constitution should convene in the city of New York on the 4th of March, 1789. On that day but eight members of the Senate and thirteen of the House of Representatives appeared in their respective halls and took their seats, and both Houses adjourned from day to day until the 1st of April, when, a quorum of the House being present, an organization was effected by the choice of Frederick Augustus Muhlenberg, of Pennsylvania, as Speaker, and John Beckley as Clerk, both gentlemen being selected by ballot. It was not until the 6th of April, however, that a quorum of the Senate was present, so that this became the natal day of Congress.[1] On the following morning, while the House was entering into a discussion of duties on imports, the Senate preferred to grapple with the question of organizing the Judiciary, and appointed a Committee to bring in a Bill, of which Ellsworth was Chairman, with Paterson, Maclay, Strong, Lee, Bassett, Few and Wingate as associates.[2] On the 12th of June, Richard Henry Lee, in behalf of this Committee, reported a bill "to establish the Judicial Courts of the United States."

---

[1] "Annals of Congress," compiled by Joseph Gales, Sr., Vol. I, p. 16. "History of Congress," Vol. I, pp. 9–24.

[2] Annals of Congress, p. 18.

It is understood that the original draft, which was modified but little, was prepared chiefly by Ellsworth, with some assistance from Paterson.[1] It provoked considerable discussion and occupied the attention of the Senate for about seventeen days.

After "much wrangling about words" it was determined that there should be district courts. Lee, unable as a Senator of the United States, to divest himself of the views he had expressed in the "Letters of a Federal Farmer," then brought forward a motion,—which would have embarrassed the Constitutional provision had it prevailed,—that the jurisdiction of the Federal Courts should be confined to cases of admiralty and maritime jurisdiction. Grayson, his colleague, supported him, but was answered by Ellsworth, and the debate became warm. As the question was about to be put, William Maclay, of Pennsylvania, a member of the Committee, a sturdy democrat, and a close adherent to the language and letter of the Constitution, arose and observed that the effect of the motion was to exclude the Federal jurisdiction from each of the States, except in admiralty and maritime cases. But the Constitution expressly extended it to all cases, in law and equity, under the Constitution and laws of the United States; treaties made, or about to be made, &c. We already had existing treaties, and were about making many laws. These must be executed by the Federal judiciary. The arguments used were inapplicable, as no amendments of the Constitution were under consideration. Inasmuch as the powers of Con-

---

[1] Mr. Flanders in his Life of Ellsworth, "Lives and Times of the Chief Justices," Vol. II, p. 159, attributes a share of the honor to William Samuel Johnson, of Connecticut, but this is an error, as Dr. Johnson was not a member of the Committee. As the original bill is in the handwriting of Ellsworth preserved among the archives of the Government, it is very clear that though reported by Lee, the laurels belong to Ellsworth.

9

gress extended to the collection of taxes, duties, and imposts; the naturalization of foreigners, the coinage, punishing counterfeiting of the coin, treason against the United States, &c., and no force of construction could bring any of these cases within the admiralty or maritime jurisdiction, it was clear that all these cases were most expressly within the province of the Federal jurisdiction, so that the question resolved itself into the simple one, Shall we follow the Constitution or not? Lee sought to parry the effect of this direct reasoning by the singular argument that the State judges would all be sworn to support the Constitution; that they must obey their oaths, and of course execute the Federal laws. To this Maclay replied that exactly the contrary could be looked for; that the Judges would swear to support the Constitution, that the Constitution placed the judicial power of the Union in one Supreme Court and such inferior Courts as might be established; and, of course, the State judges, by virtue of their oaths, would abstain from every judicial act under the Federal laws, and would refer all such business to the Federal Courts; that if any matter made cognizable in a Federal Court should be agitated in a State Court, a plea to the jurisdiction would immediately be put in, and proceedings would be stayed.[1] Lee's motion was then put and rejected.

The number of Judges to be appointed to the Supreme Court was then discussed. Grayson favored six. Maclay thought that if the Circuit Courts were established, six were

---

[1] "Sketches of Debate in the First Senate of the United States in 1789-90-91 by William Maclay, a Senator from Pennsylvania," (Harrisburg, 1880), pp. 86, 87. This Journal gives us the only insight into the debates of the First Senate that can be had, and is a very spirited record, full of characteristic touches, and portraits of the time from the pen of a conscientious democrat. It is but little known, but is deserving of close study.

too few, but that if the provision for Circuit Courts was struck out, they would be too many. Ellsworth then arose and made an elaborate argument upon the necessity of a numerous bench of judges. He enlarged upon the importance of the causes that would come before them; of the dignity it was necessary to support, and held up to view the twelve Judges of England, in the Exchequer Chamber. Maclay retorted that the whole mass of litigation in the Kingdom came before these judges—the whole judicial business of eight or nine millions of people, but in America it was wholly different; the mass of causes would remain with the State Judges. Those only arising from Federal laws would come before the Federal Judges, and there would, comparatively, be few, indeed. When they became numerous, it would be time enough to increase the judges. Grayson repeated his opinion that numbers were necessary to procure respectable decisions. Maclay replied that the way to secure respectable decisions was to choose eminent characters for judges—that numbers lessened responsibility, and, unless they were all eminent, tended to obscure the decisions. The clause providing that the Supreme Court should consist of a Chief Justice and five Associates was then passed.[1]

A debate then arose whether there should be Circuit Courts or Courts of *Nisi prius*. The distinction was started by the learned Dr. Johnson, of Connecticut. Pierce Butler adopted it and spoke for the greater part of a day. The vote was in favor of thirteen district courts.

The clause relating to oaths was then considered; Maclay moved to amend so that all persons conscientiously scrupulous of taking an oath should be permitted to affirm. Great

[1] Maclay's "Sketches of Debate," p. 88.

opposition was manifested. The Quakers were abused by Ralph Izard of South Carolina. Robert Morris and Maclay defended them, and the latter "ran Ellsworth and the other anti-affirmants so hard on the anti-constitutionalism of the clause, that they at last consented to have a question whether the clause should not be expunged; and expunged it was."[1]

Maclay then pointed out where Ellsworth in his diction in the bill had varied from the Constitution. "This bill is a child of his, and he defends it with the care of a parent, even with wrath and anger. He kindled, as he always does when it was meddled with. Lee, however, after some time, joined me. Although the President, John Adams, showed himself against us, we carried the amendment."[2]

Maclay then attacked a clause by which a defendant was required, on oath, to disclose his or her knowledge in the cause. He could not pass in silence such inquisitorial powers. Extorting evidence was a species of torture, and inconsistent with the spirit of freedom. No man should be compelled to give evidence against himself. Paterson moved to strike it out. Ellsworth defended it, now in chancery, now in common law, and now common law with a chancery side, and "then threw the common law back all the way to the wager of law, which he asserted was still in force." Strong rose and took the other side. Bassett rose; Read rose, and the rage of speaking caught the Senate. Paterson appealed to the feudal system, and pointedly denied all of Ellsworth's positions. The motion to strike out then prevailed.[3]

A clause was then taken up, "that suits in equity shall not be sustained in either of the Courts of the United States in any case where a remedy may be had at law." After a

---

[1] Maclay's "Sketches of Debate," p. 89.   [2] *Ibid.*, p. 90.   [3] *Ibid.*, p. 93.

long debate, in which all the leading lawyers participated, a motion to adopt was carried, but not without a violent assault upon Chancery proceedings by Maclay.

The bill was then taken up on third reading. Ellsworth had led in its support, backed by Strong, Paterson, Read and Bassett. At the same moment that Maclay made an entry in his Journal that he could scarcely account for his dislike of the bill, and that he really feared it would become the Gun-powder Plot of the Constitution, Chief-Justice McKean, of Pennsylvania, James Wilson, Miers Fisher, Richard Peters, Tench Coxe and other members of the bar approved in writing of its general outlines. Maclay again attacked it, ridiculing the delays of Chancery. John Adams, who was in the Chair, said that there was an instance of a cause being finished by the present Chancellor in his life-time, to which it was retorted: One swallow does not make a summer. As a general result of chancery proceedings, both parties were ruined. Plum is matched to plum. Where the parties were poor, the exhausted litigants dropped into ruin about one-fourth of the way through.

On the 17th of July the engrossed bill was read and passed by a vote of fourteen to six. Maclay could not conceal his disappointment and bitter dislike, for he entered in his Journal:

"I opposed this bill from the beginning. It certainly is a vile law system, calculated for expense, and with a design to draw by degrees all law business into the Federal Courts. The Constitution is meant to swallow all the State Constitutions, by degrees; and this to swallow, by degrees, all the State judiciaries. This, at least, is the design some gentlemen are aiming at."

In the House of Representatives the bill was supported by Fisher Ames, Theodore Sedgwick and Egbert Benson, against the assaults of Livermore of New Hampshire, and Jackson of Georgia. The former could not conceive why the system had been devised unless it be to plague mankind. He saw a foundation laid for discord, civil war and all its concomitants. To avert these evils he hoped the House would reject the bill.[1]

Inveterate prejudice and stubborn pride of State sovereignty, strange terror at the distant adumbration of the Nation; singular perplexity over what seems to us to be so clear! Posterity has not approved of these condemnatory judgments. On the contrary, the merits of the bill have been loudly applauded, and its distinguished author has been spoken of in terms of peculiar reverence by the American bar. One of his eulogists has declared that the whole Federal judicial system—"the whole edifice, organization, jurisdiction and process, was built by him as it now stands."[2] Although this must be regarded as extravagant, yet no one will deny to Ellsworth the high praise due to the fact that the judicial structure raised by him has stood the test of time, and remains to-day, in its essential features, the same as when it came from the hands of its founder.

The bill was approved by Washington on the 24th of September, 1789. It provided that the Supreme Court of the United States should consist of a Chief Justice and five Associate Justices, any four of whom should be a quorum, and should hold annually at the seat of government two sessions, commencing on the first Monday of February and the first Monday of August. The Associate Justices were to rank according to the date of their commissions, or when the com-

---

[1] Annals of Congress, Vol. I, pp. 784, 785.
[2] Wharton's "State Trials," p. 41.

missions bore date on the same day according to their respective ages.

The Court was empowered to appoint a clerk, and his oath of office was prescribed. The oath of the Justices of the Supreme Court was directed to be that they would "administer justice without respect to persons, and do equal right to the poor and to the rich," and that they would faithfully and impartially perform all the duties incumbent upon them, according to the best of their abilities and understanding, agreeably to the Constitution and Laws of the United States.

It was provided that the Supreme Court should have exclusive jurisdiction of all controversies of a civil nature where a State is a party, except between a State and its citizens; and except also between a State and citizens of other States, or aliens, in which latter case it shall have original, but not exclusive jurisdiction; and shall have exclusively all such jurisdiction of suits or proceedings against ambassadors or other public ministers or their domestic servants, as a court of law can have or exercise consistently with the law of nations; and original, but not exclusive jurisdiction, of all suits brought by ambassadors or other public ministers, or in which a Consul or Vice-Consul shall be a party.

It was expressly provided that the trial of issues in fact in the Supreme Court, in all actions at law against citizens of the United States, should be by jury.

The appellate jurisdiction of the Supreme Court from the Circuit Courts and Courts of the several States was specially provided for in the famous 25th Section, and power was given to issue writs of prohibition to the District Courts when proceeding as Courts of Admiralty and maritime jurisdiction, and writs of mandamus in cases warranted by the principles and usages of law to any Courts appointed or persons holding office under the authority of the United States.

The Supreme Court was not to issue execution in cases removed before them by writs of error, but ·was directed to send a special mandate to the Circuit Court to award execution thereupon.

The remaining provisions of the Bill related to the division of the United States into thirteen districts, and three circuits; the establishment of a District Court in each District, and provisions for the holding of special District Courts. The Circuit Courts were to consist of any two Justices of the Supreme Court and the District Judge of such District, any two of whom were to constitute a quorum, provided that no District Judge should give a vote in any case of appeal from his own decision, but might assign the reasons in support of it. The jurisdiction of the District and Circuit Courts were then regulated and distributed, and special provisions made as to matters of practice; the entry of special bail; the production of books and writings; the granting of new trials; the awarding of executions; the finality of decrees; the regulation of appeals and writs of error; the appointment of Marshals; the default of his deputies; the regulation of trials in cases punishable by death; the drawing of juries; the mode of proof; the taking of depositions *de bene esse.* Finally it was provided that parties in all Courts of the United States might personally plead and manage their own causes, or by the assistance of such counsel or attorneys at law as by the rules of the said Court should be permitted to practice therein. An attorney for the United States was to be appointed in each District, and an Attorney-General for the United States whose duty it should be to prosecute and conduct all suits in the Supreme Court in which the United States should be concerned, and to give his advice and opinion upon questions of law when required by the President, or when requested by the heads of any of the Departments touching any matters that may concern their Departments.[1]

Such were the leading features of the first Judiciary Act of the United States, and it only remained for the President to appoint, and the Senate to confirm, judges to fill the positions which had been created in order to organize the judicial department of the Government.

[1] See "Laws of the United States of America" (Phila. 1796), Vol. I, pp. 47–75.

PART III.

THE SUPREME COURT OF THE UNITED STATES.

CHAPTER XI.

THE ink was still wet upon the signature of the President to the Judiciary Act when he sent to the Senate the following names: for Chief Justice, John Jay; for Associate Justices, John Rutledge, James Wilson, William Cushing, Robert H. Harrison and John Blair. On the 26th of September the appointments were confirmed. In the order of date of commissions as actually issued, Wilson was postponed to Rutledge, Cushing and Harrison.

At the same time Edmund Randolph was appointed Attorney-General.

The motives which governed Washington in making these selections are visible in his correspondence. To his nephew, Bushrod Washington, he wrote:

" My political conduct in nominations, even if I were uninfluenced by principle, must be exceedingly circumspect and proof against just criticism; for the eyes of Argus are upon me, and no slip will pass unnoticed that can be improved into a supposed partiality for friends or relatives." [1]

---

[1] Letter dated 27 July, 1789, Sparks' " Writings of Washington," Vol. X, p. 24.

To Madison, a few days later, he expressed the utmost solicitude for drawing the first characters of the Union into the judiciary and his regret that Edmund Pendleton was too old to be appointed to the Supreme Court. For Randolph in the character of Attorney-General he declared a preference to any person with whom he was acquainted of not superior abilities, from habits of intimacy with him.[1]

To the Judges themselves he addressed letters, stating that he considered the judicial system as the chief pillar upon which our National Government must rest; that he had thought it his duty to nominate for the high offices in that department such men as he conceived would give dignity and lustre to our national character, and he flattered himself that the love which they had to their country, and a desire to promote the general happiness, would lead them to a ready acceptance of the commissions enclosed, which were accompanied by a copy of the Judiciary Act.[2] To Jay he wrote in the warmest terms, conveying the singular pleasure with which he addressed him as Chief Justice, and confessing that in nominating him he not only acted in conformity to his best judgment, but did a grateful thing to the good citizens of the United States. He begged him not to hesitate a moment in bringing into action the talents, knowledge and integrity which were so necessary to be exercised at the head of that department which must be considered as the keystone of our political fabric.[3]

We are assured by his son that Jay preferred the Chief Justiceship to the various offices tendered him, as the sphere

---

[1] Letter, 10th August, 1789, Sparks' "Writings of Washington," Vol. X, p. 5.

[2] Letter to the Judges, September 30th, 1789, *Ibid.* p. 35.

[3] Letter to Jay, 5th October, 1789, *Ibid.* p. 35.

in which for the future his talents could be most usefully exerted.[1] At that time he was acting as Secretary for Foreign Affairs. He was but little more than forty-four years of age, almost six feet in height, of thin but well-formed person, of colorless complexion, with black, or, as some say blue, penetrating eyes, aquiline nose and pointed chin. His hair was usually drawn back from his forehead, tied behind and lightly powdered. His manners were gentle and unassuming.[2] He was neither a brilliant advocate nor a profoundly learned lawyer nor a master of the technique of practice. His public duties had been too exacting to permit him to labor in the forum. He was rather a statesman and a jurist than a pleader of causes. But his character was "a jewel in the sacred treasures of national reputation, and when the spotless ermine of the judicial robe fell upon him, it touched nothing not as spotless as itself." [3]

He was judicious and prudent, rather than emotional, retired in disposition, dignified, self-controlled, conscientious, just and wise, remarkable, as his friend, Lindley Murray wrote, for strong reasoning powers, comprehensive views, indefatigable industry and uncommon firmness of mind. Judgment, discriminative, penetrating, was the characteristic of his understanding. If over his other faculties imagination had presided, the compass of his thought would have been enlarged, and grace and flexibility been imparted to his mind. He wrote at all times with great clearness and force, and occa-

---

[1] William Jay, "Life and Writings of John Jay," New York, 1833, Vol. I, p. 275.

[2] Sullivan's "Letters on Public Characters," p. 59.

[3] Webster's Speech in the City of New York, March 10, 1831.

[4] William Jay, "Life of John Jay;" Henry Flanders, "Lives and Times of Chief Justices," Vol. I, p. 429; George Pellew, "John Jay," in "American Statesmen" Series.

sionally with extreme elegance of expression. Of the gifts of the orator he had none. His paternal ancestors were French Huguenots, who had been driven from their native land by the fury of persecution which followed the revocation of the Edict of Nantes. In time they found their way to South Carolina, but subsequently, on account of the climate, thought it advisable to go to New York. There, on the 12th of December, 1745, John Jay was born, the eighth of a family of ten children. His mother was of Dutch extraction. After a preliminary course at a grammar school, and instruction from a private tutor, he entered Columbia (then King's) College, and after graduation pursued the study of the law in the office of Benjamin Kissam. After his admission to the bar he was successful in obtaining practice, but before he had an opportunity of becoming distinguished in his profession was drawn into the vortex of politics.

Notwithstanding his youth, he became one of the most active and influential spirits of the early Revolutionary period. In 1774 he was sent as a delegate to the First Continental Congress, which assembled at the Hall of the Carpenters' Company in Philadelphia, and found himself, with the single exception of Edward Rutledge, the youngest member of that august body. With none of the headlong impetuosity or fiery zeal of Henry, Rutledge and Adams, he prudently abstained from the vain effort to compete with those splendid orators; but he won world-wide renown as the author of the Address to the People of Great Britain,—a paper which drew forth the encomiums of the Earl of Chatham by its able and dignified statement of the rights, and glowing portrayal of the wrongs of the Colonies. He also served as a member of the Committee of Correspondence, and is supposed to have written the reply to the Boston Address, in which he opposed the project of non-intercourse. He wrote also the Address to the People of Canada, and, at the request of his father-in-law, Governor William Livingston, of New Jersey, an Address to the Inhabitants of Ireland. He continued to serve as a member of Congress until his recall, in May, 1776, to assist in framing a government for New York, and thus narrowly missed the immortality which glorifies the names of the Signers of the Declaration of Independence. In his own State he prepared a Bill of Rights, and took a leading part in framing the Constitution; in fact, it is claimed that he was its author. He acted as a member of the Council of Safety, and was appointed Chief-Justice of New York in September, 1776,—an office which he held until December, 1778, when he was again sent to Congress, where he presided over its deliberations as the successor of Henry Laurens. He then entered upon the wider theatre of diplomacy. He was sent to Spain to negotiate a loan of two millions of dollars and the freedom of the Mississippi. With Franklin, Adams and Laurens he negotiated the Treaty of Peace, and, returning to New York, was appointed by Congress Secretary of Foreign Affairs. In October, 1786, he drew up an elaborate report on the relations between the United States and Great Britain. Although not a member of the Federal Convention, he took a leading part in the advocacy of the new government, contributing five numbers to "The Federalist," and a pamphlet and eloquent Address to the People of the State of New York on the subject of the Constitution. He favored the national idea. In 1785 he had written: "It is my first wish to see the United States assume and merit the character of one great nation, whose territory is divided into different States merely for more convenient government, and the more easy and prompt administration of justice,—just as our several

States are divided into counties and townships for the like purposes." Ripe in experience, and thoroughly tried in many responsible and conspicuous positions, in all of which he had conducted himself with lofty disinterestedness and unyielding integrity, his calmness of temperament, accuracy of judgment, unblemished character and sound views upon public questions commended him to the sagacious choice of Washington as the publicist and jurist best fitted to elevate and adorn the judiciary of the nation and to preside over the deliberations of its supreme tribunal.

The Associate Justices were also men of national reputation. John Rutledge was the son of Dr. John Rutledge, who, with his brother Andrew, both natives of Ireland, settled in Charleston, South Carolina, where, in the year 1739, the future Associate and Chief-Justice of the United States was born. The historian, Dr. Ramsay, says: "In the friendly competitions of the States for the comparative merits of their respective statesmen and orators, while Massachusetts boasts of her John Adams, Connecticut of her Ellsworth, New York of her Jay, Pennsylvania of her Wilson, Delaware of her Bayard, Virginia of her Henry, South Carolina rests her claim on the talents and eloquence of John Rutledge." After an excellent classical education, Rutledge entered as a law student in the Temple, in London, and proceeding barrister, came out to Charleston, and began the active work of the profession in 1761. In his first cause—an action for breach of promise of marriage—his eloquence astonished all who heard him. His business became large, and he at once took rank among the able members of the bar. With Gadsden and Lynch, he was sent to the Congress at New York in 1765, and his bold denunciation of the Stamp Act filled with wonder the members of distant provinces. He returned to the bar, and for ten years devoted himself exclusively to practice. In 1774 he became a member of the First Continental Congress, and Patrick Henry called him the foremost orator of that body. He remained in this branch of public service for two years, and was then elected President and Commander-in-Chief of his native State. Thenceforth his duties were executive. The following anecdote is quoted as a sample of the spirit with which he acted. He wrote to General Moultrie, who commanded Sullivan's Island, in the harbor of Charleston, this laconic note: "General Lee wishes you to evacuate the fort. You will not without an order from me. I would sooner cut off my hand than write one." In 1778 he became the Governor of the State under the new Constitution, and made great exertions to repel the British invasions, to defend Charleston in the year 1779–80, to procure the aid of Congress and of the adjacent States, and to revive the suspended legislative and judicial powers of the State. His genius for organizing was superb. In 1782 he was again sent to Congress. The next year he was appointed Minister Plenipotentiary to Holland, but declined the office. He was then elected a Judge of the Court of Chancery in his own State, and his duties, from this time forth, were almost exclusively judicial. His legal learning is said to have been great. He was one of the most active of the Southern members of the Federal Convention, and exerted himself strenuously to induce his countrymen to ratify the Constitution. These services constituted his brief of title to the confidence which led Washington to place his name next to Jay's in the list of appointments to the Federal judiciary.

William Cushing, who was the first representative of New England upon the bench of the Supreme Court was a man of good stature, erect, graceful, and dignified, of fair com-

Wm Cushing

plexion, blue eyes, and enormous nose; in dress adhering to the style of the Revolution, wearing a three-cornered hat, wig, and small clothes, with buckles in his shoes, a gentleman of the old school, affable and courteous; in politics a Federalist of the Washington type. He was born at Scituate, in Massachusetts, on the 1st of March, 1732. His father was a member of the Supreme Court of the State, and was one of the Judges who presided at the trial of the British soldiers for the massacre of citizens in the streets of Boston on the 5th of March, 1770. The son was a graduate of Harvard, which afterwards conferred on him the degree of LL.D. He pursued his professional studies under the direction of Jeremiah Gridley, and at an early age was appointed a judge of probate. He succeeded his father as a Judge of the Supreme Judicial Court, and, at the outbreak of the Revolution, alone of all those high in office supported the rights of his country. At town meetings he was an eloquent and invincible speaker. He became the first Chief Justice of Massachusetts under the Constitution of 1780, an office which he held at the time of his promotion to the Supreme Court of the United States. His mental characteristics were eminently judicial.

Robert Hanson Harrison, though almost unknown to the present generation, was a special favorite of Washington, owing to the close and confidential relation he sustained to his chief during the war of the Revolution. He was born in Charles County, Maryland, in 1745, and was the son of Richard Harrison and Dorothy, daughter of Robert Hanson. He was bred to the law, but at the age of thirty-one preferred to leave his clientage for the service of his country. On the 16th of May, 1776, he succeeded Joseph Reed as Secretary to General Washington, with the rank of Lieutenant-Colonel, and remained a member of the military family of the Commander-

10

in-Chief until the spring of 1781. He is described in one of the letters of the General as "sensible, clear, and perfectly confidential." He was appointed by Congress a member of the Board of War, but declined the position. He participated in the Battle of Long Island, the operations near White Plains, the action at Chatterton's Hill and the Battle of Brandywine. He also served as a Commissioner for the exchange of prisoners. In March, 1781, he was appointed Chief Judge of the General Court of Maryland, an office which he held when, in the balloting for a first Vice-President in the electoral college, he received the six votes of his native State. Five days after his confirmation as an Associate Justice of the Supreme Court of the United States he was unanimously chosen Chancellor of Maryland. He hesitated for some time before making a choice between the two positions, but finally determined in favor of the latter. In a letter, dated 25th November, 1789, Washington acknowledged the return of the commission, but finding that one of the reasons that induced him to decline the appointment was an objection to the Judiciary Act, suggested that such a change in the system was contemplated as would permit him to pay as much attention to his private affairs as his present station, and declared that he thought it proper to return his commission, not for the sake of urging him to accept it contrary to his interests or convenience, but with a view of giving him a further opportunity of informing himself as to the nature and probability of the change alluded to.[1] In the end he again declined, preferring the State office. He died, however, in the following April at his seat on the Potomac, near Port Tobacco, in the

---

[1] Letter of Washington to Harrison, Nov. 25th, 1789. Sparks' "Writings of Washington," Vol. X, p. 52.

forty-fifth year of his age, and Washington wrote to Lafayette: "Poor Colonel Harrison, who was appointed one of the Associate Judges of the Supreme Court and declined, is lately dead."[1]

James Wilson was in some respects the ablest member of the first Supreme Court. He stood in the very foremost rank at the bar, and though he had been called upon on frequent occasions to discharge public duties, yet as they were all performed in the city of Philadelphia during the sessions of Congress, and the Federal and State Conventions, he was able to devote himself to an important and varied practice, without suffering as others did from a long absence from home. His attainments in the law were such as to lead the King of France to commission him as *Avocat général de la Nation Française à Philadelphie*, and bestow upon him the sum of ten thousand livres; while Washington, passing by the Wythes and Pendletons of Virginia, selected him as the preceptor of his nephew, Bushrod Washington.[2] There is evidence that he was thought of by his friends as likely to be called upon to fill the highest judicial position in the nation.[3]

[1] Letter of 3d June, 1790. Sparks' "Writings of Washington," Vol. X, p. 250.

[2] The writer is in possession of the original of the following note: "Philada., March 22, 1782. I promise to pay James Wilson Esq: or order on demand one hundred guineas, his fee for receiving my nephew, Bushrod Washington, as a Student of Law in his office. G. Washington." Endorsed: "Received 23 July, 1782, from his Excellency, General Washington, one hundred guineas in full of the within note. James Wilson." Endorsed in handwriting of Washington: "Rect. No. 135—James Wilson Esq., 100 Guineas, 23 July, 1782."

[3] In a letter of General Anthony Wayne to Wilson, dated the 20th of May, 1789, he congratulates him upon the adoption and organization of the Federal Constitution--"a business in which you took so early, so conspicuous and so effectual a part, and permit me to add that it was to a display of the perfect knowledge you entertained and the plain elucidation you gave of the component parts of that system, which caused it to be approved by the Convention of Pennsylvania, it

It is not known whether Wilson himself ever raised his eyes to the first place; certain it is that he did not permit disappointment to sour him. He accepted the position tendered with great cheerfulness, and, on the 5th of October, appeared before the Mayor of Philadelphia and voluntarily took the oath of office prescribed by the Judiciary Act.[1] His education and public experience had fully prepared him for the post. He was a native of Scotland, and had studied at Glasgow, St. Andrew's, and Edinburgh, under Dr. Blair, in Rhetoric, and in 1763, at the age of twenty-one years, had emigrated to New York, and in 1766 arrived in Philadelphia. His attainments in the classics were remarkable; the student of his literary remains cannot fail to be impressed by the evidence

---

being the first that met, and the first in consequence in the Union and perhaps its present operation may justly be attributed to the happy *turning of the scale* in that State. I therefore hope and trust that I may with propriety venture to congratulate you upon an appointment, so generally acknowledged, due to your professional and other merits, *i.e.*, the *Chief Justiceship* of the United States of America." The original of this letter, which has never been published, is in the possession of Thos. H. Montgomery, Esq., of Philadelphia, who received it from the grand-daughter of Judge Wilson. The latter part of it is characteristic and interesting. After winning Wilson's good will by this not carefully concealed flattery, he recommends a friend for office, and then asks that Wilson use his best interest to secure for himself "an appointment in the Southern Department similar to that which General St. Clair enjoys to the Westward and to which I have *some claims* as well from my past unrewarded services, as from the knowledge I have of the country and of the *Creeks*, *Choctaws* and other nations of Indians whom I have more than once defeated in the field, and afterwards concluded a treaty of peace, honorable and advantageous to this country and satisfactory to them, which may be seen among the papers of Congress and those of his Excellency, the President of the United States of America." Little did Wayne at the time dream that he would be sent into the West to retrieve the defeats which overwhelmed St. Clair, and that victory would crown him on the banks of the Miami.

[1] Original certificate under the hand and seal of the Mayor of Philadelphia, in the possession of the grand-daughter of Judge Wilson. I have not been able to find any other record of the manner in which the Chief Justice and remaining Associates were sworn. It may be that they all pursued a similar course.

James Wilson

of his familiarity with the history and philosophy of Greece and Rome. For a short time he was a tutor in the College of Philadelphia. He subsequently studied law in the office of John Dickinson, and after some years of practice at Reading, Carlisle, and Annapolis, came to Philadelphia, and was admitted to the bar of that city in December, 1778. His political experience was great. An ardent advocate of American Independence, he was for six years a member of Congress, though not continuously, and was concerned in all the measures of government both during and after the war. He was one of the signers of the Declaration. In the principles of finance and constitutional law as it then existed he was particularly learned. As an orator he held high rank both as an advocate and a parliamentary debater. He was one of the ablest and most active of the members of the Federal Convention, and his speeches in the Convention of Pennsylvania, called to adopt or reject the new Constitution will compare favorably as luminous expositions of the work he had helped to perform, with any of the arguments in its favor to be found reported in Elliott's Debates. He was a man of large and powerful frame, with an open, honest face, with bright blue eyes beaming mildly from behind a pair of heavy silver-rimmed spectacles; his mouth was large and expressive.

John Blair, the last in commission of the Associate Justices, was of slight frame, but with an astonishing breadth of brow, particularly between the eyes, which were brown in color, surmounted by a bald forehead fringed with scanty locks of red hair, which fell over his ears. His lower lip protruded in a singular way, like the bill of a bird. He was born in the City of Williamsburg, Virginia, in 1732, and was educated at William and Mary College. His family was one of fortune and powerful connections. Bred to the bar, he studied in the Temple and became a barrister; on his return he settled in his native city, where he acquired a considerable share of the current legal business. In 1766 he became a member of the House of Burgesses, and ten years later was one of the committee of the Convention which drew up a plan for the government of the State. In 1779 he was made Chief Justice of the General Court, and on the death of Judge Nicholas was appointed a member of the High Court of Chancery, and by virtue of both stations was a Judge of the first Court of Appeals. He served as a member of the Federal Convention, as well as of his State Convention; and though not aggressive in his advocacy, was a firm supporter of the Constitution. He was regarded by his contemporaries as an able man, amiable in disposition, blameless and pious, possessed of great benevolence and goodness of heart.

On the first Monday of February, being the first day of the month, 1790, in the City of New York, then the seat of the National Government, Chief Justice Jay and Justices Cushing and Wilson appeared in the Court room which had been provided at the Exchange. John McKesson acted as clerk. No quorum being present, the Court adjourned to the following day, when, Justice Blair having arrived, with Edmund Randolph, the first Attorney-General, the Court was formally opened in the presence of the Chief Justice and other judges of the Supreme Court of New York, the Hon. James Duane, United States District Judge, the Mayor and Recorder of New York City, the Marshal of the District, the Sheriff and other officers, and a great number of the gentlemen of the bar.[1]

---

[1] Gazette of the United States, Feb. 3, 1790, No. Lxxxv. New York letter dated Feb. 4th, in the Pennsylvania Journal and Weekly Advertiser, February 10, 1790.

John Blair jun.

The Jury from the District Court was also in attendance, many members of Congress and a number of respectable citizens.[1] Proclamation was made, and the commissions of the Judges and of the Attorney-General were read and published. Richard Wenman was appointed cryer.[2] The next day John Tucker, Esq., of Boston, was appointed Clerk, and it was ordered that he reside and keep his Office at the seat of the National Government, and that he do not practice either as counsellor or attorney so long as he acted as Clerk.[3]

After oath had been administered and a bond approved, the Court adjourned for the day. In the evening the Grand Jury for the United States, in the district, gave " a very elegant entertainment" in honor of the Court at Francis' Tavern in Courtlandt Street. "The liberality displayed on this occasion and the good order and harmony which presided gave particular satisfaction to the respectable guests."[4]

The next morning Elias Boudinot, of New Jersey, Thomas Hartley, of Pennsylvania, and Richard Harrison, of New York, were severally sworn as by law required, and were ad-

[1] Pennsylvania Packet and Daily Advertiser, Feb. 6, 1790.

[2] Minutes of the Supreme Court of the United States.

[3] Minutes of the Supreme Court. Mr. Tucker was selected by Jay; his character is stated to have been most exemplary. William Jay, "Life of John Jay," Vol. II, p. 201.

[4] Letter dated Feby. 10, 1790. Gazette of the United States. After dinner the following toasts were drunk: The President of the United States; The Vice-President; The National Judiciary; The Senate of the United States; The Speaker and House of Representatives; The late National Convention; The Constitution of our Country, —May it Prove the Solid Fabrick of American Liberty, Prosperity and Glory; The Memory of the Heroes who Fell in Defence of the Liberties of America; His Most Christian Majesty and the People of France; The Convention of Rhode Island,— May their Wisdom and Integrity soon introduce our Stray Sister to her Station in the Happy National Family of America.

mitted as counsellors, their names being enrolled upon parchment.[1]·

After a few moments of quiet consultation, the Judges adopted Rules, by which it was declared and established that the Seal of the Court shall be the arms of the United States, engraved on a piece of steel of the size of a dollar, with these words in the margin: "The Seal of the Supreme Court of the United States," and that the seals of the Circuit Courts shall be the arms of the United States, engraven on circular pieces of silver of the size of a half dollar, with these words in the margin, in the upper part: "The Seal of the Circuit Court," and in the lower part the name of the district for which it is intended. It was further ordered that it should be requisite to the admission of attorneys and counselors to practice in this Court that they shall have been such for three years past in the Supreme Court of the State to which they respectively belong, and that their private and professional character shall appear to be "fair." It was also ordered that counselors should not practice as attorneys, nor attorneys as counselors, and that they should be sworn to demean themselves as officers of the Court agreeably and according to law, and that they would support the Constitution of the United States. It was also ordered that all process of the Court should be in the name of the President of the United States. Thereupon the Court adjourned to the first Monday of August following, as fixed by law.[2]

Not a single litigant had appeared at their bar. The silence had been unbroken by the voice of counsel in argument. The table was unburdened by the weight of learned

---

[1] Minutes of the Supreme Court. Parchment roll in the Office of the Clerk of the Supreme Court.

[2] Minutes of the Supreme Court.

briefs. No papers were on file with the Clerk. Not a single decision, even in embryo, existed. The Judges were there; but of business there was none.

Not one of the spectators of that hour, though gifted with the eagle eyes of prophecy, could have foreseen that out of that modest assemblage of gentlemen, unheard of and unthought of among the tribunals of the earth, a Court without a docket, without a record, without a writ, of unknown and untried powers, and of undetermined jurisdiction, there would be developed, in the space of a single century, a Court of which the ancient world could present no model, and the modern boast no parallel; a Court whose decrees, woven like threads of gold into the priceless and imperishable fabric of our Constitutional jurisprudence, would bind in the bonds of love, liberty and law the members of our great Republic. Nor could they have foreseen that the tables of Congress would groan beneath the weight of petitions from all parts of the country inviting that body to devise some means for the relief of that overburdened tribunal whose litigants are now doomed to stand in line for a space of more than three years before they have a chance to be heard.

James Iredell was appointed on the day upon which the Court rose in the place of Harrison, his commission being dated February 10, 1790. He was born at Lewes, England, October 5, 1751, (N. S.), and was of Irish extraction. Tradition says that the family name was originally Ireton, and that they were collateral descendants of the son-in-law of Cromwell; and that when at the Restoration the body of the great Protector was dug up and exposed upon the gibbet at Tyburn, prudence dictated a change of name so as to escape the fury of the royalists.[1] However that might be, there was no trace of

---

[1] McRee, "Life and Correspondence of James Iredell," Vol. I, p. 1.

ancestral pusillanimity in the judge: he was ever bold and outspoken in speech and courageous in conduct. At the age of seventeen he arrived in Boston, and was deputed by the commissioners for managing the royal customs to act as comptroller at Edenton, North Carolina, where, soon after his arrival, he entered on the study of the law, under the direction of Samuel Johnston. For six years he prepared all the accounts, returns and exhibits, and kept the books of the Custom House. For an uncle, who resided in England, he sold and leased lands, collected rents and fees, remitted by bills of exchange and cargoes of corn and pork.[1] In this way he acquired a thorough knowledge of business, while devoting all his leisure moments to the law. He was admitted to the bar in 1770, and slowly but steadily forced his way to leadership. He became a deputy to the Attorney-General, and an active political writer upon the topics of the day. In 1777 he was elected to the bench of the District Court, but held his office only a year.[2] During that time he delivered addresses to grand juries which were published by request as a means of invigorating the timid, rousing the indifferent, reclaiming the disaffected and calling the united strength of the people to the support of the American cause. Shortly after this he became Attorney-General, and later a Councillor of State. In the famous State trials at Warrenton he bore a conspicuous part, and his argument, sustaining the power of a Court to declare an act of the legislature void because of an infringement of the Constitution, was a splendid instance of his bold and original methods of reasoning, and his power of illustration and statement. About this time the State was convulsed by the contest over the ratification of the Constitution, and Iredell's

[1] McRee, "Life and Correspondence of James Iredell," Vol. I., p. 54.
[2] *Ibid.*, p. 367.

"Reply to the Objections of George Mason," raised him in the opinion of competent judges to the position of the ablest legal reasoner in the State. No one contributed more than he to bring about the amazing change in the sentiments of the people which was evinced at the final election.[1] Mr. Iredell had just completed his labors as commissioner to revise the laws of his adopted State, when he was appointed to the vacant position in the Supreme Court of the United States. This appointment was made without any solicitation upon his part. He had been led to think that he would be made District Judge for North Carolina, and when the higher dignity was tendered, it was to him a matter of agreeable surprise. It is said that Washington derived his conviction of Iredell's merit from a perusal of the debates in the North Carolina Convention and the famous Reply to George Mason's Objections.[2] His confirmation by the Senate was unanimous, and Pierce Butler in a graceful letter congratulated the States that they would no longer be deprived of his aid and the benefit of his abilities.

The first service performed by the Judges was upon Circuit. The Chief Justice and his associate, Cushing, with Duane, the District Judge, held the first Circuit Court, for the Eastern Circuit, in New York City, upon April 3, 1790. Jay delivered an elaborate charge to the Grand Jury, in which he inculcated the principles of morality and advised submission to Constitutional authority. Wilson and Blair went upon the Middle Circuit, while the Southern Circuit was attended by Rutledge and Iredell.[3] It was expected that the Judges would

---

[1] Letter of Chas. Johnson (Speaker of the Senate), to Iredell, Nov. 23, 1789. McRee's "Life of Iredell," Vol. II, p. 273.

[2] *Ibid.*, Vol. II, p. 279.

[3] The Eastern Circuit embraced the Districts of New Hampshire, Massachu-

take these in rotation.[1] In traveling through New England Jay declined every invitation of his friends to lodge with them, preferring to go to public houses. To one he wrote: "As a man, and as your friend, I should be happy in accepting your invitation, but, as a judge, I have my doubts—they will occur to you without details." At New Haven he was met by a body of the citizens who escorted him as far as his inn. Boston was lavish of her civilities. Harvard University conferred upon him the degree of Doctor of Laws; Portsmouth honored him with a public entry, and on his departure attended him some distance on his journey.[2] In the autumn he again made the circuit, and held Courts at Boston, Exeter, Providence, Hartford and Albany. Although often urged to interest himself with the President and Heads of Departments in favor of applicants for office, he scrupulously avoided interference, except in the single case of Matthew Clarkson, for the office of Marshal, an office connected with his own tribunal, and in the faithful discharge of which he was officially interested.[3]

We know nothing of what occurred in the Middle Circuit,[4] but we are able to trace, through the charming letters of Judge Iredell to his wife, his journey from Camden to

setts, Connecticut and New York; the Middle Circuit, the Districts of New Jersey, Pennsylvania, Delaware, Maryland and Virginia; and the Southern Circuit, South Carolina and Georgia. Judiciary Act of 1789. Laws of United States, Vol. I, p. 50. At that time North Carolina and Rhode Island had not ratified the Constitution.

[1] Letter of Samuel Johnston to Iredell, March 11, 1790, McRee's "Life of Iredell," Vol. II, p. 285.

[2] An interesting account of "The Circuit Court for the New Hampshire District One Hundred years Ago" is to be found in a paper by Wm. H. Hackett, Esq. "The Green Bag," Vol. II., No. 6, p. 262.

[3] William Jay, "Life of John Jay," Vol. II, p. 277.

[4] No cases are reported by Dallas until April term, 1792.

Charleston and Savannah, in company with Rutledge. The nature of the business which came before them is not stated. From the latter place Iredell proceeded to North Carolina, under the impression that the Judiciary Act had been extended to that State. As this was doubtful, Rutledge remained at home. After a delay at New Berne, without information, the former traveled northward to be present at the August term of the Supreme Court.[1]

In the preceding April President Washington had addressed a letter to the Chief Justice and Associate Justices, stating his sense of the importance of having the judiciary system not only independent in its operations, but as perfect as possible in its formation, and asking them to communicate to him whatever occurred to them in the unexplored fields of their circuits, with whatever remarks they deemed expedient.[2] In reply, the Chief Justice, in a letter which does not appear to have been concurred in by Iredell, urges what he notes as deviations of the Judiciary Act from the Constitution, calling for correction: First, that under the appellate jurisdiction bestowed upon the Supreme Court there was an incompatibility and inconsistency between the offices of Judges of the Supreme Court and Judges of the Circuit Courts, and that they ought not to be held by the same persons; and second, that the assignment by Act of Congress of the Judges of the Supreme Court to Circuit Court duties was an exercise of powers which constitutionally belonged to the President and the Senate, the Constitution not having provided that the judges of the inferior Courts should be appointed "*otherwise.*"[3] No immediate result is traceable to

[1] McRee's, "Life of Iredell," Vol. II, p. 291.
[2] Sparks's "Writings of Washington," Vol. X, p 86.
[3] McRee's "Life of Iredell," Vol. II, p. 295.

this letter, and the point remained undisposed of for several years. Among the last acts of the administration of President Adams was a bill for "the more convenient organization of the Courts of the United States," which will be noticed more particularly in its proper place, by which the Judges of the Supreme Court were relieved from circuit duty entirely, and confined to attendance upon the sessions of their own tribunal. The act was repealed in the following year, and the old system restored, but the opponents of the repeal stoutly maintained that, under the Constitution, Congress could not require the Judges of the Supreme Court to sit at Circuit. Such, it seems, was the opinion of John Marshall, which he endeavored to urge upon his associates, without success. Finally, in the case of *Stuart* v. *Laird*,[1] it was held that practice and acquiescence, for a period of many years, commencing with the organization of the judicial system, had fixed the construction, and that this contemporary and practical exposition was too strong to be shaken or controverted.[2]

When the Supreme Court met for the second time in New York City, on the first Monday of August, 1790, Rutledge alone was absent. After the publication of Iredell's commission, the admission of several counsel, and directions to the clerk to prepare a seal for the Circuit Court of Rhode Island, an adjournment took place from lack of business.[3]

In the following February the Chief Justice laid before the Court a letter from James Duane, the District Judge of New York, requesting the appointment of a special Circuit Court for the trial of prisoners confined in gaol for breaches of the revenue laws, on the ground that the District Court

---

[1] 1 Cranch, p. 299 (1803).
[2] See also Van Santvoord's "Lives of the Chief Justices," p. 351.
[3] Minutes of the Supreme Court.

was excluded from jurisdiction of these offences by the extent
of the punishment, and that its criminal cognizance thus cir-
cumscribed was a burthen to the community without any cor-
responding advantage. The request was granted, and a similar
special court was ordered to be held in Philadelphia for the
trial of criminals and the relief of certain sea-faring men who
were detained as witnesses.[1]

At the same term the first instance of a suit by an individual against a State, the case of *Vanstaphorst* v. *The State
of Maryland*, appeared upon the record, the Marshal making
return that he had served the summons by copy upon the
Governor, Executive Council and Attorney-General of the
State, in the presence of witnesses. An appearance was entered, without objection of any sort, by Luther Martin as Attorney-General of the State of Maryland, and on motion of
Edmund Randolph, the Attorney-General of the United States,
the State was ordered to plead within two months.[2] A commission to take the depositions of certain witnesses in Holland,
with the consent of the counsel for the defendant State was
applied for but refused, until a commissioner was named. This
being done the motion was granted.[3] The case was subsequently discontinued, each party agreeing to pay their own
costs.

A suit was also brought by *Oswald, administrator*, v. *The
State of New York*,[4] in which after a return of service, a motion
was made for a *distringas* to compel the appearance of the
State; while the matter was under consideration, leave was
given to withdraw the motion and enter a discontinuance.
The case was again renewed, and an order made by the Court
that unless the State should appear by the following term,

[1] Minutes of the Supreme Court.   [2] *Ibid.*   [3] *Ibid.*
[4] 2 Dallas, 401 (1792).

and show cause to the contrary, judgment would be entered by default.

A question of practice also arose. A writ of error had been presented, issued out of the Office of the Clerk of the Circuit Court for the Rhode Island district, directed to that Court, and commanding a return of the judgment and proceedings therein, and a rule was moved for that the defendants rejoin to the errors assigned. It was objected to the validity of the writ that it had issued out of the wrong office, and after argument, it was unanimously determined that writs of error to remove causes from inferior courts could regularly issue only from the Office of the Clerk of the Supreme Court.[1]

On the 1st of August, 1791, John Tucker resigned as clerk, and Samuel Bayard, of Delaware, was appointed in his stead.[2]

A difference of opinion soon arose among the Judges relative to their circuits, and contrary to the expectation and the wishes of the Southern members of the Court, it was determined that the Judges should be divided into pairs, and each pair be confined permanently to one circuit.[3] Iredell, it seems, was taken by surprise, and Blair voted under a misconception. The burden of " leading the life of a Postboy" in a circuit of vast extent, under great difficulties of travel and peril of life in the sickly seasons, fell heavily upon Iredell, who applied to Congress for relief, but it was not until the Act of 13th of April, 1792, providing that the Judges should ride by turns the circuit most distant from the seat of government, that the difficulty was adjusted.[4]

In the meantime John Rutledge had resigned, preferring

---

[1] West *v.* Barnes *et al.*, 2 Dallas, 401 (1791).   Minutes of the Supreme Court.
[2] Minutes of Supreme Court.
[3] McRee's " Life of Iredell," Vol. II, p. 321.
[4] Laws of the United States, p. 234.

the position of Chancellor of his native State, to which he had been recently chosen, and Charles Cotesworth Pinckney and Edward Rutledge having declined in turn, Thomas Johnson was appointed in the recess on August 5th, 1791. In transmitting his commission Washington alluded to the opinion which prevailed against the expediency of continuing the circuits of the Associate Judges, and stated that it was expected that some alterations in the judicial system would be made, with a view of relieving them from disagreeable tours.[1]

Johnson was born in Calvert County, Maryland, in 1732. He was educated under the direction of private tutors, and subsequently studied law, in which he attained great distinction. In 1774 he was a member of the Committee of Correspondence of his State, and the following year was sent as a delegate to the Continental Congress, where he had the felicity of nominating Washington as Commander-in-Chief, a circumstance which led to the most cordial and friendly relations, which were never disturbed. His attachment to the great soldier led him to resign his membership in Congress, and go to the assistance of the American Army then in New England with a small force which he had raised by his personal exertions. He was the first Governor of Maryland under the new State Constitution, and held the position for three years. He warmly advocated internal navigation; on the establishment of the Federal government he was tendered the place of United States District Judge for Maryland, but declined it, and was active in securing the appointment of William Paca, who was one of the signers of the Declaration of Independence. He served as a member of the Board of Commissioners for Locating the District of Columbia. His relations with Wash-

---

[1] Letter of Washington to Thomas Johnson, 7 Aug., 1791, Sparks's "Writings of Washington," Vol. X, p. 182.

11

ington continued to be intimate, and he was frequently visited by the President at his estate at Rose Hill, near the city of Frederick.   When Jefferson left the Cabinet, the position of Secretary of State was tendered to him but declined.   The high order of merit due to his services was attested by John Adams who, when questioned as to how it was that so many Southern men participated in the war, replied that had it not been for such men as Richard Henry Lee, Thomas Jefferson, Samuel Chase, and Thomas Johnson there would never have been any revolution.   Johnson was regularly confirmed on the 7th of November, 1791, and took his seat in the following August term, but resigned in less than eighteen months on account of failing health.

A few months prior to this the Judges had asserted with firmness and boldness the independence of the judiciary as a coördinate branch of the government.   Congress, by an act to provide for the settlement of the claims of widows and orphans, and to regulate the claims of invalid pensioners, had imposed on the Circuit Courts certain duties, and subjected their action to the consideration and supervision of the Secretary of War, and finally to the revision of Congress.   The Chief Justice, with Cushing and Duane, the District Judges, refused to comply, and declared that neither the Legislature nor Executive branches could constitutionally assign to the Judiciary any duties, but such as were properly judicial, and to be performed in a judicial manner; that the duties assigned were not of that description, and that neither the Secretary of War nor any other executive officer, nor even the Legislature were authorized to sit as a Court of Errors.   They regarded themselves under the Act, as commissioners merely, an appointment which they might accept or decline at pleasure.   But as the objects of the act were benevolent, and did honor to the humanity and justice of Congress, out of respect to the Legislature, they declared their willingness to act as Commissioners. Similar views were declared by Wilson, Blair and Peters, District Judge, and by Iredell and Sitgreaves, District Judge, all of whom addressed joint letters to the President.[1] Wilson, however, absolutely refused at all times to act even as a commissioner. To bring the matter to a judicial determination, the Attorney General moved, *ex officio*, for a mandamus to the Circuit Court for the District of Pennsylvania, to proceed in the case of William Hayburn, who had applied to be put on the list as an invalid pensioner. An elaborate argument was made, but because of a division in opinion as to the powers of the Attorney General the motion was denied. The ground was then shifted, and a motion made at the instance of Hayburn himself, and the merits of the case, the scope of the Act of Congress, and the refusal of the Judges to carry it into effect were fully considered. No decision was ever pronounced, as Congress at an intermediate session provided, in another way, for the relief of pensioners.[2]

The progress of the Supreme Court towards a position of independent power and influence was slow and difficult. " It is much to be regretted," wrote Randolph to Washington, "that the judiciary, in spite of their apparent firmness in annulling the pension law, are not what some time hence they will be,—a resource against the infractions of the Constitution on the one hand, and a steady asserter of Federal rights on the other."[3] He denounced the crudities of the Federal judiciary system, the jealousies of State Judges of their authority, the

---

[1] See Letters *in extenso*, Hayburn's case, 2 Dallas, 409, note (1791).

[2] Act 28th Feb'y, 1793. Laws of the United States, p. 305.

[3] Edmund Randolph to Washington, 5th Aug., 1792. Sparks's "Life and Writings of Washington," Vol. X, p. 513.

ambiguities of the Constitution, and pointed out that the most probable quarter from which alarming discontents might proceed was the rivalship between the two orders of judges. Mere superiority of talent in the Federal Judges, even if admitted, would not suffice to counterbalance the real talents and popularity of their competitors. It was possible, too, that the former might not be so far forgetful of their previous connection with the State governments as to be indifferent about the continuance of their old interests there. To these causes could be traced an abandonment of the true authority of the National Government. Besides, many severe experiments, the result of which could not be foreseen, awaited the judiciary. States were to be brought into Court as defendants to the claims of land companies and of individuals. British debts still rankled deeply, and it was feared that the precedent, fixed by the condemnation of the pension law, if not reduced to its precise principles, might justify every constable in thwarting the laws.

Another opportunity was afforded the judges of defining the independence of their position. The President, disturbed by the threatening appearance of public affairs, sought to obtain from the Chief-Justice and his Associates advice upon certain legal questions most interesting and important. Twenty-nine interrogatories, carefully framed, were submitted: Whether the principles of international law or the Treaties of the United States with France gave her or her citizens the right to fit out originally in the ports of the United States vessels of war, with or without commissions, or to refit, or re-arm, or to increase the armament; whether other powers with whom the United States were at peace could fit out such vessels or exercise similar powers; whether France had a right to erect courts within the jurisdiction of the United States

for the trial and condemnation of prizes made by armed vessels in her service; whether the principle that free bottoms
made free goods, and enemy bottoms enemy goods was a part
of the law of nations.[1] To these the Judges declined to reply, asserting with great and commendable dignity that it
would be improper for them to anticipate any case which
might arise, or indicate their opinion in advance of argument.

A series of exciting State trials now taxed the energies
of the Judges upon Circuit. Chief-Justice Jay, in a charge
delivered to the Grand Jury at Richmond, laid down the
principle that by the common law, independent of any statute, the Federal Courts had power to punish offenders against
the Federal sovereignty; "that the United States are in a
state of neutrality relative to all the powers at war, and that
it is their duty, their interest and their disposition to maintain it; that, therefore, they who commit, aid or abet hostilities against these powers, or either of them, offend against
the laws of the United States, and ought to be punished."[2]

Two months later Genet, to check whom this doctrine
had been invoked, supplied an American skipper with a
French flag, who captured an English merchantman in the
Delaware. Henfield, an American citizen, without casting off
his allegiance, had enlisted in the service of the privateer.
The English minister demanded his arrest; the French minister insisted on his discharge. Mr. Justice Wilson, in a labored, but scholastic discourse, charged the Grand Jury at
Philadelphia, re-affirming the doctrine of Jay, and Henfield
was indicted, and tried before Wilson, Iredell and Peters, Dis-

---

[1] Letter of Washington to Ch. J. Jay, &c., 23rd July, 1793. Sparks's "Writings
of Washington," Appendix XVIII, Vol. X, pp. 359–360, 542 et seq.

[2] See Wharton's "State Trials of the United States," p. 49.

trict Judges. It was the joint and unanimous opinion of the Court that the acts of hostility committed by the prisoner were an offence against this country and punishable by its laws. The Jury refused to convict, while Jefferson sent the English minister a copy of the charge of the Court, as demonstrating that the Federal government had the power to punish offenders against the laws of nations. Genet gave a dinner to " Citizen Henfield," and boasted that the verdict of the Jury enabled the American people to make war upon England under the protection of the French flag.[1]

The common law jurisdiction of the United States in criminal cases was again asserted, and acted upon in several instances by different judges for a number of years, until abruptly denied by Judge Chase on the trial of Worrall, in 1798.[2] The doctrine maintained its ground, until further shaken by Judge Washington and Chief-Justice Marshall, when it was finally overthrown in *United States* v. *Hudson.*[3]

The Trials of the Western Insurgents, growing out of the Whiskey Insurrection in Pennsylvania, attracted much attention at the time, and led the President, in a speech to Congress, to call the attention of that body to the manner in which the laws of the United States had been opposed, and their execution obstructed by combinations too powerful to be suppressed by the ordinary course of judicial proceedings, or by the powers vested in the Marshal of the district.[4] Verdicts of guilty on several indictments of High Treason

[1] Wharton's " State Trials of the United States," p. 2.

[2] Compare trials of Henfield, Guinet, Villato, Isaac Williams and Worrall, *Ibid.*, also U. S. *v.* Ravara, 2 Dallas, 297 (1793).

[3] 7 Cranch, 32 (1812). See also U. S. *v.* Coolidge, 1 Wheaton, 415 (1816). State of Penna. *v.* Wheeling Bridge Co., 13 Howard, 519 (1812).

[4] See Wharton's "State Trials," 102 ; 2 Dallas, 335 (1795). Sparks' "Writings of Washington," Vol. XII, p. 46.

were obtained, after animated discussions upon the law, and gradually law and order were restored.

Such was the general character of the duties discharged by the Judges upon Circuit.[1] It is now proper to turn to the cases which came before the Supreme Court.

[1] Mr. Hackett, Clerk of the United States Circuit Court for New Hampshire, in his interesting sketch of the Circuit Court for the New Hampshire District one hundred years ago, says:

The sessions of the courts in those days were great events in the town. Perhaps no better illustration of this fact can be had than is contained in the following taken from the "United States Oracle of the Day," a newspaper published in Portsmouth. In the paper of May 24, 1800, appears this, almost the only local item, which may be regarded as a first-rate notice:

"Circuit Court. On Monday last the Circuit Court of the United States was opened in this town. The Hon. Judge Paterson presided. After the jury were empanelled the Judge delivered a most elegant and appropriate charge. The *Law* was laid down in a masterly manner: *Politics* were set in their true light by holding up the Jacobins as the disorganizers of our happy country, and the only instruments of introducing discontent and dissatisfaction among the well-meaning part of the Community. *Religion* and *Morality* were pleasingly inculcated and enforced as being necessary to good government, good order and good laws; for ' when the righteous are in authority the people rejoice.'

"We are sorry we could not prevail upon the Honourable Judge to furnish a copy of said charge to adorn the pages of the United States Oracle.

"After the charge was delivered, the Rev. Mr. Alden addressed the Throne of Grace in an excellent and well-adapted prayer."

It may well be supposed that the Judge who was Associate Justice William Paterson, of New Jersey, could hardly afford to concede the request of the New Hampshire editor, as doubtless the charge might be needed to be thereafter given in other districts by the learned judge, who probably spent more time in its preparation than was commonly required for matter which adorned the pages of Portsmouth papers nearly a hundred years ago.—*Green Bag*, Vol. II., No. 6, 264.

CHAPTER XII.

THE FIRST EPOCH: 1790–1801: EARLY DECISIONS UPON CONSTITUTIONAL QUESTIONS: ADMIRALTY CAUSES: MATTERS OF PRACTICE: CHANGES UPON THE BENCH: SKETCHES OF PATERSON, ELLSWORTH, CHASE, WASHINGTON, MOORE: CHANGES IN THE CHIEF JUSTICESHIP: INSTANCES OF POLITICO JUDICIALISM: JUDICIAL PLURALISTS: ESTIMATE OF THE SERVICES OF THE OLD SUPREME COURT.

THE first cause of note was that of the *State of Georgia* v. *Brailsford and others.* In 1782, by an Act of Confiscation, a bond which had been given, in 1774, by Kelsall and Spalding to Brailsford and others, alleged aliens, had been sequestrated to the State of Georgia. Brailsford and his copartners had brought suit on the bond in 1791, in the United States Circuit Court for the District of Georgia. The State had unsuccessfully applied for permission to assert her claim, and judgment had been entered for the plaintiffs. The State now filed her bill in Equity in the Supreme Court for an injunction to stay proceedings in the lower Court, and praying that the Marshal should be directed to pay over the moneys in his hands to the treasurer of the State.

Some difference of opinion was expressed as to whether the State had or had not an adequate remedy at law, and the Court, Johnson and Cushing dissenting, granted the injunction, so as to retain the money in the custody of the law until it should be adjudged to whom it belonged.[1]

---

[1] 2 Dallas, 402 (1792). It is remarkable that the very first opinion published in the reports of the decisions of the Supreme Court is a *dissenting* opinion, that of Mr. Justice Johnson.

A motion was subsequently made to dissolve the injunction and dismiss the bill, but it was allowed to stand until the next term, when the right of the State to the bond was tried by a special jury, upon an amicable issue, before the Supreme Court.[1] After argument the Chief Justice charged the jury that it was the unanimous opinion of the Court that the Act of Georgia did not vest the debt in the State at the time of passing it; that it was subjected, not to confiscation, but only to sequestration, and the owner's right to recover it revived after the peace.

This decision, although not elaborately expressed, involved the important principle that the Treaty of Peace, like the Constitution, was in respect to matters embraced by its terms, the supreme law, and could not be restricted in its operation by State action or State laws. The same result was reached, and the same conclusion justified after the most exhaustive examination in the far more celebrated case of *Ware* v. *Hylton*,[2] in which the splendid eloquence of Patrick Henry, the great

[1] 3 Dallas, 1 (1794). It has been asserted that this case is the only instance of trial by jury in the Supreme Court. This is an error. The Minutes of the Court disclose that in the case of Oswald *v.* The State of New York, a jury was sworn and witnesses called, and a verdict found for the plaintiff of $5,315.06. This was in February, 1795. Two years and a-half later a writ of inquiry of damages in the case of Catlin *v.* The State of South Carolina, was executed at the bar of the Supreme Court, and a verdict was given for the plaintiff for $55,-002.84. Although judgments were entered, there is no record of any steps to enforce them. In Grayson *v.* The State of Virginia, a distringas was granted to compel the State to appear, but this process was abandoned and an alias subpœna issued, upon the establishment of a general rule by which it was provided that when process at common law or equity shall issue against a State, the same shall be served on the Governor and Attorney-General, and that if process in equity by subpœna should be served sixty days before return day, and the defendant State should not appear, the plaintiff should proceed *ex parte*. Minutes. See also Grayson *v.* Virginia, 3 Dallas, 320 (1796).

[2] 3 Dallas, 199 (1796).

reasoning faculties of John Marshall at the bar, and the powerful dissenting opinion of Iredell were employed in vain to convince the Court that Congress had no power to make a treaty that could operate to annul a legislative act of any of the States, and thus destroy rights acquired under such an act. Chase, Paterson, Wilson and Cushing, impressed by the uncommon magnitude of the subject, the bitter and exciting controversies it had provoked, and the far-reaching consequences by which their decision would be attended, although differing upon some matters of detail and in the mode of their reasoning, reached the conclusion that the Treaty of 1783 was the supreme law, equal in its effect to the Constitution itself, in overruling all State laws upon the subject, and the words that British creditors should "meet with no lawful impediment" were as strong as the wit of man could devise to avoid all effects of sequestration, confiscation, or any other obstacle thrown in the way by any law, particularly pointed against the recovery of such debts. The decision expanded from a statement of the contractual liability of an individual to an assertion that the treaty obligations of the nation were paramount to the laws of individual States. Happy conclusion! A contrary result would have blackened our character, at the very outset of our career as a nation, with the guilt of treachery to the terms of the treaty by which our Independence had been recognized, and would have prostrated the national sovereignty at the feet of Virginia.

A case now came before the Court which excited an unusual degree of attention, both on account of the novelty of the questions raised and the important political consequences involved in the decision. Chisholm, a citizen of South Carolina, had brought an action in the Supreme Court against the State of Georgia, by service of process upon the Governor and

Attorney-General of that State. Georgia refused to appear, and the Attorney-General of the United States moved that unless Georgia caused her appearance to be entered by the next term, judgment should be entered against her by default and a writ of inquiry issue. Georgia refused to recognize the jurisdiction, although it had been acquiesced in in similar suits by New York, Maryland, South Carolina and Virginia, and presented, through Dallas and Ingersoll of Pennsylvania, a written remonstrance and protestation, declining to appear, even upon argument.[1]

The reasoning of Randolph, upon whom the burden fell of breaking his way without assistance into a subject full of difficulty and replete with danger, is profound and masterly. Fully conscious of the unpopularity of his motion and of the condemnation of his native State, he refused to commit an act of official perfidy by surrendering his own convictions of duty when brought face to face with a question of Constitutional right.

His contention embraced four propositions: that a State could be made a party defendant, in any case, in the Supreme Court, at the suit of a private citizen of another State; that an action of assumpsit could be maintained against a State; that service by summons upon the Governor and Attorney General of a State was a competent service; that an appearance could be enforced by process. All of these were distinctly sustained by the Court, with the exception of the latter, which for the time being was passed from motives of prudence and delicacy, but it was ordered that unless the State appeared, or showed cause to the contrary, by the next term, judgment by default should be entered.

[1] Chisholm Exrs. *v.* Georgia, 2 Dallas, 419 (1793).

Justice Blair planted himself upon the express letter of the Constitution, which extended the jurisdiction of the Court in express terms "to controversies between a State and citizens of another State."

"Is then," he asks, "the case before us one of that description? Undoubtedly it is, unless it may be a sufficient denial to say, that it is a controversy between a citizen of one State and another State. Can this change of order be an essential change in the thing intended? And is this alone a sufficient ground from which to conclude that the jurisdiction of this Court reaches the case where a State is plaintiff, but not where it is defendant? In this latter case, should any man be asked, whether it was not a controversy between a State and a citizen of another State, must not the answer be in the affirmative? A dispute between A and B is surely a dispute between B and A."

After showing that the Constitution describes generally the judicial powers of the United States, he points out that it then proceeds to speak of them distributively, and gives to the Supreme Court original jurisdiction, among other instances, in the case where a State shall be a party. He then asks:

"But is not a State a party as well in the condition of a defendant as in that of plaintiff? And is the whole force of that expression satisfied by confining its meaning to the case of a plaintiff State? It seems to me that if this Court should refuse to hold jurisdiction of a case where a State is defendant, it would renounce part of the authority conferred, and consequently part of the duty imposed on it by the Constitution."

Upon the question of sovereignty, he said:

"But we are not now in a State Court; and if sovereignty be an exemption from suit in any other than the sovereign's own Courts, it follows that when a State, by adopting the Constitution has agreed to be amenable to the judicial power of the United States, she has, in that respect, given up her right of sovereignty."

The question, said Wilson, "may, perhaps, be ultimately resolved into one, no less radical than this—'Do the people of the United States form a nation?'" Applying the touchstones of the principles of general jurisprudence; the laws and practice of States and Kingdoms, and the direct and explicit declaration of the Constitution itself, he declared that from all the combined inference was that the action would lie.

Cushing put the matter concisely:

"With respect to controversies between a State and citizens of another State, comparing all the clauses together, the remedy is reciprocal; the claim to justice equal. As controversies between State and State, and between a State and citizens of another State, might tend gradually to involve States in war and bloodshed, a disinterested civil tribunal was intended to be instituted to decide such controversies, and preserve peace and friendship; if a State is entitled to justice in the Federal Court against a citizen of another State, why not such citizen against the State, when the same language equally comprehends both? The rights of individuals and the justice due to them are as dear and precious as those of States. Indeed the latter are founded upon the former; and the great end and object of them must be to secure and support the rights of individuals, or else vain is government."

The opinion of Chief Justice Jay is the most elaborate of his judicial utterances. He pointed to the language of the Preamble of the Constitution, and to the history of the country preceding its formation, to emphasize his assertion that the sovereignty of the nation was in the people of the nation, who were "sovereigns without subjects," and that a vast distinction existed between such a condition and the sovereignty of European potentates, whose dignities, pre-eminences, and powers were personal but not official. In a country where all citizens were equal, it was agreed that one free citizen could sue another citizen or any number of citizens; nay, in certain cases one citizen might sue forty thousand; for where a corporation is sued, all the members of it are actually though not personally sued. He saw no distinction as to right between the forty thousand inhabitants of Philadelphia, associated under a charter, and the fifty thousand citizens of Delaware associated under a State government. The service of a summons on a Governor and Attorney General of a State was as easy and convenient to the public and parties, as on the Mayor or other officers of the corporation of a city. All were officers of the people, and however more exalted a Governor might be than a Mayor, yet, in the opinion of those who disliked aristocracy, that circumstance could not be a good reason for impeding justice. He saw no incompatibility between suability and State sovereignty, and declared that as one State might sue another State in the Supreme Court, it was "plain that no degradation to a State was thought to accompany her appearance in this Court." He then showed that Georgia by becoming a party to the national compact had consented to be suable by individual citizens of another State, and argued that if there was "a controversy" between them it clearly fell not only within the spirit but the very words of the Constitution He insisted that the Constitution had established a new order of rights and duties, and finally, lest his conclusions might reach too far, pointed out that there was a distinction between suits against a State and suits against the United States, because in the former the national Courts were supported in all their legal and Constitutional proceedings and judgments by the arm of the National Executive, but in the latter there was no power which the Courts could call to their aid.

From these views Iredell, alone, dissented, in an opinion of which it has been truly declared that it enunciates either directly or by implication all the leading principles of what has since become known as State Rights Doctrine, and which as a mere legal argument was far superior in closeness of reasoning to Wilson's or Jay's. He confined himself strictly to the question before the Court, whether an action of assumpsit would lie against a State, and showed by numerous illustrations that though in England certain judicial proceedings by way of petition, not inconsistent with sovereignty, might take place against the Crown, yet an action of assumpsit would not lie. Yet surely the King could assume as well as a State. If such an action could be maintained, it must be in virtue of the Constitution of the United States, or of some law of Congress conformable thereto. After closely examining the grant of judicial power, and the distribution of jurisdiction as stated in the Judiciary Act, he failed to find any delegation of authority in such a case. He challenged the construction of the Attorney General that the Supreme Court could exercise all the judicial power vested by the Constitution, by its own authority, whether the Legislature had prescribed methods of doing so or not. The Constitution was not self-enforcing; the Article could not be effectuated without legislative intervention. All the Courts of the United States must receive not merely their organization, but all their authority as to the mode of their proceeding from the Legislature only. There was no part of the Constitution that authorized the Supreme Court to take up any business where Congress had left it, and, in order to give full activity to the powers given by the Constitution, supply legislative omissions by making new laws for new cases, or by applying old prin· ciples to new cases materially different from those to which they had been previously applied. The States had not surrendered their sovereignties to the Union in this respect, and at the time of the adoption of the Constitution there was not in any State any particular legislative mode authorizing a compulsory suit for the recovery of money against a State. No new remedy having been provided, the case must be governed by the principles of pre-existing law, and a long train of precedents showed that no such action could be maintained. No debt could be due from a State, except in case of a contract with the Legislature itself, or with the Executive in pursuance of express authority, from the Legislature, or in case of a contract with the Executive without any special authority. Every man knew that he could not sue the Legislature, nor could he sue a Governor, unless the Legislature had made such a provision, and in the third case, as a Governor was possessed simply of Executive powers he could not make a contract unless specially authorized. The arguments as to corporations did not apply. Corporations were the mere creatures of sovereignty, but States were sovereigns themselves; they did not owe their origin to the Government of the United States, but were in existence before it. No fair construction of the Constitution could show that they had abdicated in favor of the General Government in such a case as this.

It is somewhat singular that no one of the Judges alluded to the views expressed by eminent public men at the time the Constitution was before the people for ratification. The authors of "The Federalist" had declared that such a jurisdiction was without "a color of foundation." John Marshall had declared in the Virginia Convention: "I hope that no gentleman will think that a State will be called at the bar of the Federal Courts. . . . It is not rational to suppose that the sovereign power shall be dragged before a Court."

The decision as soon as pronounced created much excitement and fanned anti-federal sentiment into a flame. Every

State was burdened with heavy debts. Several had been sued, and the Legislature of Georgia responded by a statute denouncing the penalty of death against any one who should presume to enforce any process upon the judgment within its jurisdiction. The decision was pronounced on the 18th of February, 1793; two days afterwards the Eleventh Amendment to the Constitution was proposed to Congress, and formally acted upon by that body in the following December. It was not declared adopted by the several States until January 8th, 1798. In the meantime the Court refused to bend to the popular fury, and after a year rendered judgment by default, and ordered an inquiry of damages.[1] The plaintiff, however, prudently awaited action upon the proposed amendment, and on the 4th of February, 1798, the case of *Hollingsworth* v. *The State of Virginia*[2] being before the Court, it was declared that in view of the amendment, jurisdiction was renounced " in any case past or future, in which a State was sued by the citizens of another State, or by citizens or subjects of any foreign State."[3]

The importance of the decision, however, remained. It was the first clear trumpet-note which had been sounded by the new nation, in striking contrast with the feeble wail against State power uttered by the Committee of the Continental Congress when dealing judicially with *Olmstead's Appeal* in the case of the sloop *Active*. As Judge Cooley has

[1] Minutes of the Supreme Court, February 14, 1794.

[2] 3 Dallas, 378 (1798).

[3] See Hollingsworth *v.* Virginia, 3 Dallas, 378–382 (1798). Minutes of the Supreme Court. Schouler's "History of the United States," Vol. II, p. 274. Pitkin's "History of the United States," Vol. II, pp. 335, 341. Van Santvoord's "Lives of the Chief Justices of the United States," pp. 51, 54. McRee's "Life of Iredell," Vol. II, p. 380. Cooley in "Constitutional History of the United States as Seen in the Development of American Law," pp. 47–71.

12

remarked, the Union could scarcely have had a valuable ex
istence had it been judicially determined that powers of sover
eignty were exclusively in the States or in the people of th
States severally.[1] The doctrine of an indissoluble Union
though not in terms declared, was in its elements containe
in this decision, which proved of priceless value in determin
ing at the very outset of our national career the true charac
ter of our government.

In *Hylton* v. *The United States*[2] the power of Congres
to lay taxes was exhaustively considered, and the principl
established that two rules must be observed: first, that of uni
formity, whenever imposts, excises or duties were laid; an
second, that of apportionment according to the census, when
ever the tax was direct. It was held that no tax could b
direct unless capable of apportionment, and it was demon
strated by an unanswerable course of reasoning that a ta
upon carriages could not be a direct tax, because apportion
ment would lead to the grossest and most arbitrary difference
in the rate in each State. Mr. Justice Chase inclined to th
opinion that the direct taxes contemplated by the Constitutio
were only two, a capitation or poll tax simply, without regar
to property, profession, or any other circumstances, and a ta
on land. He showed that a tax on carriages was a specie
of duty—a generic term, almost as comprehensive as the wor
tax, which could not be confined to taxes on importation
only. Although he did not think it necessary at that tim
to decide whether the Supreme Court possessed the power
under the Constitution, to declare an Act of Congress void
because of a conflict with the Constitution, yet he declare

---

[1] Cooley in "Constitutional History of the United States as seen in the Deve
opment of American Law," p. 49.

[2] 3 Dallas, 171 (1796).

that if the Court did have such power he would never exercise it except in a very clear case.

In *Calder* v. *Bull*,[1] although the point actually decided was that the clause in the Constitution forbiding the States to pass *ex post facto* laws related only to penal and criminal proceedings, and that therefore a retrospective law of a State, affecting property rights only, and violating no contract, was valid, yet two principles of great value in the maintenance of the rights of the States were enlarged upon; that the validity of State legislation was at all times to be presumed, and second: that where no Federal question arose, the proper authority for determining the validity of State legislation was the State judiciary. Chase declared himself "fully satisfied" that the Supreme Court had no jurisdiction to declare void a State law contrary to the Constitution of such State, and again carefully avoided the question whether it could declare void an Act of Congress contrary to the Federal Constitution. Iredell, however, while asserting that Acts of Congress or of the Legislature, violative of Constitutional provisions, were unquestionably void, admitted that as the authority to declare them void was "of a delicate and awful" nature, the Court would never resort to that authority but in a clear and urgent case.

Some years later, in *Cooper* v. *Telfair*,[2] where an act of banishment and confiscation of property was held to be not repugnant to the Constitution of Georgia, although it was admitted that a general opinion existed at the bar, and had been expressed by some of the judges upon Circuit[3] that an Act of Congress in opposition to the Constitution is void, yet, in the absence of a decision of the Supreme Court itself, it was

---

[1] 3 Dallas, 386 (1798).   [2] 4 Dallas, 14 (1800).
[3] See remarks of Paterson, J., in Van Horn *v.* Dorrance, 2 Dallas, 304 (1795).

said to be still an open question where the power resided to declare it void.

Thus, it was, with slow, timid and halting footsteps that the Supreme Court approached the doctrine of *Marbury* v. *Madison*.

In the meantime the Constitutional adoption of the Eleventh Amendment was judicially declared in *Hollingsworth* v. *Virginia*,[1] while in *Fowler* v. *Lindsey*[2] the distinction was drawn between a case in which a State was a party, and where the interests of a State might be indirectly affected by the decision in a suit relating to land between individuals claiming under a State grant, Judge Washington stating it as "a safe rule" that a case which belongs to the jurisdiction of the Supreme Court, on account of the interest that a State has in the controversy, must be one in which a State is either nominally or substantially a party to the record.

During the same period several important cases affecting the admiralty jurisdiction of the Federal Courts were determined. Of these the most important and instructive, as containing an expression of the growth of the federal idea, was that of *Penhallow* v. *Doane*,[3] in which the power of the old Federal Court of Appeals in cases of Capture, instituted by the Continental Congress under the Articles of Confederation was sustained, and its jurisdiction declared to be final and conclusive.

In *Glass* v. *The Sloop Betsey*,[4] although it was argued with much ingenuity and learning that the District Courts of the United States had no jurisdiction over questions of prize, yet it was held that they possessed all the powers of Courts of Admiralty, both upon the instance and prize sides and could

---

[1] 3 Dallas, 378 (1798).   [2] *Ibid.*, 411 (1799).   [3] 3 *Ibid.*, 54 (1795).
[4] *Ibid.*, 6 (1794).

Wm Paterson

decree restitution of a vessel belonging to a neutral, captured as British property by a French privateer and brought to a port of the United States by the captor. In the same case, it was asserted with great dignity that no foreign power could institute a Court of judicature of any kind within the jurisdiction of the United States except by treaty, and that the admiralty jurisdiction exercised by consuls of France in the United States was unwarranted. Due care, however, was exercised not to overstep the bounds prescribed by international law, and later, in the case of a capture of a vessel belonging to a citizen of the United States by a French privateer, which had been carried *infra præsidia* of the captors, the principle was sustained that all such questions belonged exclusively to the tribunals of the belligerent power, and that no vessel of war of such belligerent or the officers thereof could be seized or arrested within the United States, at the suit of individuals to answer for such capture. A writ of prohibition was accordingly issued, restraining a District Court from proceedings of a retaliatory nature.[1]

In *Talbot* v. *Jansen*,[2] the only case in the decision of which Rutledge participated as Chief-Justice, the important question of the right of expatriation was raised, but not determined, although one or two of the judges inclined, extrajudicially, to the view that a citizen did not possess the right of voluntary expatriation without the permission of his own government.

In *United States* v. *Judge Lawrence*,[3] upon an application for a mandamus directing him to issue a warrant of arrest, it was held that the Court had no power to compel a judge to decide according to the dictates of any Judgment but his own.

---

[1] United States *v.* Richard Peters, District Judge, 3 Dallas, 121 (1795).
[2] 3 Dallas, 133 (1795).   [3] *Ibid.*, 42 (1795).

Several important matters of practice were determined. The Attorney-General having asked for information relative to the system by which proceedings should be regulated, it was ordered that the practice of the Courts of King's Bench and Chancery in England afforded outlines for the practice of this Court.[1] The bar was also notified that the Court expected to be furnished with a statement of the material points of a case.[2] All evidence on motions for the discharge of prisoners on bail must be by way of deposition, and not *viva voce*.[3] The statements of facts required by Act of Congress of the Circuit Courts as the basis of their judgments in any Equity or Admiralty cause were held to be conclusive.[4] In suits against States, whether at common law or in equity, it was ordered that service should be made of process upon the Governor and the Attorney-General, and that the process of subpœna, when resorted to, should be served sixty days before return day, and on a failure of the State to appear, the complainant might proceed *ex parte*.[5]

Two questions of jurisdiction were also settled: To sustain the Federal jurisdiction, the record must show that the parties were citizens of different States;[6] the amount demanded by the plaintiff, and not the sum found to be due, was the test of jurisdiction even upon proceedings in error.[7]

During the period of the decisions which have been reviewed changes took place in the composition of the bench which it is now proper to notice. The Court, as originally

---

[1] Minutes of the Supreme Court.   [2] *Ibid.*

[3] U. S. *v.* Hamilton, 3 Dallas, 17–120 (1795).

[4] Wiscart *v.* Dauchy, 3 Dallas, 321 (1796).

[5] Grayson *v.* The State of Virginia, 3 Dallas, 320 (1796).

[6] Bingham *v.* Cabbot, 3 Dallas, 19 (1795). S. C., *Ibid.* 382 (1798). Turner, Admnr. *v.* Enrille, 4 Dallas, 7 (1799). Turner *v.* Bank, 4 Dallas, 8 (1799).

[7] Wilson *v.* Daniel, 3 Dallas, 401 (1798).

Olin. Ellsworth

constituted, consisted of Jay as Chief-Justice, and Rutledge, Cushing, Harrison, Wilson and Blair as Associates. Harrison had declined, and Iredell had taken his place. Rutledge had resigned after a few months of service on the Circuit, and Thomas Johnson had succeeded him. Johnson resigned at the end of eighteen months, with no trace of his judicial work except a short dissenting opinion in *Georgia* v. *Brailsford*, and on the 4th of March, 1793, William Paterson was commissioned. His father was an Irish immigrant to New Jersey in 1749, and, according to some accounts, the son was born in Ireland; according to others, at sea on the passage to America. He was educated at Princeton, and graduated September 27, 1763. He read law with Richard Stockton, one of the Signers of the Declaration of Independence; was admitted to the bar within a year, and became an attorney of the Supreme Court in 1769. He took an active part in public affairs, always on the patriotic side, and was a member of the First Provincial Congress of New Jersey, serving as Assistant Secretary. In 1775 he became a member of the Continental Congress, and during the following year was the Attorney-General of the State and a member of the Legislative Council. He was several times re-elected to Congress, but resigned all his public positions in 1783 to resume the practice of the law. He was a member of the Annapolis and the Federal Conventions, and in the latter offered the plan so well known as the New Jersey Plan, by which it was proposed to preserve the State sovereignties, while giving to the General Government power to provide for the common defence and general welfare. He contended that the proper object of the Convention was a mere revision and extension of the Articles of Confederation. He insisted on an equal vote of the States in the Senate, and objected to a proportional representation in either House. After the adoption of the Constitution, Mr. Paterson was chosen one of the Senators of the United States from New Jersey, his colleague being Jonathan Elmer. He was one of the tellers to count the electoral votes, and chairman of the committee to prepare the certificates of the election and to certify the elected officers. He served as a member of the Judiciary Committee, and, next to Ellsworth, took the most active share of the work of framing the Judiciary Act. On the death of Governor Livingston, in 1790, he became the Governor and Chancellor of his State, resigning his position as United States Senator, and held the former office for three years. During this time he executed, under the authority of the Legislature, the work of collecting and reducing into proper form all the Statutes of Great Britain which before the Revolution were held to be in force, and which, by the Constitution, were extended to the State, as well as all the public acts which had been passed since,—a work which has been spoken of by a competent authority as a system of statute law more perfect than that of any other State, and which has continued to this day to deserve the highest praise. Such had been the public services of the man whom Washington now raised to the Supreme Bench.

In 1795 John Jay, who had been sent during the previous year as special envoy to Great Britain, was elected Governor of New York and resigned the Chief Justiceship. Thereupon the President, notwithstanding the opposition of his cabinet whose hostility had been excited by an intemperate attack by Rutledge upon Jay's treaty, sent a commission during the recess to John Rutledge, who presided over the Court during the August term. His name came before the Senate on the 10th of December, 1795, and on the 15th was rejected, the real reason being that the mind of this illustrious patriot had become seriously impaired. William Cushing, the Senior Associate Justice, was commissioned as Chief Justice on the 27th of January, 1796, but declined, preferring to retain his former position.

Oliver Ellsworth, at that time a Senator of the United States, was then named, and commissioned on the 4th of March, 1796; a man of kingly dignity, exalted conscience, immutability of will, but slow and ponderous intellect. His name will always rank among the most distinguished statesmen and jurists of America. He was born at Windsor, Conn., on the 29th of April, 1745. He received a classical education, and graduated from Princeton in 1766. He then read law, but was not admitted to the bar until 1771. His integrity, industry, knowledge of law, careful preparation of his cases, and earnest logic, occasionally warming into eloquence, soon won for him a commanding position among his professional brethren. He rose almost at once to political distinction, and took an active part in support of the colonies in resisting the oppression of Great Britain. In 1777 he was elected a delegate to the Continental Congress, and became a leading member, serving upon important committees, conspicuous for his talents as a debater. In 1784 he was appointed a judge of the Superior Court of Connecticut. While still upon the Bench, in 1787, he was chosen a member of the Federal Convention, and exerted a powerful influence in securing substantial recognition of the State governments, which service has linked his name with that of Paterson of New Jersey, as one of the authors of our Federal system. He objected to the word "national," and preferred the title of "The United States," declaring that he wished the plan of the Convention to go forth as an amendment of the Articles of Confederation, since, under this idea, the authority of the

legislatures could ratify it.   He did not like popular conventions, as they were better fitted to pull down than build up
Constitutions.   He wished the agency of the States maintained, and urged a compromise between the large and small
States as to their vote in Congress.   He contended for an
Executive Council, and approved of a council of revision of
acts of Congress, to be composed of the President and the
Judges.   For some reason he was absent from the Convention on the last day, and his name does not appear upon the
consecrated roll of the Signers of the Constitution.   But in
his own State convention, and ever afterwards, he was among
the most earnest and zealous supporters of the new Government.   Having attached himself to the Federal party, he was
elected by the legislature of his native State to the Senate
of the United States, in which he gained great renown as a
debater, and as a pillar of Washington's administration.   His
most important work was the establishment of the Federal
Judiciary system.   In fact, it is asserted by some that he was
the sole author of the famous Judiciary Act of 1789.   "That
great Act," said Mr. Justice Field, "was penned by Oliver
Ellsworth, a member of the Convention which framed the
Constitution, and one of the early Chief Justices of this
Court.   It may be said to reflect the views of the founders
of the Republic as to the proper relations between the Federal and State courts." [1]   "He was born," says Dr. Dwight,
"to be a great man."   In one of his Senatorial speeches,
Daniel Webster referred to him as "a gentleman who has
left behind him, on the records of the government of his
country, proofs of the clearest intelligence, and of the utmost
purity and integrity of character," while a recent biographer

---

[1] *Ex parte* Virginia, 100 U. S., 313–339 (1879).

has declared that "for strength of reason, for sagacity, wisdom and sound, good sense in the conduct of affairs; for moderation of temper and general ability, it may be doubted if New England has yet produced his superior."

The next change occurred through the resignation of John Blair, his successor being Samuel Chase, a native of Maryland, who was commissioned on the 27th of January, 1796. He was born in Somerset County, on the 17th of April, 1741, and was the son of an Episcopal clergyman, by whom he was carefully educated. Devoting himself to the study of the law, he was admitted to the Bar of Annapolis in 1761, where his remarkable personal traits soon brought him distinction. His abilities were of the highest order; industry, intrepidity, intense convictions, energetic eloquence, added to a sonorous voice and imposing stature, made him conspicuous as a leader in the Colonial Legislature, where he became known as "the Maryland Demosthenes." He vehemently denounced the Stamp Act, and a few years afterwards served as a member of the Committee of Correspondence and as a delegate to Congress, retaining his position until 1779. His terrible arraignment of Zubly, of Georgia, whom he stigmatized as a Judas, compelled that traitor to flee from Congress, whose secrets he was divulging to the enemy. In 1776, with Franklin and Carroll, he endeavored, as Commissioner, to form a plan of Union between the Colonies and Canada, and on his return labored zealously and successfully to change the sentiments of Maryland so as to authorize him to vote for the Declaration of Independence, of which he became one of the Signers. Throughout the long and dark years of the war his exertions were untiring, and his spirit courageous and alert. In 1783 he interested himself in securing for his State a large sum of money which had been intrusted to the Bank of England prior to the Revolution.   In his State Convention he was in favor of the ratification of the Constitution, although many of its provisions he did not regard as sufficiently clear. In 1791 he became the Chief Justice of the General Court of Maryland, a position which he held at the time of his appointment to the Supreme Court of the United States.   Irascible, vain, overbearing and sometimes tyrannical, but learned, able, patriotic and of spotless honor, with an instinct for tumult, and a faculty for promoting insurrection at the bar, "moving perpetually with a mob at his heels," a suite from which, as Dr. Wharton writes, even the judicial office could not separate him; he trusted with general success to his fearlessness to extricate himself from the disorders which his imprudence fomented.   Averse to the assumption of jurisdiction, yet harsh in the manner of exercising that which he had, with a quick perception of the spirit of the Constitution, and an intellect conspicuous for its clearness, he presents, as an American Thurlow, one of the most singular yet striking figures in our judicial history.   He was the only member of the Supreme Court who was ever impeached for judicial misconduct, but was triumphantly acquitted.

The appointment of Bushrod Washington, of Virginia, was occasioned by the death of James Wilson, at the house of his colleague Iredell, where he succumbed, at the comparatively early age of fifty-six, to the misfortunes attending unhappy speculation in land, the dishonesty of an agent and the mortification of imprisonment for debt.   Washington was commissioned on the 29th of September, in the recess, and re-commissioned on confirmation, December 20th, 1798.   His father was John A. Washington, a younger brother of General Washington, of whom the son was a favorite nephew.   His education was received from a tutor at the house of Richard

Bush. Washington

Henry Lee, and subsequently at the College of William and Mary. During the invasion of Virginia by Cornwallis he joined a volunteer troop of horse, and served in the army under the command of Lafayette. In 1781 he came to Philadelphia, bearing a letter from George Washington to James Wilson, who had been selected as his legal preceptor, and pursued his studies with diligence and success. Returning to his native State, he practiced law with close attention to details and slowly rose to prominence. In 1787 he became a member of the House of Delegates, and in the following year stood beside Madison and Marshall in their advocacy of the Constitution of the United States in the State Convention. Removing to Alexandria, and subsequently to Richmond, he continued his practice, reporting, in two volumes, the decisions of the State Supreme Court. Of solid rather than brilliant mind, sagacious and searching, rather than quick or eager, of temperate yet firm disposition, simple and reserved in his manner, laborious in research, clear in statement, learned in discussion, accurate in reasoning, with the love of justice as his ruling passion, "fearless, dignified and enlightened," he found himself at the early age of thirty-six years called upon by President Adams to fill an office which during a long judicial life he adorned by labor, learning and wisdom.

The death of Iredell in October, 1799, occasioned another vacancy, which was filled by the appointment of Alfred Moore, whose commission was dated December 10, 1799. His birthplace was near Wilmington, North Carolina, and the day of his birth was the 21st of May, 1755. His ancestors were among the most distinguished of the early settlers of the Province, his father, Maurice Moore, being one of the three colonial judges holding office at the outbreak of the Revolution. In 1764 young Moore was sent to Boston, where he became a student at Harvard and attracted attention by his quick wit and agreeable manners. During his absence he became interested in military matters through the friendship of a British officer, who sought in vain to induce him to enter the royal service. Upon his return home, in 1774, he read law under the direction of his father, and was admitted to the bar in the following year. He soon exchanged the labors of the forum for the toils and dangers of war, participating in the defence of Fort Moultrie in Charleston Harbor, and subsequently organizing a partisan corps with which he so effectually worried the enemy that they singled him out for vengeance and plundered his plantation, carrying off his slaves and burning his residence. In 1782 he became the Attorney-General of the State, and for nine years labored with such assiduity as to achieve a reputation rarely equalled by any prosecuting officer. In 1798 he was appointed a Judge of the Superior Court, delivering opinions which have been spoken of in terms of praise by his successors. From this office he was promoted to the Supreme Court of the United States, but owing to the practice which prevailed after Marshall ascended the bench of making the Chief Justice the organ of the Court, delivered but one short opinion in the case of *Bass* v. *Tingy*.[1] He had a keen sense of humor, a brilliant wit, and an overpowering logic. His style as an advocate was lucid and direct, terse and compact. He was small in stature, neat in dress, graceful in manners; his voice was clear and sonorous, his perceptions quick and his judgment almost intuitive; his manner of speaking was animated. He had chosen Swift for his model, and his language was always plain. An eminent authority has declared that he is certainly to be ranked

[1] 4 Dallas, 37 (1800).

among the first advocates whom the American nation has produced. In politics he was a Federalist, and in 1795 had been nominated for the United States Senate, but was defeated by a single vote. A county in his native State preserves his memory and his name.[1]

For the fourth time a change was made in the head of the Court. In October, 1799, Ellsworth had been commissioned one of the three Envoys Extraordinary and Ministers Plenipotentiary to France, and resigned the office of Chief Justice from Paris, in November, 1800. Without prior notice to him, Jay was a second time nominated and confirmed, his commission being dated December 19th. "I had no permission from you," wrote President Adams, "to take this step, but it appeared to me that Providence had thrown in my way an opportunity, not only of marking to the public the spot where, in my opinion, the greatest mass of worth remained collected in one individual, but of furnishing my country with the best security afforded its inhabitants against its increasing dissolution of morals."[2] "I left the Bench," replied Jay, "perfectly convinced that under a system so defective it would not obtain the energy, weight and dignity which was essential to its affording due support to the national government; nor acquire the public confidence and respect which, as the last resort of the justice of the nation, it should possess. Hence I am induced to doubt both the propriety and expediency of my returning to the Bench under the present system. . . . Independently of these considerations, the state of my health removes every doubt."[3]

[1] For the materials of this sketch, I am indebted to the Hon. A. M. Waddell, of Wilmington, N. C.

[2] John Adams to Jay, December 19, 1800, William Jay's "Life of John Jay," Vol. II, p. 421.

[3] To President Adams, January 2, 1801, Jay MSS. Pellew's "Life of Jay," p. 338.

That such an estimate of the Supreme Court and such a despairing prophecy should be uttered by such a man as John Jay would occasion much surprise, were it not a fact that one of the vices of the day was the frequent desertion by the judiciary of its own exalted functions for other branches of the service. Doubt and uncertainty as to its true position clouded its earlier years, "when the politicians—or statesmen —of that day bivouacked in the chief justiceship on their march from one political position to another."[1] They were judicial pluralists as well. Jay himself held at the same time the offices of Chief Justice and Secretary of State for nearly six months; and afterwards, while retaining the Chief Justiceship, did not scruple to undertake the mission to England, which caused his absence from the bench for more than a year, and when at last he resigned, he did so, not because he thought the two offices incompatible, but because he had been elected to a third, that of Governor of New York.[2] Ellsworth, while Minister Plenipotentiary to France, retained the Chief Justiceship and resigned only on the ground of ill-health, and even Marshall, who was commissioned as Chief Justice on January 31, 1801, and presided during the February Term of the Supreme Court, retained his place as Secretary of State until the incoming of Jefferson's administration, discharging in the mean time the duties of the two offices concurrently, on the same day issuing reports in the one capacity, and listening to arguments in the other.[3]

[1] John M. Shirley, "The Dartmouth College Causes and the Supreme Court of the United States," p. 18.

[2] Wharton's "State Trials of the United States," Preliminary Notes, p. 46.

[3] Mr. Charles Pinckney, a Senator of the United States from South Carolina, in March, 1800, in debate upon a motion for leave to bring in a bill relating to the Judiciary, contended for the absolute independence of the Judicial department, and commented with great severity upon the appointment of Judges of the Supreme

A. Moore.

In the beginning of August, 1800, Judge Chase left the Bench to canvass the State of Maryland in behalf of the existing administration, and the result was that the Court, the Chief Justice then being in France, was left without a quorum. Charges to Grand Juries were party harangues, and the State courts adopted in its fullest development " this system of politico-judicialism." It was left for Marshall, after he had become firmly seated on the bench, to lift the Court into that serene and lofty atmosphere, which clothed it with the attributes of a sovereignty beyond the reach of sceptres and crowns. Confined within Constitutional limits, under the con-

Court as Envoys, asserting that it was contrary to the dignity of the President, and the honor and independence of the Judges, to hold out to them the temptation of being Envoys, or of giving them other offices, thus placing in the power of the one to offer, and the others to accept, additional favors. He insisted that no man ought to hold two offices under the same government, and asserted in particular that no judge ought to be absent from the United States, or be drawn from his official station, leaving an undue proportion of its duties to be performed by the remainder of the Bench. Besides this, as the Chief Justice was to preside in case of the Impeachment of the President, and there was no provision in the Constitution to supply a vacancy, therefore if an Impeachment was to take place in his absence, it must remain undecided until the Chief Justice could be sent for. He submitted with great deference that as the President was the only officer on whose trial the Chief Justice was to preside, or on whose Impeachment his absence would be a public inconvenience, it was not perhaps presuming too far on his own infallibility or incapacity to err to send the only officer to a distant country without whose presence in case of an Impeachment a Court could not be formed to try him. Besides this, a judge might be induced to accept any other appointment from the Executive of the Union, and might even accept them from individual States or even from foreign powers, and thus become the minion of the one, or the tool of the other, as circumstances or his own interest might prompt him. He contended for a provision similar to that existing in the State of South Carolina, which by her Constitution provided that no judge should hold any other office of private or public trust under the State, United States, or any other power. (Benton's Abridgment of the Debates of Congress, Vol. II, pp. 419, 421.)

It will be remembered that the New Jersey plan expressly provided that none of the judiciary should, during the time they remain in office, be capable of holding any other office or appointment during their term of service. See Ante, p. 90.

13

trol of that pure and intrepid jurist, it soon began to develop its great prerogatives as a co-ordinate and co-equal department of the government.

It must not be forgotten, however, that the earliest decisions of the old Supreme Court determined for all time the real character of the new government. They established its national features. They rescued it from State interference and control. The judges, as they entered upon the *terra incognita* of national jurisdiction, were perhaps unconscious of their awful responsibilities, but happily they yielded not to popular clamor, they swerved neither to the right nor to the left from the path in which they were guided by the hand of an overruling Providence. Had they done so, the splendid and majestic career of the nation would have been frustrated, and powers bestowed by the Constitution would have been smitten with incurable palsy. "The real importance of the Supreme Court," says Judge Cooley, "was never greater than at first. And the judges who occupied the Bench before the time of Marshall are entitled to have it said of them that what they did was of incalculable value to representative institutions, not in America alone, but throughout the world. They vindicated the national character of the Constitution; they asserted and maintained the supremacy of the national authority; they made plain for the statesmen as well as the jurists who should come after them the true path of Constitutional interpretation; and while doing so, they also justified in the States, as regards purely State questions, the same right of final judgment which they asserted for the Union in respect to questions which were national."[1]

[1] Thomas M. Cooley, LL.D., "Constitutional History of the United States as seen in the Development of American Law." "The Federal Supreme Court—Its Place in the American Constitutional System," p. 52.

J Marshall

CHAPTER XIII.

IT was a favorable omen that on the day of the first meeting of the Supreme Court of the United States at the
City of Washington as the seat of the national government—4th of February, 1801—John Marshall sat as Chief
Justice for the first time. He had been summoned to the
lofty duty of presiding over the deliberations of the American
Comitia Centuriata, and, proceeding to the holiest of temples,
had been proclaimed a magistrate *salvis auspiciis creatus.*

The appearance of Marshall upon the Bench was an epoch
in the history of the Constitution. The hours of provincial-
ism were numbered. The glory and strength of the nation
were to come, and the decisions of the great Chief Justice, in
which he explained, defended and enforced the Constitution,
were to shed upon the ascending pathway of the Republic
the combined lustre of learning, intelligence and integrity.
"The Providence of God," said Mr. Binney, "is shown most
beneficently to the world, in raising up from time to time, and

in crowning with length of days, men of pre-eminent goodness and wisdom." It was Marshall's happy lot to close the services of an active and distinguished life with the longest, most honorable and successful judicial career in the history of the most exalted of tribunals. Fortunate in his opportunities, great in his achievements, he employed his faculties in the creation of a system of jurisprudence which ranks among the admired intellectual productions of the world.

His life was one of reflection and action, of incident and character. A soldier of distinction, a legislator of commanding power, a diplomat skillful and subtle, an historian minute, impartial and accurate, a statesman enlightened and patriotic, a jurist analytical and profound, a magistrate of awful dignity, he displayed in every walk of life the highest qualities, and combined the most opposite characteristics. Born to command, he easily attained the front rank in every species of labor which he undertook, yet his modesty was as great as it was rare. His intercourse with men was graced by an engaging charm, a simplicity, a purity of sentiment, a moral loftiness, an undaunted courage that armed him with a power that not even Jefferson—his bitter enemy—could resist. Whether we view him as a youth, the son of a virtuous and sturdy sire, a child of the people and a product of the soil; or as a soldier facing the dangers of battle or sharing the privations of the camp; or as the champion of the Federal Constitution; or as an envoy outwitting Talleyrand; or as the biographer of Washington; or as an advocate of surpassing strength at the bar; or as a debater in the halls of Congress; or as a Secretary of State and the author of two of the ablest papers in our archives; or as a Judge fit to rank in creative power with Nottingham, Hardwicke, Mansfield or Stowell, we find his career marked with capacity, energy and success. With a mind mathematical and analytical, not richly stored with technical knowledge as compared with those of Taney or Story, but, conscious of its own strength, working out results with astonishing penetration, and resolving every argument into its ultimate principles; moving among the intricacies of novel questions with calm but persevering circumspection; with a marvellous instinct as to what the law ought to be, which enabled him, while other judges were "creeping timidly from cape to headland, to put boldly out to sea;" close and logical in the connection of his thoughts, clear as light itself in his demonstrations, he conquered by pure ratiocination the intellectual convictions and prejudices of his countrymen, and won by his unsullied character their absolute trust in the integrity of his tribunal. He was in close communion with the Constitution, from the hour of its birth, for a period of thirty-four years, and interpreted its provisions upon the sensible theory that they were not to be restrained in a spirit of jealousy within less than the fair dimensions of its delegated authority, nor were they to be extended beyond them in a spirit of usurpation. By a system of practical construction, and by the exercise of those qualities of lawyer, statesman and patriot, which in their triple union complete the frame of a great Constitutional Judge, he raised the government from a doubtful experiment to an assured success, and established it in the affections and confidence of the people. "He was born," said William Pinkney, "to be the Chief Justice of any country into which Providence should have cast him." His career has called forth the most striking eulogies,[1] but in none of them is the sentiment common to all more sententiously expressed than by Mr. Petigru: "Though his authority as Chief Justice

[1] Those of Wirt, Story, Kent, Webster, Binney, Sergeant, Van Santvoord, Flanders, Shirley, Magruder, Rawle, Phelps and Hitchcock.

of the United States was protracted beyond the ordinary term of public life, no man dared to covet his place, or express a wish to see it filled by another. Even the spirit of party respected the unsullied purity of the Judge, and the fame of the Chief Justice has justified the wisdom of the Constitution and reconciled the Jealousy of Freedom to the Independence of the Judiciary."

He was born at a roadside village, called Germantown, in Fauquier County, Virginia, on the 24th of September, 1755. His grandfather, of the same name, was a native of Wales, and his father, Thomas Marshall, who is described as a man of extraordinary vigor of mind, had been associated with Washington under the appointment of Lord Fairfax in surveying the western territory. As a lad, young Marshall delighted in the sports of the fields, in foot-races and quoit-pitching, in hunting and trapping, and, at a place called "The Hollow," in the midst of the picturesque beauty of the mountains east of the Blue Ridge, laid the foundation of that vigorous health which attended him through life. He was seldom studious, naturally indolent, full of poetic longings, and day dreams and romances. In after life he never lost the simple-mindedness and sensitive modesty of a child, but his ardent social nature, waggish humor and personal magnetism, combined with his physical and moral courage and activity made him the favorite leader of his play-fellows. His earliest instruction was domestic, but at the age of fourteen he was sent to a clergyman named Campbell, in whose house, with James Monroe as a fellow-student, he acquired the rudiments of grammatical and classical knowledge. A year later he received further instruction from a Scotch gentleman named Thomson, the clergyman of the parish, but soon returned home, where he received from his father, who was a practical surveyor, adequately acquainted with mathematics and astronomy, and familiar with the standard works of history, poetry and general literature, the only real, systematic training that he had as a school-boy. "My father," as he frequently said in after life, "was a far abler man than any of his sons. To him I owe the solid foundation of all my success in life." At eighteen he began the study of the law, but the impending struggle with Great Britain distracted his attention before he had obtained a license to practice. From the time that he was made a lieutenant in a militia company, in the spring of 1775, until the winter of 1779—when he attended the law lectures of Wythe, afterwards Chancellor—at William and Mary College, he was in active service, participating in the battles of Great Bridge, Iron Hill, Brandywine, Germantown, Monmouth, Stony Point, and Paulus Hook, and sharing with unflinching fortitude the sufferings at Valley Forge. In 1780 he was admitted to the bar, and after a short return to the army to meet Arnold's invasion, continued with assiduity the practice of his profession. He served as a member of the Lower House in his native State, and of the Executive Council in the course of the year 1782, and continued intermittently to discharge such public duties until 1795. In 1788 he was one of the sturdiest and most influential of the supporters of the Federal Constitution, when it was before the people of Virginia for approval, and by the side of Madison met the shock of the onslaughts of Henry, Mason and Grayson. So admirable was the temper of his arguments, and such the spirit of sincerity that they breathed that Patrick Henry pronounced upon him the short but comprehensive eulogium: "I have the highest respect and veneration for the honorable gentleman. I have experienced his candor upon all occasions." By this time Marshall's high professional reputation, great learning, and extraordinary vigor of mind, made him one of the most eminent lawyers of the State. In 1796 he argued the famous case of the British debts in the Circuit Court of the United States, in opposition to Henry, who spoke, as Judge Iredell said, "with a splendor of eloquence," but of Marshall's argument he declared that it was marked by "a depth of investigation and a power of reasoning" exceeding anything he had ever known before. About the same time, in a speech which has been represented as one of the noblest efforts of his genius, he defended the policy of the mission to England, and the treaty of peace negotiated by Mr. Jay. The fame of these admirable arguments spread through the Union, and when he came to Philadelphia in the case of *Ware* v. *Hylton* before the Supreme Court of the United States—the only case he ever argued before that tribunal—he found that his reputation had preceded him. Soon after, he was tendered the office of Attorney General of the United States, which he declined, but subsequently accepted a special mission to France with Charles Cotesworth Pinckney and Elbridge Gerry, in which he won unbounded popularity by the skill with which he snatched laurels from the brow of Talleyrand. Yielding to the persuasions of Washington he became a member of Congress, at the sacrifice of the place on the bench of the Supreme Court made vacant by the death of Iredell. In the famous debate upon the resolutions of Edward Livingston censuring President Adams for his conduct relative to the extradition of Thomas Nash, otherwise called Jonathan Robbins, Marshall delivered that elaborate and triumphant speech, which, in the language of Judge Story, settled then and forever the points of international law upon which the controversy hinged. It was, says the same high authority, one of the most consummate juridical arguments ever pronounced in the

halls of legislation; and, like Lord Mansfield's answer to the
Prussian Memorial, it was *réponse sans réplique.*   Upon the
retirement of McHenry as Secretary of War, Marshall was
appointed, but before he could insist upon the withdrawal of
his nomination, the rupture took place between the President
and Colonel Pickering, and he was appointed Secretary of
State.   Here his thorough knowledge of our foreign relations
enabled him to manage the affairs of his department with signal ability and success, until the incoming of Jefferson's administration.   In the meantime Chief Justice Ellsworth had
resigned his place.   Marshall, upon being consulted, recommended the appointment of Judge Paterson, but the President
objected lest he should wound the feelings of Judge Cushing,
an old friend and the senior Justice.   Thereupon Jay was appointed but declined.   As soon as this was known, Marshall's
name was sent to the Senate, which confirmed him unanimously,
and on the 31st of January, 1801, he was commissioned as
Chief Justice of the United States.   In after years John Q.
Adams said that if his father had done nothing else to deserve the approbation of his country and posterity, he might
proudly claim it for this single act.   Marshall was now to
crown his illustrious career by labors which have made his
name immortal.

Prior to the decision in *Marbury* v. *Madison,* which is
one of the base-stones of his reputation, Marshall, as Chief
Justice, delivered five opinions, one involving a claim to salvage turning upon an alleged recapture, in which he undertook to review elaborately our relations towards France in
1799, and declared that they were those of a partial war;[1]
one relating to the proper method of appropriating waste

---

[1] Talbot *v.* Seeman, 1 Cranch, 1 (1801).

lands in Kentucky;[1] one in which he upheld the treaty obligations of the nation, even though such a course might involve an interference with private rights vested under a decree of condemnation in an inferior court;[2] and two involving mere matters of practice,[3] the latter turning upon nice considerations of the law relating to executions.[4] In all these the conclusions are well and clearly worked out, though at a length much greater than would be deemed necessary at the present day.

In the December term, 1801, Charles Lee, late Attorney-General of the United States, moved for a rule to show cause why a mandamus should not issue addressed to Madison, then Secretary of State, commanding him to deliver a commission to Marbury, whom President Adams, before the expiration of his term, had nominated as a Justice of the Peace for the District of Columbia.[5] The nomination had been confirmed by the Senate. A commission had been filled up, signed by the President, and sealed with the seal of the United States, but had not been delivered when Mr. Jefferson came into office. Acting on the idea that the appointment was incomplete and void so long as the commission remained undelivered, Jefferson countermanded its issue. The application made to the Supreme Court was for the exercise of its original jurisdiction under the terms of the Judiciary Act, and the main question undoubtedly was whether such a writ could issue from the Supreme Court under the gift of a jurisdiction by Congress in direct violation of the terms of the Constitution in distributing original and appellate authority.

---

[1] Wilson *v.* Mason, 1 Cranch, 45 (1801).

[2] United States *v.* Schooner Peggy, *Ibid.* 103 (1801).

[3] Resler *v.* Shehee, *Ibid.* 111 (1801).   [4] Turner *v.* Fendall, *Ibid.* 117 (1801).

[5] Marbury *v.* Madison, *Ibid.* 137 (1803).

The Court held that delivery was not essential to the validity of letters patent, and that the right of the plaintiff to his office was complete, and hence he was entitled to a remedy; but as Congress could not give original jurisdiction to the Supreme Court, in cases not sanctioned by the Constitution, the application must be refused.

The importance of this decision lies in the fact that it was the first authoritative announcement by the Supreme Court that it had the right as well as the power to declare null and void an act of Congress in violation of the Constitution. It declared that the Constitution was to be regarded as an absolute limit to legislative power; that Congress could not pretend to possess the omnipotence of Parliament. And although in some respects the decision was *obiter dictum*, since the Court declared in the end that it had no jurisdiction of the case, yet it has always been understood as establishing principles which have never since been controverted, subjecting the ministerial and executive officers of the government all over the country to the control of the courts in regard to the execution of a large part of their duties.[1]

The Chief Justice, in the course of his opinion, said:

"If it had been intended to leave it in the discretion of the Legislature to apportion the judicial power between the Supreme and inferior Courts according to the will of that body, it would certainly have been useless to have proceeded further than to have defined the judicial power and the tribunals in which it should be vested. The subsequent part of the section is mere surplusage, is entirely without meaning, if such is to be the construction. If Congress remains at liberty to give this Court appellate jurisdiction where the Constitution has declared their

[1] Address of Mr. Justice Miller on the Supreme Court of the United States, delivered June 29, 1887, before the Alumni of the Law Department of the University of Michigan. See also United States *v.* Schurz, 102 United States Reports, 407 (1880).

jurisdiction shall be original, and original jurisdiction where the Constitution has declared it shall be appellate, the distribution of jurisdiction made in the Constitution is form without substance. . . . . The question whether an act repugnant to the Constitution can become the law of the land, is a question deeply interesting to the United States, but happily not of an intricacy proportioned to its interest. It seems only necessary to recognize certain principles supposed to have been long and well established to decide it. . . . . The powers of the Legislature are defined and limited; and that those limits may not be mistaken or forgotten, the Constitution is written. To what purpose are powers limited, and to what purpose is that limitation committed to writing, if these limits may, at any time, be passed by those intended to be restrained? The distinction between a government with limited and unlimited powers is abolished if those limits do not confine the persons on whom they are imposed, and if acts prohibited and acts allowed are of equal obligation. It is a proposition too plain to be contested, that the Constitution controls any legislative act repugnant to it, or that the Legislature may alter the Constitution by an ordinary act. Between these alternatives there is no middle ground. The Constitution is either a superior paramount law, unchangeable by ordinary means, or it is on a level with ordinary legislative acts, and, like other acts, is alterable when the Legislature shall please to alter it. If the former part of the alternative be true, then a legislative act contrary to the Constitution is not law; if the latter part be true, then written Constitutions are absurd attempts, on the part of the people, to limit a power in its own nature illimitable. . . . If an act of the Legislature repugnant to the Constitution is void, does it, notwithstanding its invalidity, bind the Courts, and oblige them to give it effect? Or, in other words, though it be not law, does it constitute a rule as operative as if it was a law? This would be to overthrow in fact what was established in theory, and would seem at first view an absurdity too gross to be insisted on. It shall, however, receive a more attentive consideration. It is emphatically the province and duty of the judicial department to say what the law is. Those who apply the rule to particular cases must of necessity expound and interpret that rule. If two laws conflict with each other, the Courts must decide on the operation of each. So if a law be in opposition to the Constitution; if both the law and the Constitution apply to a particular case, so that the Court must either decide that case conformably to the law, disregarding the Constitution, or conformably to the Constitution, disregarding the law,—the Court must determine which of these conflicting rules governs the case. This is of the very essence of judicial duty. If, then, the Courts are to regard the Constitution, and the Constitution is superior to any ordinary act of the Legislature, the Constitution, and not such ordinary act, must govern the case to which they both apply."

From this remorseless logic there could be no escape.

Apart from the interest which will always be taken by lawyers in this famous decision, as establishing a principle which lies at the foundation of our constitutional jurisprudence, and which places the judiciary upon an independent and lofty plane, there are certain dramatic features attached to it which grew out of the history of the times. A recent historian has pointed out that in the appointment of Marshall John Adams had intended to perpetuate the Federal principles of his administration, and that Marshall was as obnoxious to Jefferson as the most rigid New England Calvinist would have been, for Jefferson had determined upon restricting the powers of the National Government in the interests of human liberty, and Marshall was bent upon enlarging the powers of the government in the interests of justice and nationality.[1]

As the new President and the new Chief Justice stood face to face upon the threshold of their power, each could foresee that the contest between them would end only with life. The judgment of posterity has crowned Marshall as the victor.

Marbury and Madison, says another writer, were the John Doe and Richard Roe of the ejectment; the real issue was

[1] Henry Adams, "History of the United States, 1801 to 1805," Vol. I, p. 192.

between John Marshall and Thomas Jefferson—a trial of strength in their new positions.[1]

The opinion of Marshall was regarded by Jefferson as a defiance. Even the strongest admirers of the Chief Justice admit that his manner of dealing with the case was unusual. Ordinarily where a cause was to turn on a question of jurisdiction, the Court would consider that point as first and final, but instead of beginning at that point and dismissing the motion the Court reversed the order of discussion in the manner already indicated. The settled bent of Marshall's mind was towards the maintenance of the sanctity of pledged word; the Executive should be held to the performance of a contract, and although the Court could not intermeddle with the prerogative of the Executive, it might and would command the head of a department to perform a duty not depending on executive discretion, but on particular acts of Congress and the general principles of law.

It may well be, also, that Marshall smarted under a sense of wrong growing out of the suspension of the sessions of the Supreme Court by legislative artifice, under the dictation of the President, for a period of fourteen months, which delayed the delivery of the opinion until February, 1803. The Federalists, at the close of their days of power, had, by an Act of Congress, dated the 13th of February, 1801,[2] sought to entrench themselves, as their critics and political opponents alleged, in the judiciary department, by re-arranging the judicial Districts and by the establishment of separate Circuit Courts. Twenty-two Districts were established, and were

---

[1] Shirley, "Dartmouth College Cases and the Supreme Court of the United States," p. 393.

[2] Act of 13th February, 1801, Laws of the United States, Vol. III, p. 405, Ed of 1815.

divided into six Circuits. In each of the Circuits, except the sixth, there were to be three Circuit Court Judges, one of whom should be commissioned as Chief Judge, and none of whom should be judges of the Supreme Court of the United States. In the sixth Circuit the Circuit Court was to consist of a Circuit judge and the two judges of the District courts of the Districts of Kentucky and Tennessee, and the old District courts in those Districts were abolished. The number of Justices of the Supreme Court was to be reduced after the next vacancy to five, making a Chief Justice and four Associates. This new arrangement, which was intended to meet the Constitutional objections which had been raised by the Judges of the Supreme Court themselves as to their sitting at circuit, as well as to provide an intermediate court of appeal, entirely separate in its personality from that of the Court of last resort, gave to President Adams the appointment of sixteen new judges, and their commissions were signed and delivered upon the eve of his departure from office, and the incumbents were derisively styled "The Midnight Judges." The moment that Jefferson came into power a systematic and well-organized attack was made upon the Federal judiciary. The Act establishing separate Circuit Courts was repealed after a long and acrimonious debate in Congress [1] notwithstanding the Constitutional argument that was made by the Federalists in opposition, and in order to prevent Chief Justice Marshall and his Associates from interfering with the new arrangements, Congress, while destroying the new Circuit Courts, adopted the drastic remedy of suspending for more than a year the sessions of the Supreme

---

[1] Act of March 8, 1802, Laws of United States, Vol. III, p. 450, Ed. of 1815. Also Act of April 29, 1802, *Ibid.* p. 479. See Adams' "History of the United States," Vol. I, pp. 274, 298, Vol. II, p. 143.

Court itself by abolishing the August term. This Congressional assault was followed up by the impeachment of Judge Pickering who had become insane from habits of drinking, and by the impeachment of Justice Chase, an Associate Justice of the Supreme Court, whose violent partisan harangues from the Bench, and whose conduct upon the trial of Fries six years before, were seized upon as pretexts, the real object being to establish the point that the bench could be reached through impeachment for high crimes and misdemeanors. These movements were intended to be the forerunners of a general attack upon those members of the judiciary, including Marshall himself, who seemed bent upon the consolidation of the government through the judiciary department.

Pickering, the United States District Judge for the District of New Hampshire, was found guilty, although clearly insane, a fact which robbed his conviction of its significance, while the triumphant acquittal of Chase, through the extraordinary skill and ability of his counsel, Luther Martin, Robert G. Harper and Joseph Hopkinson, in compelling John Randolph and his fellow-managers to admit that the phrase "high crimes and misdemeanors" in the Constitution meant indictable offences, proved the safety of the Supreme Court, and rescued the Judiciary from the dangers of its position. Thenceforth John Marshall was safe, and he proceeded at his leisure to establish the principles of Constitutional law.

John Randolph, in a rage, submitted an amendment to the Constitution: "The Judges of the Supreme Court and all other Courts of the United States shall be removed by the President on the joint address of both Houses of Congress." But he could not command sufficient support. The bitterness of Jefferson had not died out when, fifteen years later, he wrote to a friend:[1] "The judiciary of the United States is the subtle corps of sappers and miners constantly working underground to undermine the foundations of our confederated fabric. They are construing our Constitution from a co-ordination of a general and special government to a general and supreme one alone. . . . Having found from experience that impeachment is an impracticable thing, a mere scarecrow, they consider themselves secure for life; they skulk from responsibility. . . . An opinion is huddled up in conclave, perhaps by a majority of one, delivered as if unanimous, and with the silent acquiescence of lazy and timid associates, by a crafty chief judge who sophisticates the law to his mind by the turn of his own reasoning."

Once more did Marshall have an opportunity of reflecting upon the President. In *Little* v. *Barreme et al.*,[2] a commander of a ship-of-war was held answerable in damages to a person injured, even though he had acted under the instructions of the President. "Instructions not warranted by law," said the Chief Justice sententiously, "cannot legalize a trespass."

Some years elapsed before a second question of national importance arose. In the meantime a variety of cases were decided, to which a general reference will be sufficient to indicate their extent and character. Presumption of payment;[3] application of payments;[4] commercial paper;[5] indorsements;[6]

---

[1] Letter of Thomas Jefferson to Thomas Ritchie, December 25, 1820, "Jefferson's Works," Vol. VII, p. 192.

[2] 2 Cranch, 170 (1804).

[3] Dunlop & Co. *v.* Ball, 2 Cranch, 180 (1804).

[4] Field *et al. v.* Holland *et al.*, 6 Cranch, 8 (1810).

[5] French's Exr. *v.* Bank of Columbia, 4 Cranch, 142 (1807).

[6] Clark *v.* Young & Co., 1 Cranch, 181 (1803). Wilson *v.* Lenox, *Ibid.*, 194 (1803). Mandeville & Jameson *v.* Riddle & Co., *Ibid.*, 290 (1803). Yeaton *v.* Bank of Alexandria, 5 Cranch, 49 (1809). Dulany *v.* Hodgkin, *Ibid.*, 333 (1809).

14

insurance;[1] salvage;[2] prize;[3] violations of the embargo or non-intercourse act;[4] patent rights;[5] chancery jurisdiction in cases of dower;[6] tacking;[7] equity pleading;[8] pleading at law;[9] devise;[10] abatement of legacies;[11] evidence;[12] usury;[13] set-off;[14] land laws;[15] the ownership of slaves;[16] statutes of limitation;[17] wills, executors and trustees [18]—these and kindred subjects, argued at length with the most profuse display of learning, were patiently and exhaustively considered. Several points of jurisdiction were determined: Federal jurisdiction being sustained in a case between citizens of the same State, where the plaintiffs were only nominal plaintiffs for the use of an alien,[19] and declined where all the parties were aliens.[20] It was also held that a citizen of the District of Columbia

---

[1] Head & Amory *v.* Providence Ins. Co., 2 Cranch, 128 (1804). Church *v.* Hubbart, *Ibid.*, 187 (1804). Graves & Barnewall *v.* Boston Marine Ins. Co., *Ibid.*, 419 (1805). Marine Ins. Co. of Alexandria *v.* Wilson, 3 Cranch, 187 (1805).

[2] Mason *v.* Ship Blaireau, 2 Cranch, 240 (1804).

[3] Armitz Brown *v.* The United States, 8 Cranch, 110 (1814). Talbot *v.* Seeman, 1 Cranch, 1 (1801). Murray *v.* Schooner Charming Betsey, 2 Cranch, 64 (1804).

[4] United States *v.* Brig Eliza, 7 Cranch, 113 (1812). Brig Penobscot *v.* United States, *Ibid.*, 356 (1813).

[5] Tyler *et al. v.* Tuel, 6 Cranch, 324 (1810).

[6] Herbert *et al. v.* Wren and wife *et al.*, 7 Cranch, 370 (1813).

[7] Fitzsimmons *v.* Ogden, 7 Cranch, 2 (1812).

[8] Milligan, Admr. *v.* Milledge and wife, 3 Cranch, 220 (1805).

[9] Cooke *v.* Graham's Admr., 3 Cranch, 229 (1805).

[10] Lambert's Lessee *v.* Paine, 3 Cranch, 97 (1805).

[11] Silsby *v.* Young & Silsby, 3 Cranch, 249 (1806).

[12] Wilson *v.* Speed, 3 Cranch, 283 (1806).

[13] Levy *v.* Gadsby, 3 Cranch, 180 (1805).

[14] Winchester *v.* Hackley, 2 Cranch, 343 (1804).

[15] Huidekoper's Lessee *v.* Douglass, 3 Cranch, 1 (1805).

[16] Scott *v.* Negro Ludlow, 3 Cranch, 325 (1806).

[17] Faw *v.* Roberdeau's Excr., 3 Cranch, 175 (1805).

[18] Griffith *v.* Frazier, 8 Cranch, 11 (1814).

[19] Browne *v.* Strode, 5 Cranch, 303 (1809).

[20] Montalet *v.* Murray, 4 Cranch, 47 (1807).

was not a citizen of a State within the meaning of the Constitution, and could not sue a citizen of Virginia in the Circuit Court for the Virginia District. "It is extraordinary," said the Chief Justice, "that courts open to aliens, and to the citizens of every State in the Union, should be closed upon them, but this is a subject for legislative and not judicial consideration."[1] It was also ruled that where there are two or more joint plaintiffs, and two or more joint defendants, each one of the plaintiffs must be capable of suing each of the defendants to support Federal jurisdiction.[2] Where the decision of a State Court was in favor of the privilege claimed under an Act of Congress, it was held that the Supreme Court had no jurisdiction on a writ of error to a State Court under the 25th Section of the Judiciary Act.[3]

In *McIlvaine* v. *Coxe's Lessee*[4] the question was twice argued whether a person born in the colony of New Jersey before the war with Great Britain, and who resided there until 1777, and then joined the British army, and afterwards went to England, where he resided ever afterwards, and always claimed to be a British subject, could take lands in New Jersey by descent from a citizen of the United States. Although the Court declined, as they had done twice before, to pass directly upon the question of expatriation,[5] yet they held that he could

---

[1] Hepburn and Dundas v. Ellzey, 2 Cranch, 445 (1805). This was in accordance with the result reached in Reily v. Lamar et al., 2 Cranch, 344 (1805), where it was held that the inhabitants of the District of Columbia by its separation from Virginia and Maryland ceased to be citizens of those States respectively. A similar disability rests upon a citizen of a Territory, who cannot sue a citizen of a State in the Courts of the United States. A Territory is not a State in the sense intended by the Constitution. Corporation of New Orleans v. Winter, 1 Wheaton, 92 (1816).   [2] Strawbridge v. Curtiss, 3 Cranch, 267 (1806).

[3] Gordon v. Caldcleugh, 3 Cranch, 269 (1806).   [4] 2 Cranch, 280 (1804).

[5] See Talbot v. Jansen, 3 Dallas, 133 (1795). The Charming Betsey, Circuit Ct. of Penna., 26th May, 1802, S. C. 2 Cranch, p. 64 (1804).

take and hold such lands, as New Jersey as a sovereign State had the right to compel her inhabitants to become citizens thereof, as she had endeavored to do by an act of 1776, nor could the State allege alienage in one over whom she had asserted authority; nor did the Treaty of Peace diminish her sovereignty.[1] In contrast with this was the decision that a person born in England before the year 1775, and who always resided there and never was in the United States, is an alien, and could not, in the year 1793, take lands in Maryland by descent from a citizen of the United States.[2]

Federal supremacy was sustained in a series of interesting cases, in several of which the Chief Justice speaks in a tone of conscious pride and strength. In sustaining the claim of the United States to a preference in all cases of insolvency or bankruptcy[3] he says:

"This claim of priority on the part of the United States will, it has been said, interfere with the right of the State sovereignties respecting the dignity of debts, and will defeat the measures they have a right to adopt to secure themselves against delinquencies on the part of their own revenue officers. But this is an objection to the Constitution itself. The mischief suggested, so far as it can really happen, is the necessary consequence of the supremacy of the laws of the United States on all subjects to which the legislative power of Congress extends."

The paramount obligations of the Treaty of Peace were again asserted, and it was held that the Virginia statute of limitations could not operate upon debts contracted before the date of the treaty.[4] In *Jennings* v. *Carson*,[5] in affirmance of

---

[1] McIlvaine *v.* Coxe's Lessee, 4 Cranch, 211 (1808).
[2] Dawson's Lessee *v.* Godfrey, 4 Cranch, 321 (1808).
[3] U. S. *v.* Fisher *et al.*, 2 Cranch, 358 (1804).
[4] Hopkirk *v.* Bell, 3 Cranch, 454 (1806).
[5] 4 Cranch, 2 (1807).

Penhallow v. *Doane*,[1] it was held that the District Courts of
t'ie United States were courts of prize, and had power to carry
into effect the sentences of the old Continental Courts of Appeal in cases of Capture. About the same time it was ruled,
with some display of offended dignity, that the Courts of the
United States will not enforce an agreement entered into in
fraud of a law of the United States, even though the parties
to the agreement were public enemies and the agreement was
a mere stratagem of war.[2]

We now encounter a signal instance of the growth of
Federal power. As has been seen,[3] in the case of the sloop
Active, the State of Pennsylvania was able to resist successfully the execution of a decree entered by the Standing Committee of Appeals in Cases of Capture, reversing the judgment of her own Court of Admiralty sustaining as final the
verdict of a jury distributing prize money. The Continental
Congress, although defending their jurisdiction by the most
pointed and unanswerable logic, had cowered before the authority of the State and shrunk timidly from any prospect of
collision, abandoning the appellants to their fate. Quietly
awaiting the course of events, Olmstead, whose original appeal
had been brought in 1779, watched the collapse of the Confederation, the adoption of the Constitution and the establishment of the new government, and then availing himself of the
doctrine of *Penhallow* v. *Doane*, filed his libel in the District
Court for the District of Pennsylvania and obtained a decree
in his favor. Upon the refusal of Judge Peters to grant an
attachment, who for prudential reasons deemed it best to avoid
embroiling the government of the United States and that of
Pennsylvania, an application was made to the Supreme Court

[1] 3 Dallas, 54 (1795).   [2] Hannay *v.* Eve, 3 Cranch, 242 (1806).
[3] *Ante*, Chap. IV., p. 53.

in 1808, for a mandamus to be directed to the Judge.[1] The writ was awarded by the Chief Justice in one of his most characteristic judgments. "With great attention and serious concern" he examined the question of jurisdiction, and after a calm but convincing course of reason in support of Federal power, solemnly declared:

"If the legislatures of the several States may at will annul the judgments of the Courts of the United States, and destroy the rights acquired under those judgments, the Constitution itself becomes a solemn mockery, and the nation is deprived of the means of enforcing its laws by the instrumentality of its own tribunals. So fatal a result must be deprecated by all, and the people of Pennsylvania not less than the citizens of every other State must feel a deep interest in resisting principles so destructive of the Union, and in averting consequences so fatal to themselves." . . . "The State of Pennsylvania can possess no Constitutional right to resist the legal process which may be directed in this case. It will be readily conceived that the order which this Court is enjoined to make by the high obligations of duty and of law is not made without extreme regret at the necessity which has induced the application. But it is a solemn duty and therefore must be performed."

There could be but little doubt as to the result when John Marshall sounded such a note, but the State still maintained an attitude of defiance. The subsequent proceedings though not occurring in the Supreme Court, are interesting as showing that the national gristle had hardened into bone. Service of the attachment was resisted by the State militia under General Bright, who had been called out by the Governor, under the sanction of the Legislature. The Marshal retired, naming a day for the service of the warrant, and summoned a posse of two thousand men. Bloodshed was imminent. The Governor appealed to President Madison

[1] U. S. *v.* Judge Peters, 5 Cranch, 115 (1809).

begging him to discriminate between factious opposition to the laws of the United States and resistance to the decree of a Judge founded on a usurpation of power, but Madison replied that he was not only unauthorized to prevent the execution of a decree of the Supreme Court, but was specially enjoined by statute wherever any such decree was resisted to aid in its enforcement. The State then beat a retreat. The Legislature appropriated money to pay the decree, and Olmstead, after a struggle for justice which had lasted thirty years, obtained the fruits of his valor. But the conflict had not ended. General Bright and his men were brought to trial, for forcibly obstructing Federal process, before Mr. Justice Washington, and after a sharp contest were convicted and sentenced to fine and imprisonment.[1] These were remited by the President on the ground that the prisoners had acted under a mistaken sense of duty, but the priceless principle had been established that the Constitution and laws of the United States were the supreme law of the land, and that the Judges in every State were bound thereby, anything in the Constitution or laws of any State to the contrary notwithstanding.

In the important and interesting case of *Ex parte Bollman and Ex parte Swartwout,*[2] the Chief-Justice dealt with the power of the Court to issue the writ of habeas corpus, as well as with the law of treason. Colonel Swartwout was the Chief of Staff of Aaron Burr, and had borne a letter in cipher from Burr to General Wilkinson, then Commander-in·

---

[1] Trial of General Bright, in the Circuit Court of the United States, for the District of Pennsylvania, printed at Philadelphia, 1809. Richard Peters, Jr., "The whole Proceedings in the case of Olmstead v. Rittenhouse," Philadelphia, 1809. United States v. Peters, 5 Cranch, 115 (1809). Ross et al. Executors v. Rittenhouse, 2 Dallas, 160 (1792). Journals of Continental Congress, Vol. 5, 372.

[2] 4 Cranch, 75 (1807).

chief of the Army of the United States, and the Military
Governor of the newly-acquired territory of Louisiana. The
letter disclosed the particulars of an intended movement down
the Ohio and Mississippi, *en route* to New Orleans, and
thence to Mexico. Wilkinson, who succeeded in weaving a
web of mystery about his real attitude towards the enterprise
pretended to hesitate as to his conduct, but finally disclosed
the treasonable conspiracy to the President, who issued a
proclamation denouncing it. Wilkinson then seized Swartwout, Bollman and others, as emissaries of Burr, and sent
them under guard to Washington, where they were committed by the Circuit Court of the District of Columbia on the
charge of treason. Motions were made in their behalf for
writs of habeas corpus, and the question of the power of the
Court to issue such a writ was elaborately argued. Mr. Justice Chase doubted the jurisdiction of the Court in any case
although he agreed that any of the Judges might issue the
writ at chambers if the application were made within the
proper Circuit. Mr. Justice Johnson thought that the power
was given to the Judges merely as auxiliary to some other
jurisdiction, but could not be exercised by the Court collect-
ively. His views were clearly and ably stated, and a most
skillful use made of *Marbury* v. *Madison.* He insisted that
no original powers could be vested by Congress in the Supreme Court beyond those to which the Court was restricted
by the Constitution, and that the principle of that decision
applied as much to the issuing of a habeas corpus in a case
of treason as to the issuing of a mandamus in a case no
more remote from the original jurisdiction of the Court
Marshall, at the very outset of his opinion, expressly dis-
claimed all jurisdiction not given by the Constitution or by
the laws of the United States, and refused to yield to the

argument which had been made by Harper that the writ might issue at common law; but he considered that the Fourteenth Section of the Judiciary Act contained a substantive grant of the power, and pointed out that the terms of the .grant must include the Supreme Court, because a denial would involve a denial of power to every other Court:

"Whatever motives might induce the Legislature to withhold from the Supreme Court the power to award the great writ of habeas corpus, there could be none which would induce them to withhold it from every Court in the United States; and as it is granted to all in the same sentence and by the same words, the sound construction would seem to be, that the first sentence vests this power in all the Courts of the United States; but as those Courts are not always in session, the second sentence vests it in every judge or justice of the United States."

The second point he treated briefly:

"In the mandamus case it was decided that this Court would not exercise original jurisdiction except so far as that jurisdiction was given by the Constitution. But so far as that case has distinguished between original and appellate jurisdiction, that which the Court is now asked to exercise is clearly appellate. It is the revision of a decision of an inferior Court by which a citizen has been committed to jail."

The motion being granted, the Court, after argument, considered whether there was sufficient evidence to justify a holding to bail, and in the course of a most elaborate opinion discussed the law of treason. After quoting the language of the Constitution, Marshall rules:

"To constitute that specific crime for which the prisoners now before the Court have been committed, war must. be actually levied against the United States. However flagitious may be the crime of conspiring to subvert by force the government of our country, such conspiracy is not treason. To conspire to levy war, and actually to levy war, are distinct offences. The first must be brought into operation by the assemblage of men for a purpose treasonable in itself, or the fact of levying war cannot be committed. . . . It is not the intention of the Court to say that no individual can be guilty of this crime who has not appeared in arms against his country. On the contrary, if war be actually levied,—that is, if a body of men be actually assembled for the purpose of effecting by force a treasonable purpose,—all those who perform any part, however minute, or however remote from the scene of action, and who are actually leagued in the general conspiracy, are to be considered as traitors. But there must be an actual assembling of men for the treasonable purpose to constitute a levying of war.''

Whatever might have been the connection of the prisoners with Burr and the operations set on foot by him, yet the offence of treason was not established to the satisfaction of the Court, and they were discharged. Upon the trial of Burr, over which Marshall presided, it was found necessary to explain and defend these doctrines. Upon the struggle to connect Burr with the transactions at Blennerhassett's Island, which proved the turning-point of the case, the Chief Justice, while still adhering to the rule laid down in the case of Bollman and Swartwout, which had been severely criticized as countenancing constructive treason, ruled out as irrelevant and inadmissible all the testimony offered by the United States to connect the prisoner, who it was admitted was at a great distance in a different State, with the alleged levying of war on the island.

These rulings were bitterly assailed. "Marshall," said Wirt, "has stepped in between Burr and death." Burr himself, when subsequently held to bail upon a charge of misdemeanor, declared it was "a sacrifice of principle to conciliate Jack Cade." Giles, a Senator of the United States from Virginia, introduced a bill at the next session of Congress to define treason, exclaiming with great warmth: "I have learned that judicial opinions on this subject are like changeable silks, which vary their colors as they are held up in political sunshine." At this time, when the passions and prejudices of the hour have perished, it is possible to form a calm judgment of the matter, and it is not too much to assert that the august figure of Marshall presented the impersonation of unbending, inflexible justice.

" The impartiality which marked the conduct of those trials was never excelled in history. . . . No greater display of judicial skill and judicial rectitude was ever witnessed. . . . The Judge was unmoved by criticism, no matter from what quarter, and was content to await the judgment of posterity, that never, in all the dark history of State trials, was the law, as then it stood and bound both parties, ever interpreted with more impartiality to the accuser and the accused." [1]

"Why did you not tell Judge Marshall that the people of America demanded a conviction?" was the question put to Wirt after the trial. "Tell *him* that!" was the reply. "I would as soon have gone to Herschel, and told him that the people of America insisted that the moon had horns, as a reason why he should draw her with them." [2]

The case of *Fletcher* v. *Peck*[3] will be always memorable as the first of that long line of instances in which the statutes of a State repugnant to the Constitution have been held to be void. It is the first judicial determination of a constitutional restriction upon the powers of the States. It towers above the decisions of a period of many years, important and imposing though they are, and, with *Marbury* v. *Madison*, stands as an outspur of that magnificent range of adjudications which bear to our Constitutional jurisprudence the relative

---

[1] Oration by Wm. Henry Rawle, LL.D., at the unveiling of the Statue of Chief Justice Marshall at Washington, May 10, 1884.

[2] Van Santvoord's "Lives of the Chief-Justices," p. 379.

[3] 6 Cranch, 87 (1810).

strength and majesty of the Rocky Mountains to our physical geography. The State of Georgia had sought by legislative enactment to destroy rights acquired under a previous statute of the same State, granting lands to an individual. It was held that a grant was a contract executed, the obligation of which continued; and since the Constitution drew no distinction between contracts executed and executory, the Constitutional clause must be so interpreted as to comprehend both.

"A law annulling conveyances between individuals and declaring that the grantors should stand seized of their former estates notwithstanding these grants," said the Chief-Justice, "would be as repugnant to the Constitution as a law discharging the vendors of property from the obligation of executing their contracts by conveyances. It would be strange if a contract to convey was secured by the Constitution, while an absolute conveyance remained unprotected."

Nor was the sovereignty of a State too exalted for the restrictions of this clause:

"Whatever respect might have been felt for the State sovereignties, it is not to be disguised that the framers of the Constitution viewed with some apprehension the violent acts which might grow out of the feelings of the moment; and that the people of the United States, in adopting that instrument, have manifested a determination to shield themselves and their property from the effects of those sudden and strong passions to which men are exposed. The restrictions upon the legislative power of the States are obviously founded in this sentiment, and the Constitution of the United States contains what may be deemed a bill of rights for the people of each State."

The same great principle of the sanctity of rights vested under legislative grants was illustrated and enforced within a few years afterwards, as against a similar course of action on the part of New Jersey, Virginia and New Hampshire.[1]

---

[1] The State of New Jersey *v.* Wilson, 7 Cranch, 164 (1812). Terrett *v.* Taylor, 9 Cranch, 43 (1815). The Town of Pawlet *v.* Daniel Clark *et al.*, 9 Cranch, 292 (1815).

It was only after a most cautious examination, however, that such results were reached. The language of the Court was solemn and dignified; no trace of passion or vindictive heat is discernible:

"The question whether a law be void for its repugnance to the Constitution is at all times a question of much delicacy, which ought seldom, if ever, to be decided in the affirmative in a doubtful case. The Court, when impelled by duty to render such a judgment, would be unworthy of its station could it be unmindful of the solemn obligations which that station imposes. But it is not on slight implication and vague conjecture that the Legislature is to be pronounced to have transcended its powers, and its acts to be considered as void. The opposition between the Constitution and the law should be such that the Judge feels a clear and strong conviction of their incompatibility with each other." [1]

In the case of a corporation suing as plaintiff, it was held that a corporation aggregate, composed of citizens of one State, might sue a citizen of another State in the Federal Courts; but where the jurisdiction depended, not on the character of the parties, but upon the nature of the case, the Judiciary Act could confer no jurisdiction on the Circuit Courts except where a controversy arose between citizens of the same State claiming lands under grants from different States.[2] It was also determined that, though the appellate powers of the Supreme Court had been given by the Constitution, yet they were limited and regulated by the Acts of Congress.[3] While adjusting the relations of Federal and State tribunals, it was held that a Court of the United States could not enjoin proceedings in a State Court,[4] nor had a State

[1] Fletcher *v.* Peck, 6 Cranch, 87 (1810).
[2] The Bank of the United States *v.* Deveaux, 5 Cranch, 62 (1809).
[3] Durousseau and others *v.* The United States, 6 Cranch, 308 (1810).
[4] Diggs & Keith *v.* Wolcott, 4 Cranch, 179 (1807).

Court jurisdiction to enjoin a judgment of the Circuit Court of the United States,[1] nor could a State tribunal interfere, by process of replevin, injunction or otherwise, with a seizure of property made by revenue officers under the laws of the United States.[2]

Another most important matter of jurisdiction was settled at this time, although long settled, as Judge Johnson said, in public opinion. It was held that the Courts of the United States could not exercise a Common law jurisdiction in criminal cases,—a doctrine in striking opposition to the views of Jay and his Associates.[3]

The law of Prize and Admiralty Jurisdiction now began to assume shape and prominence. The slender body of decisions pronounced by the early judges of the Court could scarcely be said to constitute a system. This branch of the law was then in its infancy; but the non-intercourse and embargo acts and the War of 1812 created a new class of cases, which called for the establishment of general principles. The conflicting rights of captors, of neutrals and belligerents, trading under licenses or privateering under letters of marque and reprisal, were to be adjusted.[4] One of the most important of the earliest decisions of Marshall was that of *Rose* v. *Himely*,[5] which involved the question whether the Courts of this country could examine into the authority of a foreign tribunal acting as a prize court, and disregard its sentence of condemnation, and if so, whether such sentence of a foreign tribunal is valid, when the vessel at the time was actually

---

[1] McKim *v.* Voorhies, 7 Cranch, 279 (1812).

[2] Slocum *v.* Mayberry, 2 Wheaton, 1 (1817).

[3] The United States *v.* Hudson & Goodwin, 7 Cranch, 32 (1812). **See early cases, *ante*, p. 166.**

[4] See "Life and Letters of Joseph Story," Vol. I, pp. 226–227.

[5] 4 Cranch, 241 (1808).

lying in an American port. Several cases depended upon this decision, and they were all elaborately argued by the most eminent practitioners of the day, Charles Lee, Robert G. Harper, A. J. Dallas, William Rawle, Jared Ingersoll, P. S. Duponceau, Edward Tilghman and Luther Martin, the latter speaking for three days, until the spectators, as we are assured by Judge Story, then present as a visitor, were "fatigued almost to death."[1] The decision was pronounced by the Chief Justice—clear, luminous, argumentative, pointed and brief—affirming the right, upon principle, to examine into the jurisdiction of the foreign tribunal, and disregard its sentence, if inconsistent with the law of nations. As in the case at bar the captured vessel had not been carried within the jurisdiction of the French Court at St. Domingo, the sentence of that tribunal was held invalid. The majority of the Court concurred in holding that, though the rights of war might be exercised by a country on the high seas, yet that the legislation of every country being territorial, its rights of sovereignty in the execution of a mere municipal law must be exercised within its own territory, and therefore that the seizure of a vessel not belonging to a subject, made on the high seas, for the breach of a municipal regulation, was an act which the sovereign could not authorize, and such seizure was invalid. To this last proposition Justices Livingston, Cushing and Chase did not accede. The question occurred again in *Hudson* v. *Guestier,*[2] and the Court, through

---

[1] The mode of arguing cases in the Supreme Court at that day was excessively tedious and prolix. The two-hour rule was not then in force. Long chancery bills, with overloaded documents, and long common law records, with scores of bills of exceptions attached to them, crowded the docket. Speeches consumed several days, and sometimes a week, on each side. See "Life and Letters of Joseph Story," Vol. I, p. 217. Van Santvoord's "Lives of the Chief-Justices," p. 384.

[2] 6 Cranch, 281 (1810).

Mr. Justice Livingston, the Chief Justice dissenting, overruled the doctrine. In the later case of *Williams and others* v. *Armroyd*,[1] it was said to be settled that the sentence of a competent court proceeding *in rem* is conclusive with respect to the thing itself. No Court of co-ordinate jurisdiction can examine the sentence; and though a foreign tribunal should condemn American neutral property under an edict unjust in itself, contrary to the law of nations, and in violation of neutral rights, as declared by the Executive and Legislative authority of the United States, yet the Courts of this country cannot lend their aid to the owner to recover such property, because they cannot revise, correct, or even examine the sentence of the foreign tribunal.

The *Exchange*,[2] an American merchantman, had been captured by a French vessel, under one of the decrees of Napoleon. Having been armed and commissioned in the French service, she was sent with despatches to the East Indies and put into the port of Philadelphia in distress, where she was proceeded against by the American owners. The French minister claimed that as she was a French national vessel she was not amenable to judicial process. It was held that her original ownership had been changed by her capture; that her nationality had been duly changed, and having entered an American port from necessity, where she had demeaned herself in a friendly way, she was entitled to be treated in the same manner as any other public armed vessel of the French Emperor, with whom we were at peace, and therefore was exempt from the jurisdiction of the United States.

The celebrated case of the *Nereide*[3] came before the Court

---

[1] 7 Cranch, 423 (1813).
[2] The schooner *Exchange* v. McFadden and others, 7 Cranch, 116 (1812).
[3] 9 Cranch, 389 (1815).

in 1815. The claimant, Mr. Pinto, a merchant and native of Buenos Ayres, being in London, had chartered the vessel, which had been armed and commissioned by Great Britain, to carry his own goods and the property of his family to his home. He took passage on the vessel, which sailed under British convoy, and having been separated from the squadron, was captured off the island of Madeira, after a short action, by an American privateer. The claim had been rejected in the District Court, and the goods condemned upon the ground that they were captured on board of an armed enemy's vessel, which had resisted the exercise of the right of search. The case was argued in the Supreme Court with the most extraordinary eloquence, particularly on the part of Mr. Pinkney, whose dazzling rhetoric, although unsuccessful, so heated the calm mind of Marshall as to lead him to express himself in the following exalted strain:

"The *Nereide* was armed, governed and conducted by belligerents. With her force or her conduct the neutral shippers had no concern; they deposited their goods on board the vessel, and stipulated for their direct transportation to Buenos Ayres. It is true, that on her passage she had a right to defend herself, and might have captured an assailing vessel; but to search for the enemy would have been a violation of the charter party and of her duty. With a pencil dipped in the most vivid colors, and guided by the hand of a master, a splendid portrait has been drawn, exhibiting this vessel and her freighter as forming a single figure, composed of the most discordant materials, of Peace and War. So exquisite was the skill of the artist, so dazzling the garb in which the figure was presented, that it required the exercise of that cold, investigating faculty, which ought always to belong to those who sit on this bench, to discover its only imperfection,—its want of resemblance. The *Nereide* has not that Centaur-like appearance which has been ascribed to her. She does not rove over the ocean hurling the thunders of war while sheltered by the olive-branch of peace. She is not composed in part of the neutral character of Mr. Pinto, and in part of the hostile

15

character of her owner. She is an open and declared belligerent; claiming all the rights and subject to all the dangers of the belligerent character. She conveys neutral property which does not engage in her warlike equipments, or in any employment she may make of them; which is put on board solely for the purpose of transportation, and which encounters the hazard . . . of being taken into port, and obliged to seek another conveyance, should its carrier be captured. In this, it is the opinion of the majority of the Court, there is nothing unlawful. The characters of the vessel and cargo remain as distinct in this as in any other case.''

From this conclusion Justices Story and Livingston dissented, the former, a master of prize law, delivering a very able, and, as has been thought by many, a very conclusive opinion. In a letter to a friend, written at the time, he remarks that never in his whole life was he more thoroughly satisfied that the judgment of the Court was wrong. In the case of the *Atalanta*[1] the same point was raised, and again argued, but the Court refused to reverse its doctrine, observing that the rule was correct—that enemy bottoms did not make enemy goods—and was the most liberal and honorable to the jurisprudence of this country. About the same time Sir Wm. Scott in the English High Court of Admiralty, held that though neutral property on board a merchant vessel of a belligerent was protected, yet if placed on an armed belligerent ship, it would be liable, on sound and just principles, to condemnation with the captured vessel.[2]

Another class of cases, few in number, arose, represented by *United States* v. *Crosby*,[3] by which it was decided that the title to land can be acquired and lost only in the manner prescribed by the law of the place where it is situated. In

[1] 3 Wheaton, 409 (1818).
[2] Case of the *Fanny*, 1 Dodson's Adm. Report, 443 (1814)
[3] 7 Cranch, 115 (1812).

Green v. *Liter*,[1] which is interesting as a legal fossil, like the tooth of a mastodon in a hillside, it was held in an elaborate opinion by Story that whenever there exists a union of title and seisin in deed, either by actual entry and livery of seisin, or by intendment of law, as by conveyance under the Statute of Uses, the esplees are knit to the title, so as to enable the party to maintain a writ of right.

The cases just reviewed cover the period between Marshall's appearance on the bench in 1801 and 1815. During this time several changes had taken place in the personnel of the Court. Mr. Justice Moore had resigned, owing to ill health, and William Johnson, of South Carolina, was commissioned as his successor on the 26th of March, 1804.

Mr. Justice Johnson was born in Charleston, S. C., on the 27th of December, 1771. His father, who bore the same name, had removed from New York, and, according to Christopher Gadsden, was the first to set the ball of Revolution rolling in his adopted State. The family, though originally English, had removed to Holland after 1660, and some of its members, under the name of Jansen, settled in New Amsterdam. The future Justice was educated at Princeton and graduated in 1790, at the early age of nineteen with the highest honors of his class. He chose the law as his profession, and pursued his studies under the direction of Charles Cotesworth Pinckney. He was admitted to the bar in 1793, and soon rose to eminence. He was thrice elected to the Legislature of his native State, and during his last term served as Speaker of the House of Representatives. In a short time he became a judge of the Court of Common Pleas, and while in this position at the age of thirty-three was ap-

---

[1] 8 Cranch, 229 (1814).

pointed by Jefferson to the bench of the Supreme Court. His
judicial service covered a period of thirty years. With
Washington and Story he sat beside Marshall during the
greater part of the latter's long term as Chief Justice. He
had a strong mathematical head and considerable soundness
of erudition, reminding Story of Jefferson's Attorney-General,
Levi Lincoln, although with "less of metaphysics and more
of logic." His tastes were quiet and unpretentious. His
scholarship was marked, but his opinions vary much in character. Some of them, as his dissenting opinions in Bollman
and Swartwout, and Fletcher and Peck, are strong and able,
the latter containing the germ of that spirit of dissatisfaction with the doctrines of the Dartmouth College case which
afterwards became common. Others are confused and wanting in exactness and precision, and indicate, as Mr. Shirley
has observed, that the writer was unable to put his opinions
on grounds satisfactory to himself. His legal instincts out-
ran his powers of expression. Although originally an ardent
supporter of Jefferson, he became involved in 1808 in a
discussion with the Administration over his conduct as a
Judge at Circuit. The collector of the port of Charleston,
under the authority of the Embargo Act, and the direct instructions of the President, had refused clearances to several
vessels, and on a motion for a mandamus, which was granted,
the Judge undertook to comment on the illegality of the instructions. The matter was referred to Cæsar A. Rodney,
then Attorney-General of the United States, who bitterly
assailed the Judge, and warmly contended for the independence of the Executive. The Judge was provoked into a heated
reply, which was widely published. His tendency upon Constitutional questions was that of mild Federalism; he rarely
approved of the strong national views of Marshall, and shrunk

B. Livingston

from the extreme views of Story. He stoutly resisted the extension of the admiralty jurisdiction so ably maintained and carried forward by the latter. But in the days of nullification, finding his sympathies strongly arrayed against those of a majority of his fellow-citizens, and believing that his judicial position required him to be neutral, he removed to Pennsylvania. In 1822 he attempted authorship and published the "Life and Correspondence of General Nathaniel Greene," in which he made an unfortunate attack upon the memory of James Wilson, an Associate Justice of the Supreme Court, charging him with complicity in the Conway Cabal for the removal of Washington and the substitution of Gates as Commander of the Army. The charge was completely disproved by papers in the possession of Judge Peters, of the United States District Court for Pennsylvania, and the venerable Bishop White,[1] and a public retraction was promptly made. He was the first to break in upon the practice, followed for many years, of permitting the Chief Justice to act as the organ of the Court, and restored the ancient habit of *seriatim* opinions, wherever there was any marked difference of judgment. The old system had given great dissatisfaction, as owing to the age and infirmities of Chase and Cushing, and the frequent absences of Todd, two judges sometimes practically became a majority of six, and three a majority of seven.[2]

Mr. Justice Paterson died on the 9th of September, 1806, after a service of more than thirteen years, and on the 10th of November of the same year, Brockholst Livingston was commissioned in the recess, and recommissioned upon confirmation by the Senate on the 16th of January, 1807. He was

---

[1] Wilson Papers in Library of the Historical Society of Pennsylvania.
[2] John M. Shirley, " The Dartmouth College Cases," p. 311.

the son of Governor William Livingston, of New Jersey, and the brother of Robert R. Livingston, the Chancellor of New York, who administered the oath of office to George Washington as the First President of the United States. He was also the brother of Edward Livingston, the firm friend and famous Secretary of State of Andrew Jackson, and was the brother-in-law of John Jay. He was born in New York on the 25th of November, 1757, and was educated at Princeton, but before taking his degree joined the staff of General Schuyler in 1776. He attached himself subsequently to the suite of Arnold, with the rank of major, and shared in the capture of Burgoyne. He was promoted for good conduct to a colonelcy, but in 1779 abandoned military pursuits to accompany John Jay to Spain as private Secretary. On his return home he was captured by a British vessel and was thrown into prison, but secured his release upon the arrival of Sir Guy Carleton. In 1782 he devoted himself to the study of law under Peter Yates at Albany, and was admitted to the bar in the following year. He acquired a large practice and his name appears frequently in the earlier New York Reports. In 1802 he was appointed a *puisne* Judge of the Supreme Court of New York, of which Morgan Lewis was then Chief Justice, and Smith Thompson, James Kent and Ratcliffe *puisnes.* This place he held until his elevation to the Supreme Court of the United States. As a scholar he was intensely interested in historical studies, and was one of the first Vice-Presidents of the New York Historical Society. He was prominent also as one of the organizers of the public school system of New York. He had, said Story, "a fine Roman face; an aquiline nose, high forehead, bald head and projecting chin, indicating deep research, strength and quickness of mind." ... "He evidently thinks with great solidity and seizes on the strong points of argument. He is luminous, decisive, earnest and impressive on the bench." As a judge he was candid and modest, learned, acute and discriminating. He devoted himself principally to maritime and commercial law, and his judgments were enhanced in value by the gravity and beauty of his judicial eloquence.

On the 24th of February, 1807, Congress authorized the appointment of an additional Associate Justice of the Supreme Court, to reside in the seventh Circuit, which was established for the Districts of Kentucky, Tennessee and Ohio. The Supreme Court was thus made to consist of a Chief Justice and six Associates. This act was in answer to the demands of the increasing business and population of the Western States, and the necessity of bringing to the deliberations of the Supreme Court some one well versed in the peculiar land laws of that vast region.

Thomas Todd, of Kentucky,[1] was duly nominated and confirmed for the place thus created, his commission being dated March 3, 1807. It is said that Jefferson, in making this selection, requested each member of Congress from the States composing the Circuit to communicate to him a nomination of their first and second choice. As the name of Todd appeared in every list he secured the appointment, although personally unknown to many of his supporters. He was born in Virginia, in King and Queen County, on the 23d of January, 1765. He lost his parents at a very early age, but was kindly provided for by his guardian, who afforded him an opportunity of acquiring a good English education with a little knowledge of the classics. While he was still a boy his guardian became embarrassed and he was thrown upon

[1] For much of the material relating to Judge Todd I am indebted to the Hon. H. I. Todd, of Frankfort, Ky.

his own resources. During the closing days of the war of the Revolution he was in the army, but upon receiving an invitation to become an inmate of the household of Hon. Henry Innes, a relative, he acquired a knowledge of surveying and book-keeping, and was remarkable for his accurate and methodical detail. In 1783 Judge Innes removed to Kentucky, and young Todd accompanied him, teaching the daughters of his friend by day, and prosecuting, at night, the study of the law by the light of the fire. He was soon admitted to practice and made his first effort at Madison old Court-House. His slender outfit at the beginning of the term consisted of his horse and saddle and thirty-seven and a half cents in money, but when the Court rose he had enough to meet his current expenses, and returned home with the bonds for two cows and calves, the usual fees of that day. From 1792 to 1801 he served as Clerk of the House of Representatives, and for a time was Clerk of the Federal Court for the District of Kentucky. On the erection of the State Government he was chosen Clerk of the Court of Appeals. In 1801 he was appointed one of the Judges of that Court, and in 1806, on the resignation of Judge Muter, became Chief Justice. He laid the foundation of the land laws of his State, and his perfect familiarity with questions of this character gave him a controlling influence with his brethren of the Supreme Court of the United States when considering claims such as that of The Holland Land Company. At the time of his appointment to the Supreme Court he was forty-two years of age. Patient and candid in investigation, clear and sagacious in judgment, with a just respect for authority, and at the same time, with well-settled views of his own as to the law; never affecting to possess that which he did not know, but with learning of a solid and useful cast, diffident and retiring in his habits, attentive to arguments, he won, says Mr. Justice Story, the enviable respect of his associates. Although bred in a different political school from that of Chief Justice Marshall, he steadfastly supported his Constitutional doctrines, and was warmly attached to the Union of the States.

During the latter part of the year 1810 the venerable Associate Justices Chase and Cushing died. The place of the former was filled by Gabriel Duvall, of Maryland, and that of the latter by Joseph Story, of Massachusetts, their commissions being dated November 18, 1811. The place filled by Story had been offered in turn to Levi Lincoln and John Quincy Adams, both of Massachusetts. Commissions were regularly issued to both—on the 7th and 22d of January, 1811, respectively, but both had declined the post; one because of approaching blindness, the other because he preferred the Russian mission.

Gabriel Duvall was born in Prince George County, Maryland, on the 6th of December, 1752, and after receiving a classical education studied law, was admitted to the bar and soon became interested in political life. For many years he was clerk of the Maryland Legislature. He took no active part in public affairs during the Revolution, and his name, though well known and always respected, does not occur prominently. In fact he dwindles by the side of Chase, the mighty propugnator. Although chosen as a member of the Federal Convention, for some reason he wholly ignored his appointment, and thus stripped himself by inaction of a claim which might have been his, to share in the glory which belongs to the framers of the Constitution of the United States. He was elected to the Congress of the United States in November, 1794, to fill a vacancy, and was re-elected, serving until March, 1796, when he resigned to take his place upon the bench of the Supreme Court of Maryland. In December, 1802, he was appointed Comptroller of the Currency and held the office until the 18th of November, 1811, when he was appointed by President Madison an Associate Justice of the Supreme Court. His opinions as a Judge are not characterized by either remarkable learning or great reasoning powers, but are respectable. He was the only dissentient in the Dartmouth College case. Owing to the infirmity of deafness he was compelled to resign his place in 1836.

Joseph Story, "the Lope de Vega or the Walter Scott of the Common Law," to whose vast professional labors even those of Coke and Eldon must yield in extent, whose name was as well known in Westminster Hall and in the Judicatories of Paris and Berlin as in the Courts of the United States, was one of the brightest ornaments of his profession and his age. Whatever judgment posterity may pass upon the value of his work as an author, it is certain that his labors at the side of Marshall in developing and expanding the principles of our national jurisprudence entitle him to the ceaseless gratitude of his countrymen. As a logician and a Constitutional judge he must yield to Marshall, whom he far surpassed in general legal scholarship, but as the rival of Stowell in admiralty and the peer of Kent in equity jurisprudence, as the sleepless and persistent force that urged others to the amendment and enlargement of our national code, as the Commentator upon the Constitution, as a teacher and law lecturer without an equal, as a judge urbane and benign, and as a man of spotless purity, he wrought so long, so indefatigably, and so well that he did more, perhaps, than any other man who ever sat upon the Supreme Bench to popularize the doctrines of that great tribunal and impress their importance and grandeur upon the public mind.

He was born at Marblehead, in the county of Essex, Massachusetts, on the 18th of September, 1779. His father, Elisha Story, was a native of Boston, and a sturdy Whig who had taken a very early and active part in all the Revolutionary movements, and who was one of the Indians who helped to destroy the tea in the famous Boston exploit. His mother, Mehitable Pedrick, was a woman of ardent temperament and admirable tact and method. After displaying some diligence at school and a disposition to scribble verses, young Story entered Harvard College, from which he graduated in 1798. Upon leaving Cambridge he immediately entered upon the study of the law in the office of Mr. Samuel Sewall, then a distinguished advocate at the Essex bar, a member of Congress, and afterwards Chief Justice of the Supreme Court of Massachusetts. For a time he dallied with the Muses, and seems to have left them with regret for the hard and forbidding features of the Common law. In 1801 he removed to Salem, and read with Judge Putnam, and in July was admitted to the Bar. At this time he was the only lawyer in his neighborhood who was either openly or secretly a Democrat. He found himself surrounded by Federalists, and encountered many discouraging obstacles to success. His industry and his exclusive devotion to his profession brought him clients and in the course of three or four years he could boast of a good business and an increasing reputation. In 1803 he declined the post of naval officer at the port of Salem, being persuaded that it would interfere with his prospects. In 1805 he was chosen a member of the Legislature, and supported several important measures with marked ability. Three years afterwards he was sent to Congress, and during his brief term of service distinguished himself in urging the repeal of the embargo and the augmentation of the navy. Declining re-election, he was again chosen a member of the Legislature, and became Speaker of the House. His professional ability now won recognition, and in 1810 he argued before the Supreme Court of the United States the great case of the Georgia claim known as *Fletcher* v. *Peck*. About this time he edited a new edition of Chitty on Bills of Exchange and Promissory Notes, an American edition of Abbott on Shipping, and Lawes on Assumpsit. On the 18th of November, 1811, he was commissioned as an Associate Justice of the Supreme Court of the United States to fill the vacancy created by the death of Mr. Justice Cushing, who had occupied the place since the organization of the government. The appointment was a surprise, made, it seems, at the suggestion of Mr. Bacon, a member of Congress from Massachusetts. As the annual salary was then but three thousand five hundred dollars, its acceptance involved no slight pecuniary sacrifice. The opportunity of pursuing juridical studies, the high honor of the place, the permanence of the tenure, and the prospect of meeting the great men of the nation, were considerations which he could not resist.

Story was then but thirty-two years of age—the youngest judge, except Mr. Justice Buller, who was ever called to the highest judicial station either in England or America. His labors upon Circuit were onerous indeed, owing to the immense accumulation of business in consequence of the age and infirmities of his predecessor. The commercial and maritime interests of the New England States, and the large proportion of capital invested in shipping generated curious questions of admiralty law, respecting the rights, duties and liabilities of ship owners, mariners and material men, while controversies involving salvage and insurance arose from cases of wreck and loss upon those bleak and dangerous shores. In this way the attention of Judge Story was directed, at the

Thomas Todd

very outset of his judicial career, to questions of this character. He made himself a thorough master of this branch of
jurisprudence as well as of Prize and Instance Law. From
this day his labors in every field of legal science were tire-
less and unremitting. He soon interested himself in the reform of the criminal code of the United States, and sent to
Mr. Pinkney sketches of improvements. He denounced the
existing code as grossly and barbarously defective; the courts
were crippled, and offenders, conspirators, and traitors were
enabled to carry on their purposes almost without check. He
begged his friends to induce Congress to give the Courts of
the United States power to punish all crimes and offences
against the Government, as at Common law. He pleaded for
the extension of the national authority over the whole extent
of power given by the Constitution; for great military and
naval schools; an adequate regular army; a permanent navy;
a national bank; a national system of bankruptcy; a great
navigation act; a general survey of all our ports, and appointments of port wardens and pilots; courts which should embrace
the whole Constitutional powers; national notaries; public and
national justices of the peace, for the commercial and national
concerns of the United States. By such enlarged and liberal
institutions, he argued, the Government of the United States
would become endeared to the people, and the factions of the
great States be rendered harmless. The possibility of a division would be prevented by creating great national interests
which would bind us in an indissoluble chain. He delivered
eulogies, and historical and literary addresses; published several volumes of reports of his decisions at Circuit; drafted a
Bankrupt law, the Crimes Act, a Judiciary Act, and wrote for
the use of a friend in Congress an argumentative comment
thereon. He wrote elaborate notes for Mr. Wheaton: "On the

Principles and Practice of Prize Courts," "On Charitable Bequests," "On the Patent Laws," "On Piracies," "On the Admiralty Jurisdiction," "On the Rule of 1756," and prepared a large portion of a Digest. He edited an edition of the Laws of the United States, contributed articles to "The American Jurist," reviewed books and professional treatises, corresponded with Lord Stowell, Lord Eldon, Sir James Mackintosh, Chancellor Kent, and most of the public men of his day; published verses; founded a Law School; surrendered his library to Harvard; lectured upon Equity, Equity Pleading, Commercial and Constitutional law; published treatises upon a dozen different subjects, which have become standard authorities in England as well as in this country; wrote the ablest work extant on the "Conflict of Laws;" declined the Chief Justiceship of Massachusetts, and at the same time did his fair share of the labors of the Supreme Court, as attested by more than thirty-five volumes of Reports. His mental activity was ceaseless, and as a Judge, author and teacher of Jurisprudence, he exercised in each of these characters a peculiar influence. He became a jurist of world-wide reputation, and the echoes of his fame returned to his native shores from those of England, France, Germany, Italy, Russia and Spain. As familiar with Justinian as with Coke, he swept the bounds of jurisprudence with comprehensive glance, and poured forth the rich accumulations of his industry with flowing pen. · His position in legal literature is unique, and the impression he made upon his contemporaries was profound. Yet it may be doubted whether his reputation will stand the test of time. "His power of synthesis," writes a most competent critic, "was considerable; but when you have heard his opinions and text books dissected by analytical men at the bar as often as I have, you will come to the conclusion that his mind was de-

ficient in accuracy, that its discipline was not strict, nor its investigations patient. His reputation, which was in a good degree a reflected one from England, where he took great pains to make himself known, has not, I think, stood firm in the professional mind to this day. And I much doubt whether he had any accurate knowledge of the Civil law."[1] Another writer says: "Whole chapters of some of his books seem to be little more than windrows of head notes, raked together as the farmer rakes his hay in the mow field; but when we survey the ground, the wonder is, not that they contain so many imperfections, but that his work was so well performed. His opinions will probably stand higher in the hereafter than his text books, except his works on 'The Conflict of Laws' and the 'Constitution.'"[2]

A glance at the bar of the Supreme Court may be permitted. The earliest sessions of the Court had been held in an upper room in the Exchange, New York. No arguments were made there; but on the removal of the seat of Government to Philadelphia, where the Court sat for ten years—from 1791 to 1801—its sessions were held in the South Chamber, up-stairs, of the City Hall, at the corner of Fifth and Chestnut Streets.[3] Here Edmund Randolph, William Bradford and Charles Lee appeared as Attorney-Generals of the United States, with Alexander Hamilton, John Marshall, Alexander Campbell, James Innes, John Wickham and Thomas Swann as opponents, and all the active practitioners of the Philadelphia Bar. When the Court

---

[1] Letter of John William Wallace, Esq., Reporter of the Supreme Court of the United States, to the writer, January 31st, 1876.

[2] John M. Shirley, "Dartmouth College Causes," p. 330.

[3] Discourse of John Wm. Wallace, Esq., before the Historical Society of Pennsylvania, 1872.

removed to Washington, the leaders of the old Bar of Philadelphia followed, and maintained their ascendancy: the eloquent Dallas, the accomplished Rawle, the rough and rugged
Lewis; the elder Tilghman and the elder Ingersoll,—the former, strong, pointed and logical; the latter, a perfect drag-
net in the law. "My bar," as Judge Washington affection-
ately called them, as they entered the room in a body, after
four days of tedious and dangerous riding in the middle of
February, over rough roads.

We catch delightful glimpses of the olden days and van-
ished states of society in the reminiscences of Peter S. Duponceau, himself one of that famous band, as he describes
how they all went down together to argue the causes arising
out of the British Orders in Council and the Berlin and Mi-
lan decrees; how these grave counsellors, as soon as they
were out of the city and felt the flush of air, acted like
schoolboys on a holiday; how flashes of wit shot their corus-
cations on all sides; how puns of the genuine Philadelphia
stamp were bandied about, and old college stories were revived; how macaronic Latin was spoken, and songs were
sung, among which was the famous Bacchanalian of the
archdeacon of Oxford: *Mihi est propositum in taberna mori.*
In Washington they met Charles Lee, "whom no one would
suspect of having been Attorney-General;" Harper, graceful
and flowing, though somewhat artificial; Key, Swann and
Martin, of Maryland—"that singular compound of strange
qualities, whom you should hear of, but should not see,"—
Jeremiah Mason, and John Quincy Adams, rugged and strong,
and Dexter, relying upon the deliberate suggestions of his
own mind, and finding himself supported by the authority of

[1] P. S. Duponceau, "A Memoir of William Rawle." Memoirs of the Historical
Society of Pennsylvania, Vol. IV., p. 95.

Mansfield when he least suspected it. A younger generation soon succeeded, and in the room which now serves as the law library of Congress—a basement chamber approached by a small hall, having an eastern door of entrance from the grounds of the Capitol, flanked by pillars of novel design of Indian-corn stalks with ears half open at the top,—a room spared by the conflagration kindled in 1814 by British soldiers,—sat the most august tribunal of the land hearing solemn argument. In "this cave of Trophonius," as John Randolph spitefully called it, John Marshall sat for thirty-four years, in the midst of six Associates, listening to the most profound and brilliant arguments from Pinkney, foppish, vehement, overwhelming, but always well prepared; Wirt, florid and classical, but of considerable legal attainments; Emmett, the interesting exile; Binney, the consummate lawyer; Clay, dashing and magnetic, and Webster, inspiring and profound. Such are the associations of this unimposing chamber; and while wandering beneath its solemn arches, and recalling the mighty figures of the heroic past who there labored for the establishment of a national Constitutional government, the visitor cannot fail to yield to emotions of awe, while in the holiest, but now abandoned sanctuary of Justice, upon whose altars once burned "the gladsome light of jurisprudence."

16

CHAPTER XIV.

THE THIRD EPOCH: 1816–1835: THE LATTER HALF OF MARSHALL'S CAREER: THE
GOLDEN AGE OF THE SUPREME COURT: APPELLATE JURISDICTION OF THE SU-
PREME COURT UNDER THE 25TH SECTION OF THE JUDICIARY ACT: MARTIN
v. HUNTER'S LESSEE: COHENS *v.* STATE OF VIRGINIA: THE TERM OF 1819:
M'CULLOCH *v.* STATE OF MARYLAND: TRUSTEES OF DARTMOUTH COLLEGE *v.*
WOODWARD: STURGES *v.* CROWNINSHIELD: OSBORN *v.* BANK OF THE UNITED
STATES: POWER OF CONGRESS TO REGULATE COMMERCE: GIBBONS *v.* OGDEN:
WILSON *v.* BLACKBIRD CREEK MARSH CO: BROWN *v.* STATE OF MARYLAND:
CONSTITUTIONAL RESTRICTIONS UPON THE POWERS OF THE STATES: CRAIG *v.*
STATE OF MISSOURI: POSITION AND INFLUENCE OF THE SUPREME COURT:
RIGHTS OF THE STATES: PROVIDENCE BANK *v.* BILLINGS: BARRON *v.* MAYOR
OF BALTIMORE: POWERS OF STATES TO PASS BANKRUPT LAWS: OGDEN *v.*
SAUNDERS: BOYLE *v.* ZACHARIE: WHAT CONSTITUTES A STATE: CHEROKEE
NATION *v.* STATE OF GEORGIA: WORCESTER *v.* STATE OF GEORGIA: LAST
CONSTITUTIONAL DECISION OF MARSHALL: PRINCIPLES OF CONSTITUTIONAL IN-
TERPRETATION: SKETCHES OF JUSTICES THOMPSON, TRIMBLE, McLEAN, BALD-
WIN AND WAYNE: GENERAL REVIEW OF THE WORK ACCOMPLISHED BY THE
SUPREME COURT UNDER MARSHALL.

IN the last chapter we reached a period which marks the
termination of the first half of Marshall's judicial career.
Beneath the strong and steady rays cast by his mind
the mists were rising, and the bold outlines of our national
system were gradually revealed. To keen eyes the destina-
tion of the Ship of State was visible, although from most
men still concealed by haze. Greater questions than any yet
determined were to be met. The decisive battle for national
sovereignty was still to be fought. The true method of interpreting the Constitution was still unsettled. Whether the
right of Congress to pass all laws "necessary and proper" for
the Federal government was not restricted to such as were
indispensable to that end; whether the right of taxation could

be exercised by a State against creations of the Federal Government; whether a Federal Court could revise the judgment of a State Court in a case arising under the Constitution and laws of the United States; whether the officers of the Federal Government could be protected against State interference; how far a State could impair the obligation of a charter; how far extended the power of Congress to regulate commerce among the States; how far to regulate foreign commerce as against State enactment; how far extended the prohibition to States against emitting bills of credit—these and like questions were awaiting consideration by the master mind. In this wide realm he was to be crowned as sovereign. And for the Court, there lay before it the universal empire of jurisprudence; the ancient and subtle learning of the law of real estate; the criminal law; the niceties of special pleading; the refined doctrines of contracts; the enlightened system of commercial and maritime law; the principles and practice of admiralty and prize; the immense range of chancery; the ever spreading bounds of jurisdiction over patents, copyrights and trademarks; and that higher region, rising into noble eminences, from which wide views could be obtained of the great themes of public, international and constitutional law— these fields though already entered upon were still to be subdued. With Marshall, Story and Washington upon the bench as a triumvirate, whose policy was harmonious and steadfast; with Johnson, Livingston, Todd and Duvall as intelligent advisers and critics; with men at the bar of the expansive power and propulsive energy of Pinkney and Webster, roused to the noblest exertions of their genius by the rivalry of Wirt, Emmett, Dexter and Jones, the labor of building up our Constitutional jurisprudence and of establishing its national character was carried forward by the wisest heads, the most sagacious judgments and the most patriotic hearts. In a moment of inspired prophecy, Pinkney exclaimed: "I meditate with exultation, not fear, upon the proud spectacle of a peaceful judicial review of these conflicting sovereign claims by this more than Amphictyonic Council. I see in it a pledge of the immortality of the Union, of a perpetuity of national strength and glory increasing and brightening with age,—of concord at home and reputation abroad." It was an age of great arguments at the bar, and great opinions from the bench. There were time and opportunity for both. The mercantile necessities of the people had not yet compelled the use by Judex of an hour-glass, nor the substitution of citations of the latest authorities for a discussion of principles. Dialectics might still be wedded unto Fancy; and neither was doomed to celibacy. Every argument was alive and in motion—the statue of Pygmalion inspired with vitality. It was the Golden Age of the Supreme Court.

A succession of great questions arose. In 1816 a most important matter called for determination, presenting an instance of collision between the judicial powers of the Union, and one of the greatest States on a point the most delicate and difficult to be adjusted. The Constitution of the United States had not in terms granted to the Supreme Court appellate power over courts of the States, and although silently acquiesced in at an early day, this jurisdiction was finally not only seriously questioned but absolutely denied by the State of Virginia. It required a repetition of instances, in which the Supreme Court vindicated its authority within certain well-defined limits, to convince the country that this power existed.[1]

[1] Curtis, "Jurisdiction of the United States Courts," pp. 26–27. See also Gelston *v.* Hoyt, 3 Wheaton, 246 (1818), and Houston *v.* Moore, *Ibid.*, 433 (1818), for

The 25th section of the Judiciary Act of 1789 had provided that—

"A final judgment or decree in any suit, in the highest court of law or equity of a State in which a decision in the suit could be had, where is drawn in question the validity of a treaty or statute of, or an authority exercised under, the United States, and the decision is against their validity; or where is drawn in question the validity of a statute of, or an authority exercised under any State, on the ground of their being repugnant to the Constitution, treaties or laws of the United States, and the decision is in favor of such their validity; or where is drawn in question the construction of any clause of the Constitution, or of a treaty or statute of, or commission held under the United States, and the decision is against the title, right, privilege, or exemption specially set up or claimed by either party, under such clause of the said Constitution, treaty, statute or commission,—may be re-examined and reversed or affirmed in the Supreme Court of the United States upon a writ of error." [1]

This Act was a triumph of Federalist centralization, and was a cession of power to the Supreme Court of more consequence to the States than the "necessary and proper" clause itself. Its critics believed that it had been dictated by a wish to make the State judiciaries inferior courts of the central government, because the powers of the General Government might be 'drawn in question' in many ways and on many occasions. Mr. Henry Adams asserts that Chief Justice Marshall achieved one of his greatest victories by causing Justice Story, a Republican, raised to the Bench in 1811 for the purpose of contesting his authority, to pronounce the opinion of the Court in the case of *Martin* v. *Hunter's Lessee*,[2] by which the position of the Virginia Court of Appeals was overruled

instances of acquiescence of the States in the appellate power of the Supreme Court under the 25th Section of the Judiciary Act.

[1] Act 24th of September, 1789, 1 United States Statutes at Large, p. 85.
[2] 1 Wheaton, 304 (1816).

upon the question of constitutionality raised by the State Court in regard to this section of the Judiciary Act.[1]

The case was argued on the one side by Walter Jones, who maintained for many years a proud pre-eminence at the bar of the District Court of Columbia, and on the other by Tucker, of Virginia, and Dexter, of Massachusetts; Dexter, while conceding that he had long inclined to the belief that the Government was not strong enough and that the centrifugal force was greater than the centripetal, asserted that he would not strain or break the Constitution itself in order to establish a national power. The opinion of Mr. Justice Story, which is the first Constitutional judgment ever delivered by him, differs from most of his opinions in the fact that it is a closely-reasoned argument without the citation of authority. It displays many of the peculiar merits of the best judgments of Marshall, compactness of fibre and closeness of logic. It develops the relations of the States to the Federal government, and establishes that although their sovereign authority is only impaired so far as it is ceded, yet that the Constitution does not operate to create a mere confederation and aggregation of separate sovereignties, but contains in itself paramount and supreme powers surrendered by the States and the people for the common and equal benefit of all over whom this government extends,—and that among the powers thus ceded is the appellate jurisdiction of the Supreme Court over all cases enumerated in the clause vesting the judicial power.

"The appellate power," said he, "is not limited by the terms of the third article to any particular Courts. The words are,—'The judicial power' (which includes appellate power) 'shall extend to all cases,' etc., 'and in all other cases before mentioned, the Supreme

---

[1] See Adams's "History of the United States," Vol. I, p. 260.

Court shall have appellate jurisdiction.' It is the case, then, and not the Court, that gives the jurisdiction. If the judicial power extends to the case, it will be in vain to search in the letter of the Constitution for any qualification as to the tribunal where it depends. It is incumbent, then, upon those who assert such a qualification to show its existence by necessary implication. If the text be clear and distinct, no restriction upon its plain and obvious import ought to be admitted, unless the inference be irresistible. If the Constitution meant to limit the appellate jurisdiction to cases pending in the Courts of the United States, it would necessarily follow that the jurisdiction of these Courts would, in all the cases enumerated in the Constitution, be exclusive of State tribunals. How otherwise could the jurisdiction extend to all cases arising under the Constitution, laws and treaties of the United States, or to all cases of admiralty and maritime jurisdiction? If some of these cases might be entertained by State tribunals, and no appellate jurisdiction as to them should exist, then the appellate power would not extend to all, but to some cases. If State tribunals might exercise concurrent jurisdiction over all or some of the other class of cases in the Constitution without control, then the appellate jurisdiction of the United States might, as to such cases, have no real existence, contrary to the manifest intent of the Constitution. Under such circumstances, to give effect to the judicial power, it must be construed to be exclusive, and this not only when the *casus fœderis* should arise directly, but when it should arise incidentally in cases pending in State Courts.''

From this reasoning Mr. Justice Johnson dissented, viewing the question as one of the most momentous importance, and quoting with approval the language of Patrick Henry: "I rejoice that Virginia has resisted." He concurred in the result, however, and exerted himself most ingeniously to save the State from any sense of humiliation.

The entire subject, though fully discussed by Mr. Justice Story, was not finally settled until the case of *Cohens* v. *The State of Virginia*,[1] in which the Supreme Court, with

[1] 6 Wheaton, 264 (1821).

decisive effect, and in a manner which has always been acquiesced in by the country since that time, vindicated and sustained its jurisdiction. A complete view of the nature of the judicial powers of the Federal Government is to be obtained by reading, in this connection, the opinion of the Chief Justice in the case of the *Bank of Hamilton* v. *Dudley's Lessees*,[1] in which it was held that the State Courts have exclusive power to construe the Constitution and legislative acts of their respective States. "The judicial department of every government," said he, "is the rightful expositor of its laws, and emphatically of its supreme law."

The term of 1819 became distinguished in the annals of the Court not alone by the importance of the causes which came before it relating to the general business interests of the country, but by the occurrence of several cases of more than ordinary gravity as connected with the political affairs of the nation. The principles discussed were of the most momentous character, and the decisions announced were destined to guide and control the most distant posterity. At this time Mr. Monroe was President; the fierce heat of party passion had cooled; it was an era of good feeling. The Court had become the centre of observation for its august power, dignity and public trust. It was no longer an unknown or an untried tribunal. It had become well established. Marshall had been Chief Justice for eighteen years; Washington had been on the bench for twenty-one years, Johnson for fifteen, Livingston and Todd for twelve, Story and Duvall for eight; all had won for themselves and for the court a distinctive position of eminence and influence. Whatever determinations they might reach would carry great

---

[1] 2 Peters, 492 (1829).

weight. The bar, too, had won a position of authority. Wirt as Attorney-General, and Pinkney as an ex-Attorney-General had now ascended to the highest levels of their professional careers; Martin had just begun to lag superfluous on the stage, but Jones, Hopkinson and Webster were fast approaching the zenith of their fame as advocates. Diligent study, solid accumulations of strength, long experience, varied knowledge, a widely extended reputation for eloquence and logic, kindled moreover by intense personal rivalry, and a cheerful but sanguine ambition—these were sufficient to produce at the bar arguments distinguished for perspicacity, comprehensive and philosophic views of every subject, and the most convincing power of demonstration.

The first case to arise was that of *M' Culloch* v. *The State of Maryland*[1] involving the double question of the constitutionality of the act incorporating the Bank of the United States, and of the power of a State to tax an agency of the general Government.

Congress, by an Act passed in April, 1816, had incorporated the Bank of the United States, which had been originally established under an Act of 1791, but whose charter had expired in 1811. A branch of this Bank was established at Baltimore, and in 1818 the Legislature of Maryland imposed a stamp duty on the circulating notes of all banks or branches thereof, located in that State, not chartered by the Legislature. The Maryland Branch refused to pay the tax, and M'Culloch, the Cashier, was sued for it. Judgment was recovered against him in the State Court, and he carried it, on writ of error, to the Supreme Court. The decision of the appellate tribunal was looked for with eager interest.

[1] 4 Wheaton, 316 (1819).

Pinkney, Wirt and Webster appeared for the Bank, and Martin, Hopkinson and Jones for the State. "I never in my whole life," says Judge Story, in writing of Pinkney's effort, "heard a greater speech. It was worth a journey from Salem to hear it. His elocution was excessively vehement, but his eloquence was overwhelming. His language, his style, his figures, his arguments were most brilliant and sparkling. He spoke like a great statesman and patriot, and a sound Constitutional lawyer. All the cobwebs of sophistry and metaphysics about State rights and State sovereignty he brushed away as with a mighty besom."[1]

It was in the course of his argument that Pinkney exclaimed: "I have a deep and awful conviction that upon that judgment it will depend mainly whether the Constitution under which we live and prosper is to be considered like its precursor, a mere phantom of political power, to deceive and mock us—a pageant of mimic sovereignty calculated to raise up hopes that it may leave them to perish—a frail and tottering edifice that can afford no shelter from storm, either foreign or domestic—a creature half made up, without heart or brain, or nerve, or muscle,—without protecting power or redeeming energy—or whether it is to be viewed as a competent guardian of all that is dear to us as a nation."[2]

The institution of a national bank, as being of primary importance to the prosperous administration of the finances, and of the greatest utility in the operations connected with the support of public credit, had been recommended originally by Alexander Hamilton as Secretary of the Treasury. The constitutionality of the exercise of such a power had been debated with extraordinary ability in both houses of Congress, and in

---

[1] Story's Life and Letters, Vol. I, p. 325.
[2] Wheaton's "Life of Pinkney," pp. 163–166.

the Executive Cabinet, where Jefferson, as Secretary of State, and Randolph, as Attorney-General, had declared that they saw no warrant in the language of the Constitution, even under the clause relating to incidental powers, for such a corporation. The opposite view was maintained by Hamilton, with overwhelming ability and ardor, and prevailed with Washington. The question, therefore, was not new to the thoughts of the nation, and counsel at the bar availed themselves of all that had been previously said and written upon the subject.

The opinion delivered by Marshall has always been considered as one of the most elaborate and masterly of his efforts, and Chancellor Kent[1] has said that a case could not be selected superior to this for the clear and satisfactory manner in which the supremacy of the laws of the Union have been maintained by the Court, and an undue assertion of State power overruled and defeated. A close observer of Marshall's language cannot fail to remark that much is borrowed from Hamilton. In considering the extent of the "necessary and proper" clause in the Constitution, the Chief Justice said:

"We admit, as all must admit, that the powers of the government are limited, and that its limits are not to be transcended; but we think a sound construction of the Constitution must allow to the national legislature that discretion with respect to the means by which the powers it confers are to be carried into execution, which will enable that body to perform the high duties assigned to it in the manner most beneficial to the people. Let the end be legitimate, let it be within the scope of the Constitution, and all means which are appropriate, which are plainly adapted to that end, which are not prohibited, but consist with the letter and spirit of the Constitution, are constitutional."

This language was in harmony with that which had been used some years before in the case of the *United States* v.

[1] 1 Kent's Commentaries, 428.

Fisher.[1] At the same time an expression was added of the unwillingness of the Court to assume any power to pass upon the expediency of the exercise of the power conferred upon Congress.

"Where the law is not prohibited, and is really calculated to effect any of the objects entrusted to the government, to undertake here to inquire into the degree of its necessity would be to pass the line which circumscribes the judicial department, and to tread upon legislative ground. The Court disclaims all pretensions to such a power."

In dealing with the power of a State to tax an agency of the national government, he made it clear:

"That the power to tax involves the power to destroy; that the power to destroy may defeat and render useless the power to create. . . . If the States may tax one instrument employed by the Government in the execution of its power, they may tax any and every other instrument; they may tax the mail; they may tax the mint; they may tax patent rights; they may tax the papers of the Custom House; they may tax judicial process; they may tax all the means employed by the Government to an excess which would defeat all the ends of government. This was not intended by the American people. They did not design to make the Government dependent on the States . . . The question is, in truth, a question of supremacy, and if the right of the States to tax the means employed by the General Government be conceded, the declaration that the Constitution and the laws made in pursuance thereof shall be the supreme law of the land is empty and unmeaning declamation."[2]

The famous case of the *Trustees of Dartmouth College* v. *Woodward*[3] also came before the Court at this term, estab-

---

[1] 2 Cranch, 358 (1805).

[2] The same conclusion was reached in Osborn *v.* Bank of the United States, 9 Wheaton, 738 (1824), in which the State of Ohio imposed an annual tax of $50,000 upon each office of discount and deposit maintained by that Bank in the State, and Weston *v.* Charleston, 2 Peters, 449 (1829), in which a municipal tax was imposed upon stocks of the United States owned by citizens of Charleston, S. C.

[3] 4 Wheaton, 518 (1819).

lishing the inviolability of charters and their protection by the power of the Federal Government, and is perhaps better known to laymen, both in name and in principle, than any other decision of the Court. The tide of national power was rising fast, and each successive billow marked a higher line upon the beach. Of this case, containing one of the most celebrated of Marshall's judgments, Mr. Binney says: "If I were to select, in any particular, from the mass of judgments for the purpose of showing what we derived from the Constitution, and from the noble faculties which have been applied to its interpretation, it would be that in which the protection of chartered rights has been deduced from its provisions. The case of Dartmouth College is the bulwark of our incorporated institutions for public education, and of those chartered endowments for diffusive public charity which are not only the ornaments, but among the strongest defences of a nation."[1] And Mr. Justice Miller has said: "It may well be doubted whether any decision ever delivered by any Court has had such a pervading operation and influence in controlling legislation as this. The legislation, however, so controlled, has been that of the States of the Union."[2]

The case has been the subject of much criticism, and has provoked much dissatisfaction as well as praise and admiration. The actual controversy, as the Chief Justice himself remarked, turned upon the question whether the charter of the College was a grant of political power which the State could resume or modify at pleasure, or a contract for the security and disposition of property bestowed in trust for

---

[1] An Eulogy on the Life and Character of John Marshall, delivered at the request of the Councils of Philadelphia, on the 24th of Sept., 1835, by Horace Binney.

[2] An Address delivered before the Alumni Society of the Law Department of the University of Michigan on the Supreme Court of United States, June 29, 1887.

charitable purposes. It was held to be the latter, and for that reason inviolable under Section 10 of Article I of the Constitution, which declares that—"No State shall make any law impairing the obligation of contracts."

The main stress of adverse criticism is upon the point that the corporation existed under a charter granted by the British Crown to its Trustees in New Hampshire in the year 1769. It was, therefore, a royal charter, and not a legislative grant.[1]

The Charter conferred upon the trustees the entire governing power of the College, and among others that of filling all vacancies occurring in their own body, and of removing and appointing tutors. It also declared that the number of trustees should forever consist of twelve, and no more. After the Revolution, the Legislature of New Hampshire passed a law to amend the charter, to improve and enlarge the corporation, to increase the number of trustees, giving the appointment of the additional members to the Governor of the State, and creating a Board of Overseers of twenty-five persons, of whom twenty-one were also to be appointed by the Governor. These overseers had power to inspect and control the most important acts of the trustees.

The opinion, to which there was but one dissent—that of Mr. Justice Duvall—establishes the doctrine that the act of a government, whether it be an act of the Legislature or of the Crown which creates a corporation, is a contract between the State and the corporation, and that all the essential franchises, powers and benefits conferred by the charter become, when accepted by the corporation, contracts within the meaning of the Constitutional clause.

[1] John M. Shirley, "The Dartmouth College Causes and the Supreme Court."

"This is plainly a contract," said Marshall, "to which the donors, the trustees and the crown (to whose rights and obligations New Hampshire succeeds) were the original parties. It is a contract for the security and disposition of property. It is a contract on the faith of which real and personal estate has been conveyed to the corporation. It is then a contract within the letter of the Constitution and within its spirit also, unless the fact that the property is invested by the donors and trustees for the promotion of religion and education, for the benefit of persons who are perpetually changing, though the objects remain the same, shall create a particular exception, taking this case out of the prohibition contained in the Constitution. . . . On what safe and intelligible ground can this exception stand? There is no expression in the Constitution, no sentiment delivered by its cotemporaneous expounders which would justify us in making it. In the absence of all authority of this kind, is there, in the nature and reason of the case itself, that which would constrain a construction of the Constitution not warranted by its words? Are contracts of this description of a character to excite so little interest that we must exclude them from the provisions of the Constitution as being unworthy of the attention of those who framed the instrument, or does public policy so imperiously demand their remaining exposed to legislative alteration as to compel us, or rather permit us to say that these words which were introduced to give stability to contracts, and which in their plain import comprehend this contract, must yet be so construed as to exclude it?"

In this reasoning Justices Washington and Story concurred in separate opinions, Justice Johnson in the reasons stated by the Chief Justice, while Justice Livingston concurred in the reasons stated by all.

The opinion of Mr. Justice Story was one of the most learned and able of his efforts, containing a most elaborate and exhaustive review of English and American decisions upon the nature of charities and of the power of visitation. In conclusion he says:

"In my judgment it is perfectly clear that any act of a legislature which takes away any power or franchise vested by its charter in a private corporation, or its corporate officers, or which restrains or controls the legitimate exercise of them, or transfers them to other persons without its assent, is a violation of the obligations of that charter. If the Legislature mean to claim such an authority, it must be reserved in the grant.''

It is true that the Supreme Court, as will be seen, has been compelled, of late years, to insist upon the existence of an express contract by the State with a corporation, when relief is sought against subsequent legislation, in order to guard against the evils flowing from too sweeping an abdication of sovereign powers by implication. But the main feature of the case remains, and probably will remain, that a State can make a contract by legislation, and that in such a case no subsequent legislative act can interpose any effectual barrier to its enforcement. The result of this principle has been to make void innumerable acts of State Legislatures intended, in times of disastrous financial depression and suffering, to protect the people from the hardships of a rigid enforcement of their contracts, and to prevent States from impairing, by legislation, contracts entered into with other parties. The decision has stood as a great bulwark against popular efforts, through State legislation, to avoid the payment of just debts, and the general repudiation of the rights of creditors.[1]

The same question recurred in *Green* v. *Biddle*,[2] where it was held that the Constitutional prohibition embraced all contracts, executed or executory, between private individuals, or a State and individuals, or corporations, or between the States themselves, the main question being that a compact between two States was a contract entitled to protection. An-

---

[1] Mr. Justice Miller's Address, *ut supra*.   [2] 8 Wheaton, 1 (1823).

other aspect of the same controversy was considered in the case of *Sturges* v. *Crowninshield*,[1] in which the power of the States to pass bankrupt laws was exhaustively considered, and it was held that a State has full authority to pass such a law until Congress has acted on the subject, provided such State law does not impair the obligation of contracts by discharging the debtor.

The particular act, the Constitutionality of which was assailed in this case, was held to be void, inasmuch as it not only liberated the person of the debtor, but discharged him from all liability for any debt contracted previous to his discharge upon surrender of his property, and was, therefore, held to be a law impairing the obligation of contracts within the meaning of the Constitutional clause. At the same time the Chief Justice was careful to draw the distinction which exists, and has been recognized ever since, between the obligation of a contract and the remedy given by the Legislature, and it was held that so long as the former exists unimpaired, the latter may be modified as the wisdom of the Legislature shall direct.

In the great case of *Cohens* v. *Virginia*[2] the Chief Justice had an opportunity of again asserting the supremacy of the Federal judiciary over State Courts under the 25th section of the Judiciary Act, and of interpreting the Eleventh Amendment, which had forbidden suits against a State by citizens of another State. The Cohens had undertaken to sell lottery tickets in Virginia, under the authority of an Act of Congress establishing a lottery in the District of Columbia for national purposes. They were indicted under a State statute, making the selling of lottery tickets an offence. They were convicted

---

[1] 4 Wheaton, 122 (1819). See also McMillan *v.* McNeill, *Ibid.*, 209 (1819). Farmers and Mechanics' Bank of Pennsylvania *v.* Smith, 6 Wheaton, 131 (1821).

[2] 6 Wheaton, 264 (1821).

17

and fined, and the lower Court was of opinion that they had exclusive jurisdiction of the case.

In overruling the judgment, upon the point of jurisdiction, the Chief Justice pointed out that this was not a suit against the State of Virginia, but a prosecution by the State to which a defence under the laws of the United States had been set up, and that the writ of error merely removed the record for the purpose of enabling the supreme tribunal of the nation to re-examine the Constitutional question involved. He impaled the argument of counsel for the State, by reducing their propositions to manifest absurdities. Thus he said:

"They maintain that the nation does not possess a department capable of restraining peaceably and by authority of law any attempts which may be made by a part against the legitimate powers of the whole; and that the government is reduced to the alternative of submitting to such attempts or of resisting them by force. They maintain that the Constitution of the United States has provided no tribunal for the final construction of itself, or of the laws or treaties of the nation, but that this power may be exercised in the last resort by the Courts of every State in the Union. That the Constitution, laws and treaties may receive as many constructions as there are States, and that this is not a mischief, or if a mischief, is irremediable."

To these propositions there could be but one answer. He sustained the conviction, however, on the ground that the Act of Congress did not authorize a violation of the criminal laws of the State.

In the case of *Osborn* v. *The Bank of the United States*[1] the Eleventh Amendment was again fully considered, and it was held that the criterion of a suit against a State was whether the State was a party to the record, on the ground that if the jurisdiction were held to depend, not upon that plain fact, but

[1] 9 Wheaton, 739 (1824).

upon the supposed or actual interest of the State in the result of the controversy, no rule was given by the Constitution by which that interest could be measured.[1]

A case now arose of the greatest importance and of the most lasting consequences, which gained great celebrity, and determined for the first time the true construction of the powers of Congress to regulate commerce among the several States. It is known as *Gibbons* v. *Ogden.*[2] An injunction had been granted by Chancellor Kent, which was sustained by the highest Appellate Court in New York, restraining Gibbons from navigating the Hudson River by steamboats duly licensed for the coasting trade under an act of Congress, on the ground that he was thereby infringing the exclusive right granted by the State of New York to Robert Fulton and Livingston, and by them assigned to Ogden to navigate all the waters of that State with vessels moved by steam. The decision of the lower Court rested upon the doctrine that the internal commerce of the State by land and water remained entirely and exclusively within the scope of its original authority, and that the coasting license, while giving to the steamboat an American character for the purpose of revenue, was not intended to confer a right of property, or a right of navigation or commerce. "To-morrow week," wrote Wirt to a friend, "will come on the great steamboat question from New York. Emmett and Oakley on one side, Webster and myself on the other. Come down and hear it. Emmett's whole soul is in the case, and he will stretch all his powers. Oakley is said to be one of the first logicians of the age; as much a Phocion as Emmett is a Themistocles, and Webster is as am-

[1] Henry Hitchcock, LL.D., "Constitutional Development in the United States as Influenced by Chief Justice Marshall."

[2] 9 Wheaton, 1 (1824).

bitious as Cæsar. He will not be outdone by any man if it is within the compass of his power to avoid it. It will be a combat worth witnessing."[1]

The proposition contended for was that Congress had exclusive authority to regulate commerce in all its forms, on all the navigable waters of the United States, their bays, rivers and harbors, without any monopoly, restraint or interference created by State legislation. This the Supreme Court sustained in an opinion of great length. In construing the power to regulate commerce, it was held that the term meant, not only traffic, but intercourse, and that it included navigation, and the power to regulate commerce was a power to regulate navigation. Commerce among the several States meant commerce intermingled with the States, and which might pass the external boundary line of each State and be introduced into the interior. It was admitted that it did not extend to commerce which was purely internal, carried on between different parts of the same State, but in the case at bar it was held that the statute on the part of the State was an exercise of the power of regulating commerce among the States which had been confided to Congress by the Constitution, and that inasmuch as Congress had passed laws authorizing the licensing of vessels for the coasting trade, which authorized them to navigate all the waters within the jurisdiction of the United States capable of being used for that purpose, this act was an exercise of the power conferred by the clause of the Federal Constitution concerning commerce among the States, and that this necessarily excluded the action of the State upon the subject, Congress having occupied the field by its own legislation.

It was a point left undecided whether the power of Congress

---

[1] Kennedy's "Life of Wirt," Vol. II, p. 142.

to regulate commerce was exclusive only where exercised, or whether a State might exercise the power in the absence of Congressional action. In the subsequent case of *Wilson* v. *Blackbird Creek Marsh Co.,*[1] it was held that in a class of cases local in their character, regulations affecting inter-State commerce may be enacted by the States in the absence of the exercise of that power by Congress, and a State law was held valid which authorized a dam across a creek navigable from the sea within the ebb and flow of the tide on the ground that it did not conflict with any act of Congress. It is only recently that the controversy which has divided the Judges for many years upon the validity of laws passed by the States as police regulations and which do not amount to regulations of commerce has become in any manner fixed or settled.[2]

In *Brown* v. *The State of Maryland,*[3] the same interesting question arose as to the regulations of foreign commerce: whether a State could lawfully require the importer of foreign articles to take out a license from the State before being permitted to sell a bale or package so imported. Said the Chief Justice:

"There is no difference in effect between a power to prohibit the sale of an article, and a power to prohibit its introduction into the country. The one would be a necessary consequence of the other. No goods would be imported if none could be sold. No object of any description can be accomplished by laying a duty on importation, which may not be accomplished with equal certainty by laying a duty on the thing imported in the hands of the importer. . . . It is sufficient for the present to say generally that when the importer has so acted upon the thing imported

[1] 2 Peters, 245 (1829).
[2] The Passenger Cases, 7 Howard, 283 (1849); Wabash Railway Co. *v.* Illinois, 118 U. S., 557 (1886). Philadelphia Steamship Co. *v.* Pennsylvania, 122 U. S., 326 (1886). Fargo *v.* Michigan, 121 U. S. (1886) 230.
[3] 12 Wheaton, 419 (1827).

that it has become incorporated and mixed up with the mass of property in the country, it has perhaps lost its distinctive character as an import, and has become subject to the taxing power of the State; but while remaining the property of the importer in his warehouse in the original form or package in which it was imported, a tax upon it is too plainly a duty on imports to escape the prohibition in the Constitution."[1]

In the case of *Craig* v. *The State of Missouri*[2] the Constitutional prohibition addressed to the States in relation to the emission of bills of credit was fully considered. An act of that State establishing loan offices and authorizing the issue of certificates of stock was declared void. The Chief Justice showed that the certificates of stock, which were signed by the auditor and treasurer of the State, to be issued by them to the amount of hundreds of thousands of dollars, of denominations not exceeding ten dollars nor less than fifty cents, purporting on their face to be receivable at the Treasury, or at any loan office of the State of Missouri, in discharge of taxes or debts due to the State, were undoubtedly intended to perform the same office as Bills of Credit.

"Had they been termed Bills of Credit," said he, "instead of certificates, nothing would have been wanting to bring them within the prohibitory words of the Constitution. And can this make any real difference? Is the proposition to be maintained that the Constitution meant to prohibit names and not things? That a very important act, big with great and ruinous mischief, which is expressly prohibited by words most appropriate for its description may be performed by the substitution of a name? That the Constitution in one of its most important provisions may be openly evaded by giving a new name to an old thing? We cannot think so."

---

[1] Compare the License Cases, 5 Howard, 504 (1847), and Leisy *v.* Hardin, 135 U. S., 100 (1890).

[2] 4 Peters, 410 (1830).

This case was decided by a divided Court, Justices Johnson, Thompson and McLean dissenting.

The precise question again arose, four years later, in the case of *Byrne* v. *State of Missouri*,[1] in which this decision was reviewed and confirmed.[2]

By this time it was quite apparent that the energy of the Court in upholding the provisions of the Constitution, in expounding its language, in applying its principles, and in vindicating its supremacy, had built up a national system of jurisprudence upon foundations so broad and deep that little else than revolution could shake it. " The importance of that Court," wrote William Wirt, as Attorney-General to President Monroe, "in the administration of the Federal Government, begins to be generally understood and acknowledged. The local irritations at some of their decisions in particular quarters (as in Virginia and Kentucky for instance) are greatly overbalanced by the general approbation with which those same decisions have been received throughout the Union. If there are a few exasperated portions of our people who would be for narrowing the sphere of action of that Court and subduing its energies to gratify popular clamor, there is a far greater number of our countrymen who would wish to see it in the free and independent exercise of its Constitutional powers as the best means of preserving the Constitution itself. . . . It is now seen on every hand, that the functions to be performed by the Supreme Court of the United

---

[1] 8 Peters, 40 (1834).

[2] These cases, as will be seen hereafter, conflict with that of Briscoe *v.* The Bank of the Commonwealth of Kentucky, 11 Peters, 257 (1837), one of the earliest Constitutional cases decided by Chief Justice Taney, in which it was held that an act incorporating the Bank of the Commonwealth of Kentucky was a Constitutional exercise of power by that State, and that the notes issued by the Bank were not bills of credit within the meaning of the Constitution.

States are among the most difficult and perilous which are to be performed under the Constitution. They demand the loftiest range of talents and learning and a sort of Roman purity and firmness. The questions which come before them frequently involve the fate of the Constitution, the happiness of the whole nation, and even its peace as it concerns other nations." [1]

Four years later the venerable Charles Carroll, of Carrollton, the last survivor of the Signers of the Declaration of Independence, and then upon the verge of the grave, wrote to Judge Peters: "I consider the Supreme Court of the United States as the strongest guardian of the powers of Congress and the rights of the people. As long as that Court is composed of learned, upright and intrepid judges, the Union will be preserved, and the administration of justice will be safe in this extended and extending empire." [2]   Although some of the school of Jefferson might feel apprehensive of results, when viewing the strides of the nation towards power, yet there was no real cause for alarm, even on the part of those most opposed to consolidation, for in the case of the *Providence Bank* v. *Billings*,[3] the just powers of the States were carefully guarded. It was held that a law of Rhode Island imposing a tax upon a bank chartered by that State was valid, it being an exercise of sovereignty with which the Federal Constitution did not interfere.

The bank had been chartered in 1791, and in 1822 the Legislature had passed an act imposing a duty on licensed

---

[1] Wirt to Monroe, May 5, 1823. Kennedy's "Life of Wirt," Vol. II, p. 134.

[2] Letter of Charles Carroll, of Carrollton, to Hon. Richard Peters (U. S. District Judge at Philadelphia) 28th June, 1827, unpublished, in possession of the Historical Society of Pennsylvania. Peters' Papers.

[3] 4 Peters, 514 (1830).

persons and others, and bodies corporate within the State. The Bank resisted the payment of the tax on the ground that this act was repugnant to the Constitution of the United States, inasmuch as it impaired the obligation of the contract created by the charter. It was alleged that the cases of *Fletcher* v. *Peck*, and of *Trustees of Dartmouth College* v. *Woodward*, had established the principle that a legislative grant to a corporation was a contract within the meaning of the Constitution, and that the cases of *M'Culloch* v. *Maryland*, and *Weston* v. *City of Charleston*, had decided that the power of imposing a tax upon a corporation involved the power of destroying it. The act complained of was therefore contrary to the Constitutional prohibition.

The Chief Justice, however, in a very closely reasoned opinion, draws the distinction between the action of a State operating upon its own creatures, and the action of a State coming in conflict with a Constitutional law of Congress. Conceding that the charter of such a corporation was a contract, it was clear that the charter contained no stipulation exempting the bank from taxation. The power of taxation was one of vital importance. It was an incident of sovereignty essential to the existence of the State government and the relinquishment of such a power could never be presumed. It might be exercised, therefore, in all cases by a State unless it conflicted with an Act of Congress, the supremacy of which was always to be recognized. The sovereignty of a State extends to everything which exists by its own authority, or is introduced by its own action, although it does not extend to those means which are employed by Congress to carry into execution powers conferred upon that body by the people of the United States. The act was, therefore, held to be Constitutional and valid.

Another instance of careful guardianship of the rights of the States is to be found in *Barron* v. *The Mayor of Baltimore*,[1] where it was held that the provision in the Fifth Amendment to the Constitution that private property shall not be taken for public use without just compensation, was a restriction upon the power of Congress alone, and not upon the States. It was shown by a simple but conclusive argument that each State was independent within its own sphere and free from the power of the United States.

In the case of *Ogden* v. *Saunders*[2] the Chief Justice for the first time found himself in a minority upon a question of Constitutional law, and was obliged to dissent from the opinion of the Court, and in this was supported by the views of Duvall and Story. The question raised involved another phase of that which had arisen in *Sturges* v. *Crowninshield*, the majority of the Court holding that the municipal law in force when a contract is made is part of the contract itself, and that if such a law provides for the discharge of the contract upon prescribed conditions, its enforcement upon those conditions does not impair the obligation of the contract of which that law itself was a part.

The dissenting judges maintained that, however an existing law may act upon contracts when they come to be enforced, it does not enter into them as part of the original agreement, and that an insolvent law which released the debtor upon conditions not in effect agreed to by the parties themselves, whether operating upon past or future contracts, impaired their obligation. But it was also held by a divided Court, Marshall concurring, that the State law, if a part of the contract, was such only as between citizens of that State,

[1] 7 Peters, 243 (1833).   [2] 12 Wheaton, 213 (1827).

and since the creditor in this case was a citizen of Louisiana, he was not bound by the New York insolvent law, and the debtor was not discharged.

These doctrines were again recognised in *Boyle* v. *Zacharie*,[1] in which the Chief Justice declared that inasmuch as they had been established by a majority of the Court they must be viewed as well-settled law.

A case now arose, closely connected with one of the most romantic and eventful chapters in the history of the nation. The controversy between the State of Georgia and the Cherokee tribe of Indians is memorable for its excitements, its influence upon the feelings of a large section of the Union, and for the extraordinary proceedings to which it gave rise. It marks a distinct stage of the process by which, one after another, the tribes of aborigines have melted away before a civilization which inevitably extinguishes whatever it cannot absorb. We can deal only with the legal aspect of the case.[2] A motion was made in the Supreme Court for an exercise of its original jurisdiction to restrain by injunction the execution of certain laws of the State of Georgia, in the territory of the Cherokee nation, the tribe claiming that they had the right to proceed as a foreign State, under the Constitutional provision which gave to the Court exclusive jurisdiction in controversies in which a State, or the citizens thereof, and a foreign State, citizens or subjects thereof, were parties. Although the anger of the American people was kindled in behalf of the unfortunate Indians, whose clear and undeniable rights had been wrested from them by the State without reference to the obligations owed to them by the Government of the United States, under the Treaty of · Hopewell, yet it was

[1] 6 Peters, 348 (1832).
[2] Cherokee Nation *v.* The State of Georgia, 5 Peters, 1 (1831).

held that, though no case could be presented to the Court better calculated to excite their sympathies, yet the Court had no jurisdiction of the cause, inasmuch as the Cherokee nation was not a foreign State in the sense in which that term was used in the Constitution.

The Chief Justice showed, from the language of the Constitution, from the habits and usages of the Indians, from their relations to the whites, and their appeal to the tomahawk instead of courts of justice, that the statesmen who formed the Constitution could not have meant to designate them by the term *foreign State.* Besides this they were as clearly contradistinguished by a name, appropriate to themselves, from foreign nations, as from the several States composing the Union. In addition, the interposition of the Court would savor too much of the exercise of political power to be within the proper province of the judiciary. In these views Justices Johnson and Baldwin concurred, each in separate opinions, in which it was declared that neither politics nor philanthropy should ever impel the Court to assume such a judicial power, full of awful responsibilities. A powerful dissenting opinion, concurred in by Mr. Justice Story, was delivered by Mr. Justice Thompson. It is understood that the opinion of Chancellor Kent, in favor of the jurisdiction, had been obtained by counsel before the bill in equity was filed, and an effort was made, with what success is not known, to obtain from Chief Justice Marshall, in advance, his impressions in regard to the political character of the tribe.[1]

The subject at last became a matter of loyalty or disloyalty to the administration of President Jackson, which favored the removal of the Indians, and "a chord of insanity to

---

[1] See Letter of William Wirt to Judge Carr, June 21, 1830, Kennedy's "Life of Wirt," Vol. II, pp. 253, 257, 264.

many." The most intemperate abuse was showered upon the counsel for the Indians, William Wirt and John Sergeant, who reappeared, undaunted and ardent, in the case of *Worcester* v. *Georgia*,[1] in which it was held that a law of the State of Georgia, under which a missionary had been convicted of the crime of preaching to the Indians, and residing among them without a license from the governor, was unconstitutional and void.

"The treaties and laws of the United States," said the Chief Justice, "contemplate the Indian Territory as completely separated from that of the State, and provide that all intercourse with them shall be carried on exclusively by the Government of the Union." . . . "The Cherokee Nation is a distinct community, occupying its own territory with boundaries accurately described, in which the laws of Georgia can have no force, and in which the citizens of Georgia have no right to enter but with the assent of the Cherokees themselves, or in conformity with treaties or the acts of Congress. The whole intercourse between the United States and this nation is, by our Constitution and law, vested in the Government of the United States. The act of the State of Georgia under which the plaintiff in error was prosecuted is, consequently, void and the judgment a nullity."

The State of Georgia treated this decision with defiance. The missionary was still imprisoned in the penitentiary doomed to hard labor, the Governor declaring that he would rather hang him than liberate him under the mandate of the Supreme Court. The Federal Government gave no hope of interfering in the controversy. On the contrary Jackson is reported to have said: "John Marshall has made the decision, now let him execute it." At the end of eighteen months, however, cooler judgment and more moderate counsels prevailed; the contest had grown hopeless to the weaker party, and the prisoner was released.[2]

[1] 6 Peters, 515 (1832).   [2] See Kennedy's "Life of Wirt," Vol. II, p. 323.

Within a short time the Court had occasion, in the case of *The State of New Jersey* v. *The State of New York*,[1] to consider the method of procedure in the exercise of original jurisdiction in suits between States. Congress had passed no act for the special purpose of prescribing the mode in which suits should be conducted, and as has been seen,[2] Mr. Justice Iredell in his remarkable dissenting opinion in *Chisholm* v. *The State of Georgia* had contended that an Act of Congress was necessary to enable the Court to exercise its jurisdiction, but after a careful review of all the early cases in which States had been made defendants, and the rules respecting process, the Chief Justice announced that it had been settled, on great deliberation, that the jurisdiction might be exercised under the authority conferred by the Constitution. An order was therefore made, the complainant having observed the rule as to the service of process on the Governor and Attorney-General of the defendant State, that the cause might proceed *ex parte*, and be prepared for a final hearing.

In the case of *Watson et al.* v. *Mercer et ux.*,[3] it was held that the Supreme Court had no right to pronounce an act of a State Legislature void as contrary to the Constitution from the mere fact that it divested rights which had vested antecedently. Retrospective laws were not forbidden. The Constitutional prohibition was confined to *ex post facto* laws, and it had been determined that this phrase applied solely to penal and criminal laws.

With this case, the review of the decisions of the Court upon Constitutional questions during the time of Chief Justice Marshall is completed. The principles which governed the Court, during that time, in interpreting the Constitution, were

---

[1] 5 Peters, 284 (1831).   [2] See *Ante*, p. 175.

[3] 8 Peters, 88 (1834).

well expressed in the case of the *United States Bank* v. *Deveaux*,[1] where it is said:

"The Constitution and the law are to be expounded without leaning one way or the other, according to those general principles which usually govern in the construction of fundamental laws."

And in *Ogden* v. *Saunders*,[2] where it is declared—

"That the intention of the instrument must prevail; that this intention must be collected from its words; that its words are to be understood in that sense in which they are generally used by those for whom the instrument was intended; that its provisions are neither to be restricted into insignificance, nor extended to objects not comprehended in them nor contemplated by its framers."

The rule is stated in another form in *Gibbons* v. *Ogden*[3] by the Chief Justice:

"The enlightened patriots who framed our Constitution and the people who adopted it must be understood to have employed words in their natural sense, and to have intended what they said. . . . We know of no rule of construing the extent of such powers other than is given by the language of the instrument which confers them, taken in connection with the purposes for which they were conferred. . . . What do gentlemen mean by a strict construction? If they contend only against that enlarged construction which would extend words beyond their natural and obvious import, we might question the application of the term, but should not controvert the principle. If they contend for that narrow construction which, in support of some theory not to be found in the Constitution, would deny to the government those powers which the words of the grant, as usually understood, import, and which are consistent with the general views and objects of the instrument; for that narrow construction which would cripple the government, and render it unequal to the objects for which it is declared to be instituted, and to

---

[1] 5 Cranch, 62 (1809).   [2] 12 Wheaton, 213 (1827).
[3] 9 Wheaton, 1 (1824).

which the powers given, as fairly understood, render it competent, then we cannot perceive the propriety of this strict construction, nor adopt it as the rule by which the Constitution is to be expounded."

Such were the principles of construction applied during a period of thirty-four years. There was no violent effort to stretch or strain the language of the Constitution, or make a cloak of the contents to cover usurpations of power. But all attempts to strangle the instrument itself, or impede the fair exercise of its delegations of authority, were promptly crushed. A steady, but scarcely noticeable application of a liberal and enlightened view, long continued, wrought marvels. "Stronger than he who makes the laws is he who can construe them for a long time." As was finely said in *Osborn* v. *The Bank of the United States*: "The judicial department has no will in any case. Judicial power is never exercised for the purpose of giving effect to the will of the judge, but always for the purpose of giving effect to the will of the law." And as it was the purpose of the people of the United States, in ordaining and establishing the Constitution for the government of themselves and their posterity, that the nation should be supreme, an impregnable wall of precedents was built up by slow degrees, which proved to be the bulwark and safety of the nation, when, in after years, the integrity of the Union was assailed by the armed legions of Secession.

During the period covered by the decisions which have been reviewed, death invaded the precincts of the Court and struck down several of the Associate Justices. The first victim of the insatiate archer was Mr. Justice Livingston, who had held his place for seventeen years since 1806. His successor was Smith Thompson, of New York, who was commissioned in the recess, September 1, and recommissioned, on confirma-

tion by the Senate, December 8, 1823. At this time he was serving as Secretary of the Navy, under Monroe, and prior to that time had held for fourteen years, in the Supreme Court of New York, a place at the side of Chief Justice, afterwards Chancellor Kent, with Spencer and Tompkins, as Associates, and had distinguished himself at a time when that tribunal might claim in point of talent and learning to rank with any State Judiciary in the Union. He was born, according to some authorities, in Amenia, New York, in the year 1767, and, according to others, at Stanford, in Duchess County, upon January 17, 1768. He received a common school education, and subsequently went to Princeton, graduating in his twentieth year, in 1788. He entered immediately upon the study of the law under Kent, supporting himself in the meantime by teaching school at Poughkeepsie, was admitted to the Bar in 1792, and began to practice at Troy. Pursuing his vocation with diligence, at the end of six years he became interested in politics and was sent to the State Legislature, serving also as a delegate to the State Constitutional Convention, and as attorney for the middle district of New York. In 1801 Governor Clinton appointed him an Associate Justice of the Supreme Court of the State, and in 1814 Kent having become Chancellor, Thompson became Chief Justice. He was called by President Monroe, four years later, to the position of Secretary of the Navy. Prior to this he had declined the Mayoralty of New York City. In 1823 he became the successor of the lamented Livingston in the highest court in the Union.

His acceptance of the latter place was not immediate, and there is evidence to show that he felt called upon to decline it. In the meantime the President was urged by his Attorney-General, William Wirt, to disregard political considerations

18

and confer the appointment upon James Kent. Thompson's subsequent determination prevented the association of one of the most illustrious names in American jurisprudence with the history of her highest tribunal. He held the place until his death in 1843.

His character as a Judge is best described by his associate, Mr. Justice Nelson, at the meeting of the Court held upon the occasion of his death. "From the time of his appointment to the Supreme Bench, he laboriously fulfilled all the obligations of his elevated station, which, it is no exaggeration to say, he illustrated and adorned, distinguished as he was for everything that can give a title to reverence. Of the assiduity, the patience, the energy and singleness of purpose with which he discharged his arduous official duties, his judicial associates made full acknowledgments; whilst of his genius, his attainments and his intellectual vigor, the recorded judgments of the Court during the whole term of his service furnish permanent attestation." Yale and Princeton in 1824, and Harvard in 1835, conferred upon him the degree of LL.D. He was interested in many benevolent enterprises, and at his death was the oldest Vice-President of the American Bible Society.

In February, 1826, Mr. Justice Todd succumbed to long continued illness, expressing a desire before his death that his place should be filled by Robert Trimble, then United States District Judge in the District of Kentucky. His preference and that of the President coincided, and Judge Trimble was commissioned an Associate Justice of the Supreme Court on the 9th of May, 1826. He was born in Augusta County, Virginia, in 1777, and was the son of William Trimble, one of the earliest settlers in Kentucky, a man of bold, firm and enterprising character, who encountered the dangers and hardships

R. Trimble

of a new settlement. Young Trimble, at the age of three years, accompanied his father at the time of his emigration, and the early years of his life were devoted to agriculture. He was called upon to take part in movements against Indian invasion, and distinguished himself by the display of courage and sagacity.

He had a powerful mind, developed by self-training, which prompted him to secure an education which would fit him for higher duties. By teaching an English school he procured the means of entering Bourbon Academy, and afterwards became a student in the Kentucky Academy, in Woodford County, where he completed his classical course. He then studied law, and in 1800 began its practice at Paris, in Bourbon County, where he married. In 1802 he was elected to the House of Representatives, but declined a re-election in the following year, preferring to devote himself to his profession. In 1807 he became a Judge of the Supreme Court of Kentucky, a position which he filled with increasing reputation. Three years afterwards he relinquished the office, to return to the Bar, and in 1810 refused a commission as Chief Justice of the State. He declined the same office in 1813, and continued to distinguish himself at the bar until 1817, when he received the appointment of District Judge of the United States for the District of Kentucky. He was a man learned in the law, just and discriminating in judicial investigation, and his decisions are characterized by great legal accuracy, research and perspicuity, and by a large and liberal equity. He was clear and comprehensive in his statements, and illustrated and enriched his discussions by abundant legal learning. His period of service in the Supreme Court was short, as in less than two years he was removed by death. Of him it has been said that perhaps no Associate Justice of the Supreme Court of the United States occupying the position for so short a time, placed the result of his labor in so conspicuous a form. In *Montgomery* v. *Hernandez*[1] he defined a Federal question, declaring also that the party must claim the right under the Constitution for himself. In *Mallow* v. *Hinde*[2] he asserted the right of a United States Court to retain jurisdiction of a cause on an injunction bill as between the parties before it, until the plaintiffs could litigate their controversy with other parties in another tribunal, whereupon the United States Court would proceed with its adjudication. And in *United States* v. *Nichol*,[3] he settled the rights of sureties upon official bonds as against the United States.[4]

The place vacated through Trimble's death was filled by the appointment of John McLean, of Ohio, who was commissioned upon the 7th of March, 1829. Although his genius was not brilliant, yet his talents were great, and his mind was able to comprehend the largest subject and did not shrink from the minutest analysis. He was eminently practical, ever zealous in the pursuit of truth, and his faculties were so well ordered that he could always utilize and control his ideas. He was born in Morris County, New Jersey, March 11, 1785, and at the early age of four years was taken by his father to Morgantown, Virginia, and afterwards to Nicholasville, Kentucky, from which the family removed, in 1799, to Ohio, where they settled in Warren County, clearing their farm by their own labor. His early education was slight, but at the age of sixteen years he studied under a private tutor. At this time his ambition to study law was aroused, and he en-

---

[1] 12 Wheaton, 129 (1827).   [2] 12 Wheaton, 193 (1827).

[3] 12 Wheaton, 505.

[4] See an admirable biographical sketch prefixed to the First Volume of the Indexed Digest of the United States Supreme Court Reports, published by the Lawyers' Co-operative Publishing Co.

John Adams

gaged as a deputy in the Clerk's office in Cincinnati, maintaining himself in this manner while pursuing his legal studies under Arthur St. Clair. In 1807 he was admitted to the Bar, beginning practice at Lebanon, and in 1812 was sent to Congress, defeating two opposing candidates. In political principles he adhered to the Democratic Party, was an ardent supporter of the war, and of President Madison's administration. During his Congressional term he became the author of the law to indemnify individuals for property lost in the public service, and introduced resolutions of inquiry into the expediency of pensions for widows of officers and soldiers who fell in the service of their country. In 1814 he was re-elected by a unanimous vote, a rare distinction; and in the following year declined a nomination to the Senate of the United States. Shortly after this he was chosen by the Legislature to the position of Judge of the State Supreme Court, and to accept this position resigned his seat in Congress at the close of the session of 1816. His judicial career was marked by the ability and eloquence of his charges to grand juries, and the vigor and clearness of his opinions. In 1822 President Monroe appointed him a Commissioner of the General Land Office, and by efficiency and diligence he introduced order and economy into that department. In the following year he was appointed Postmaster-General, and continued to hold the same place under John Quincy Adams. When General Jackson became President he expressed a wish to retain him in this position, but as McLean differed with him on the question of official appointments and removals, and had little or no sympathy with the spoils system, he refused the portfolio. He was then offered successively the offices of the War and the Navy Departments, both of which he declined, but finally accepted the appointment of Justice of the Supreme Court of the United

States, as more in accord with his tastes and talents, and entered upon its duties during the January Term of 1830.

His term of judicial service continued until 1861. He is best known to the country as one of the dissenting judges in the Dred Scott case, but his opinions are well and favorably known to the profession for their clearness and vigor of expression; that in *Prigg* v. *Commonwealth* being remarkable for the subtlety of its analysis and power of reasoning. Although not in entire harmony upon the questions raised in the Passenger and License cases with the majority of his brethren, yet his views are expressed with uncommon and persuasive force. His sentiments upon the question of slavery were in effect that it had its origin merely in power, and was against right, and was sustained in this country by local law only. He became identified in sympathy with the party opposed to its extension, and his name came before the Free Soil Convention at Buffalo in 1848 as a candidate for the Presidency. In the Republican National Convention held in Philadelphia in 1856 he received, for the same nomination, 196 votes against 359 for John C. Fremont, and in 1860, at the Republican Convention in Chicago, he received several votes. Harvard University conferred upon him in 1839 the degree of Doctor of Laws. He published seven volumes of Reports of his decisions at Circuit, and pronounced an eulogy upon James Monroe in 1831. He was a man of commanding appearance, of fine and noble presence, gentle and courteous in manner, and affectionate in his intercourse with the members of the Bar. He died at the age of seventy-six, much beloved and respected. His devotion to duty was marked. Of him Chief Justice Taney said: "He held a seat on this bench for more than thirty years, and until the last two years of his life, when his health began to fail, was never absent from his duties here for a single day. The reports are the recorded evidence of a mind firm, frank and vigorous, and full of the subject before him. He displayed in the office of Postmaster-General administrative talent hardly ever surpassed, with a firmness of character and uprightness of purpose never questioned."

Mr. Justice Washington died upon the 26th of November, 1829, and his vacant place was conferred upon Henry Baldwin of Pennsylvania, who was commissioned on the 6th of January, 1830. Baldwin, who was a man of extraordinary intellectual power, was a native of New Haven, Connecticut, where he was born on the 14th of January, 1780. He was a graduate of Yale College, studied law, and removed to Pittsburgh, and thence to Meadville, in Crawford County, Pennsylvania. His rise at the bar was rapid. He acquired early a position of eminent distinction, which he never lost, due to strong reasoning powers, retentive memory, and profound and varied knowledge. His arguments were characterized by singular fullness of illustration of authority; his language was fluent, ardent and eloquent. After several years of successful practice, and a career of activity in politics, he was sent to Congress in 1817, remaining a member of that body until 1822. In 1819 he acted as the Chairman of the Standing Committee on Manufactures, and distinguished himself as an advocate of the encouragement of American industries; he was one of the small minority of the delegation from Pennsylvania who sustained, on its final passage, the bill for the admission of Missouri into the Union. So high were his professional attainments, and so great was the legal ability displayed in his Congressional career, and such the reputation he had acquired for superior talents and extensive information and learning, that he was selected by President Jackson as an Associate Justice of the Supreme Court. Upon the bench he soon attracted to himself the attention of the Bar and the country by challenging the Constitutional views of Chief Justice Marshall and Mr. Justice Story. He construed the Constitution as the grant of the people of the several States, and not as the grant of the people of the United States in the aggregate, and constantly dissented from the judgments of his associates, particularly upon questions involving the Constitutionality of State laws alleged to impair the obligation of contracts. He was one of the dissenting Judges in *Craig v. Missouri*, maintaining an opposite view to that of the Chief Justice upon the nature of Bills of Credit, and in other cases always inclined to a construction which would sustain a State law as a police regulation, rather than overturn it as an attempt to regulate commerce. Each State, according to his theory, was a single sovereign power in adopting the Constitution, and he held that the operation of the Constitution must, of necessity, be like that of a treaty of cession by a foreign State to the United States. It has been asserted that he largely over-estimated the impression which his repeated dissents had produced upon other members of the Supreme Court, and this overweening self-reliance led him to prepare "A General View of the Origin and Nature of the Constitution and Government of the United States," embracing in large part his dissenting opinions, and published after Mr. Taney had become Chief Justice. He frankly admitted that his views might be deemed "peculiar," and "founded on a course of investigation different from that which is usually taken." No more graphic statement of the complete want of cohesion among the judges at this period upon questions of Constitutional law can be found than that given by Baldwin: "In the case of the Commonwealth Bank of Kentucky

I was in the minority; in the Charles River Bridge case it now appears that I stood alone after the argument in 1831; the Tennessee boundary case hung in doubtful scales, and in the New York case I was one of the bare majority. By changes of judges and of opinions there is now but one dissentient in three of the cases; and though my opinion still differs from that of three of my brothers who sat for the fourth, six years ago, it is supported by the three who have been since appointed. Placed in a position as peculiar now as it was then, and since, I feel called upon to defend it, and to explain the reasons why it was then assumed and is now retained."

His labors upon the circuit were marked by the same extraordinary grasp and vigor of mind. In 1833 he delivered an opinion in the case of *McGill* v. *Brown*,[1] in construction of the will of Sarah Zane, upon the subject of a bequest for pious and charitable uses, which, in the judgment of the late United States District Judge, John Cadwalader, himself a jurist of extraordinary learning, was the greatest legal opinion ever delivered. He discussed the question with a degree of industry, learning and research that can scarcely be paralleled in the annals of jurisprudence. Towards the close of his life his intellect became deranged, and he was violent and ungovernable in his conduct upon the bench. His death occurred in Philadelphia upon the 21st of April, 1844, at the age of sixty-five years. He died from paralysis, and in such abject poverty that a subscription among his friends was required for his burial.

In August, 1834, Mr. Justice William Johnson, of South Carolina, died, after a judicial service of more than thirty

---

[1] Published with note to Blenon's Est., Brightly's Rep. (Pa.) 346.

years. His place was filled by the appointment of James M. Wayne, of Georgia, who was commissioned on the 9th of January, 1835. He was a native of Savannah, where he was born in 1790. He received an excellent preliminary education from a private tutor, and entered Princeton College so early that he became a graduate in 1808. Returning home, he read law, and was called to the Bar within two years, practicing in his native city. In 1813 he was elected a member of the General Assembly as an opponent of the Relief Law, which had created much feeling in the State. He was twice re-elected, and subsequently declined to become a candidate. In 1823 he was chosen Mayor of his native city, and in the following year was placed upon the bench of the Superior Court, holding this office for five years, and acquiring an honorable distinction as a judge. From 1829 until 1835 he was a member of Congress, where he took an active share in debate, and supported General Jackson in his Anti-Nullification acts. The President expressed his appreciation of Wayne's services by appointing him an Associate Justice of the Supreme Court. In Congress he favored free trade, opposed internal improvements by Congress, except of rivers and harbors, was conspicuous in his opposition to the rechartering of the United States Bank, claiming that it would confer dangerous political powers upon a few individuals. He took an active part in the removal of the Cherokee Indians to the West. He presided in two conventions held for the revision of the Constitution of Georgia, and was for many years President of the Georgia Historical Society, and one of the Trustees of the University of Georgia, taking an active part in promoting and extending education in his native State. He was the last member of the Supreme Court as constituted under Chief Justice Marshall, a fact which was one of the felicities of his career, and while it was the remarkable fortune of President Jackson to fill a majority of the seats upon the bench of the Supreme Court by appointments to vacancies occurring during his term, it was the lot of Mr. Justice Wayne to be the last survivor of these appointees. As a judge he was learned, able and conscientious, and during an era of strict construction he inclined to the support of national views. His opinions are especially valued upon questions of admiralty. At the outbreak of the Civil War his sympathy and efforts were all with the cause of the Union, and his opinions indicate his fidelity to the Constitution, as interpreted by the principles of Marshall. He lived to see the triumph of his views and the restoration of Peace under conditions which promised to be permanent.

We have now reached the close of a distinct epoch in the history of the Court. The career of Chief Justice Marshall was over. He had seen Washington, his associate for thirty years, stricken down by death, and Johnson, his fellow-laborer for the same period of time, disabled by age and infirmity. He had seen Duvall, at the age of eighty-two, retire from the consultation-room, and had followed Livingston and Todd to their graves. Of all the Judges who had shared with him the grandeur and glory of his unexampled career Story alone remained. New doctrines and new men were pushing for place and recognition. The Executive was distinctly hostile, and was resolved upon revolutionizing the Court. Five vacancies had occurred during the past ten years, and men had been appointed, who gradually broke away from the old doctrines. Thompson, McLean, Baldwin and Wayne, although full of personal reverence for the exalted character of the aged Chief Justice, had but little sympathy with that school of Federalists whose principles had become the adamantine foundations of our jurisprudence. They belonged to a later generation and were the representatives of new forces. Substantial unanimity of opinion upon a Constitutional question became a thing of the past. A cloud no larger than a man's hand had arisen, and its shadow was felt in the cases of *Briscoe* v. *The Bank of the State of Kentucky*, and *The City of New York* v. *Miln*.[1] It was a solemn and ominous announcement that in cases involving Constitutional questions unless four judges should concur, no judgment would be delivered, except in cases of necessity, and as four judges had not concurred in those cases, that they should stand over for re-argument.

But however anxious Marshall might be as to the future, the past was secure, and he could reflect with serene satisfaction upon what had been accomplished. The clouds that gathered about his dying head burned with the unquenchable glories of his matchless day. He and his associates had considered jointly many of the most important powers of Congress; they had established and sustained the supremacy of the United States; their right as a creditor to priority of payment; their right to institute and protect an incorporated bank; to lay a general and indefinite embargo; to levy taxes; to preempt Indian lands; to control the State militia; to promote internal improvements; to regulate commerce with foreign nations and among the States; to establish a uniform rule of naturalization and uniform laws on the subject of bankruptcy; they had dealt with a mass of implied powers incidental to the express powers of Congress; they had enforced the Constitutional restrictions upon the powers of the States; they had stricken down pretentious efforts to emit bills of credit,

[1] 8 Peters, 118 (1834).

Henry Baldwin

to pass *ex post facto* laws, to control or impede the exercise of Federal powers; to impair the obligations of contracts; to tax national agencies; to exercise power over ceded territory; to cripple commerce, and to defy the lawful decrees of the Federal Courts. They had faced the frowns of Jefferson and Jackson, and conquered both by invincible logic. They had subjected the ministerial officers of the Executive Department to the control of the judiciary, and had shivered into atoms the pretensions of Congress to override the Constitution. They had defined the jurisdiction of the Federal Courts, both original and appellate, and had sustained against the most stubborn resistance of sovereign States the right of the supreme tribunal to supervise decrees of State courts, when denying a right conferred by the Constitution. They had dealt with all those lofty questions of international law which grew out of the War of 1812; they had developed the admiralty and maritime jurisdiction of the District Courts, as well in matters of prize as on the Instance side of the Court, and had extended the application of the principles of commercial law. They had swept through the domain of chancery, and placed the law of trusts and charities upon a stable basis. They had reared a solid and magnificent structure, destined "at no distant period of time to cast a shadow over the less elevated and the less attractive and ambitious systems of justice in the several States." In doing this, they entitled themselves forever to the gratitude and veneration of posterity. These results had been accomplished solely through the moral force which belonged to the independent position of the Judiciary. With no direct control over the sword or purse of the nation, with no armed force behind them, surrounded by no halo of military achievements to dazzle the people, supported by no party obedient to their behests, with no patronage to distribute, and with no appropriations to attract a crowd of camp followers, the Judges of the Supreme Court, placed by the Constitution beyond the reach of partisan influences, and protected by the life tenure of their offices from sudden gusts of passion, wrought on in the quiet performance of their duty, without fear or favor, and relied for the results upon the reverence of the people for the majestic and final utterances of the Law, with a proud consciousness of their authority.

The judgments of Marshall carried the Constitution through the experimental period, and settled the question of its supremacy. "Time has demonstrated their wisdom. They have remained unchanged, unquestioned, unchallenged. All the subsequent labors of that high tribunal on the subject of Constitutional law have been founded on, and have at least professed and attempted to follow them. There they remain. They will always remain. They will stand as long as the Constitution stands. And if that should perish, they would still remain to display to the world the principles upon which it rose, and by the disregard of which it fell."[1]

NOTE.

The amount of work done by the Supreme Court during the time of Marshall has been estimated as follows: 1106 opinions were filed, of which 519 were delivered by Marshall, the remainder being unequally divided among the fifteen judges who were his Associates. Eight dissenting opinions were filed by Marshall, only one of which involved a question of Constitutional law; Ogden *v.* Saunders. From 1801 to 1835 sixty-two decisions were given upon Constitutional questions, in thirty-six of which the opinion was by Marshall, the remaining twenty-six being by one of seven Justices. These decisions are reported in 30 volumes

---

[1] Address of Hon. E. J. Phelps, at the Second Annual Meeting of the American Bar Association, Aug. 21, 1879.

Sames M. Wayne

of Reports from 1 Cranch to 9 Peters inclusive. (See note and table to a lecture on Constitutional Development in the United States as Influenced by Chief Justice Marshall, by Henry Hitchcock, LL.D. "Constitutional History as Seen in American Law," pp. 118–120. "The Supreme Court of the United States," by W. W. Willoughby, p. 90.)

An effort has been made to depreciate this work. Mr. Shirley, in his book on the Dartmouth College Causes, p. 386, says: "The extent of the business of the Supreme Court during the time of Marshall has been much exaggerated. Less than 1300 cases were decided by it, and in those, Marshall delivered about five hundred opinions, or on an average about fifteen a year. During the first two years after he came to the bench, but five causes were decided, in four of which he delivered the opinion. His first term lasted five days. The average number of causes decided per year was less than forty. But a few years ago the Supreme Court of Pennsylvania, under Chief Justice Agnew, held a term of seven weeks, and in that time disposed of 425 out of 450 cases on his docket. The contrast is apparent."

This is captious criticism; the substitution of quantity for quality. Let the curious reader compare the exhaustive and profoundly reasoned opinions of the one period, with the *Per Curiam* decrees of the other, and decide whether he prefers breathless haste to careful argument and judicial deliberation.

CHAPTER XV.

Fourth Epoch: 1835–1850. The First Half of Taney's Judicial Career: General Character of Questions Discussed: Sketch of Chief Justice Taney: Sketches of Justices Barbour, Smith, Catron, McKinley, and Daniel: Leading Cases: Change in the Principles of Constitutional Interpretation: State of New York *v.* Miln: Briscoe *v.* Bank of the Commonwealth of Kentucky: Charles River Bridge Case: Limitations upon the Doctrine of the Dartmouth College Case: Lament of Justice Story: Miscellaneous Cases: Kendall *v.* United States: Rhode Island *v.* Massachusetts: Corporation Cases: Limitations upon the Powers of the States: Florida Land Claims: Martin *v.* Waddell: Swift *v.* Tyson: The Establishment of the Doctrine of a General Commercial Jurisprudence: The Fugitive Slave Law: Prigg *v.* Commonwealth of Pennsylvania: Cases Relating to Slavery: Miscellaneous Cases: The Girard Will Case: The Myra Clark Gaines Case: Cases of Inter-State Commerce: The License Cases: The Passenger Cases: Admiralty Cases: Waring *v.* Clark: Cases Affecting the Relations of the State to the Union: Luther *v.* Borden: General Review of Work Accomplished by the Court at this Time: Sketch of the Bar of the Supreme Court.

W E now enter upon the fourth great epoch in the history of the Court; an era of individual views, of doubts and queries, of numerous dissenting opinions, of strict construction of the Constitution, of State ascendency, of final submission to what Von Holst has called the "Slaveocracy," an epoch bearing bitter fruit, and serving, at the end of a quarter of a century, to bring into striking prominence the value of Marshall's work, and the necessity of appealing to his principles of interpretation if the integrity of the Union was to be preserved.

A change in the constitutional doctrines of the Court was to be expected. It was the natural and legitimate outgrowth of the times. The country was upon the verge of that wonderful physical advance which was checked, but not stifled, by civil war. Steam was about to be applied to loco-motion on land as well as water. The sumpter mule, the pack horse, and the Conestoga wagon were to be supplanted by railroads; coal was mined; canals were dug; new high-ways were constructed and old ones improved; bridges were thrown across streams and rival corporations contended about tolls; post routes were extended; newspapers were distributed. The energies of the States in the direction of internal im-provements were fully aroused; banking institutions multi-plied. The growth of cotton manufacture stimulated slavery in the South and the factory system in the North. New and vast regions were rescued from the wilderness; immense ac-cessions of national territory were made: the tide of foreign immigration was more than doubled; commercial or police regulations were attempted. Jealousy of national institutions became rife. The slave power contended for the mastery.

Amid the conflict of these forces old questions assumed new aspects, or new questions crowded out the old. The legal-ity and utility of the Bank of the United States, which had been sustained in *M'Culloch* v. *Maryland*, were now denied. President Jackson vetoed the Bill to recharter the Bank, and denied the binding effect of that immortal judgment. " If the opinion of the Supreme Court," said he, " covered the whole ground of this act, it ought not to contest the co-ordinate authorities of this government. The Congress, the Executive and the Court must each for itself be guided by its own opinion of the Constitution. Each public officer who takes an oath to support the Constitution swears that he will support it as he understands it, and not as it is understood by others."[1]

---

[1] The question whether the Departments of the Government are independent of each other, and can construe the Constitution for themselves is one which has led

19

In this view he was supported by the advice of his Attorney-General, who, in a few months, was to become Chief Justice of the United States as the immediate successor of John Marshall.   The right of the States to make regulations as to passengers from foreign ports; to incorporate banks to do business in behalf of the State; to grant franchises, such as bridges, ferries and the like, notwithstanding previous grants, unless the first charter was exclusive in its terms; and the right of the State corporations by comity to make contracts and carry on business in other States—these and other questions arose, and were determined in such a manner that Judge Story wrote that he was convinced that the doctrines and opinions of the old court were losing ground, and that new men and new opinions had succeeded.

Much of what was done, however, has proved of imperishable value.   It was well that certain doctrines, particularly those relating to legislative grants, should not be permitted to run to dangerous extremes.   It was well that the "Commerce clause" should be critically discussed, lest the powers of the States to protect themselves against disease, pauperism, disorder and crime should be too closely shorn.   In this field, Chief Justice Taney wrought better than he knew, and

---

to much interesting discussion. Attorney-General Bates, in a memorable opinion written in 1861 (Opinions Attys.-General, Vol. X, p. 74) reached the conclusion that the President was independent, and therefore, could lawfully suspend the privilege of the writ of *habeas corpus* and refuse to obey the writ when issued by the Courts. Mr. Robert G. Street, of Texas, in a paper read before the American Bar Association in August, 1883 (6 Report Amer. Bar Assn. 17), reaches the same conclusion, and his views are reviewed in a paper of great ability by Mr. Wm. M. Meigs, of Philadelphia (19 "Amer. Law Review," 190 *et seq.*), which exhausts the learning of the question. The results reached by these writers have not been accepted without adverse comment, and an interesting discussion, in which several important distinctions are drawn, is to be found in a paper by Mr. Sydney G. Fisher, of Philadelphia (21 "Amer. Law Review," 210 *et seq.*).

was singularly possessed of "that insight, that unconscious sympathy with human progress, which induces a judge, while scrupulously administering existing law, to expand and advance and develop it, commensurate with human needs."[1]

Roger B. Taney was commissioned as Chief Justice upon the 15th of March, 1836. At this time he was nearly sixty years of age, and, with the exception of a few brief periods of public service, had devoted his great abilities with unrelaxed attention to active practice. In knowledge of technical details in all departments of legal learning, in the mastery of principles derived from constant and varied occupation in the argument of causes in Courts of inferior and superior jurisdiction, both State and national, he excelled every one of his predecessors. He ascended the bench at a much later period in life than they, and had long before his promotion attained the rank of a veteran leader of the bar. Unlike many of his associates, he had not the advantage of a previous judicial experience, but gave ample compensation in his long familiarity with the tribunal over which he was called to preside, having argued many important causes in opposition to Wirt, Webster, Berrien and Jones. Delicate in health, but vehement in his feelings and passionate in temper, he expressed himself at times with extraordinary vigor, and acted with promptitude and decision. He was a man of the highest integrity and of great simplicity and purity of character. By watchfulness of himself he had acquired perfect self-control; his courage was unflinching; his industry was great; and his power of analysis was unusual, even among men remarkable for such a gift. His judicial style was admirable, lucid and logical, and, like his arguments, displayed

[1] Address of Hon. Clarkson N. Potter at 4th Annual Meeting of American Bar Association, August 18, 1881.

a thorough knowledge of the intricacies of pleading and niceties of practice, as well as a thorough comprehension of un-
derlying principles. Wirt dreaded his "apostolic simplicity,"
and on one occasion spoke of him as a man of "moon-light
mind,—the moon-light of the Arctics, with all the light of
day without its glare." He adhered closely to the language
of the Constitution, never extending the words of the grant
upon the ground of convenience or necessity. He was always
anxious to protect the States in the full and unfettered exercise of their reserved powers. The Union, in his apprehension, was one of States which had ceded great prerogatives of
sovereignty for purposes either expressly stated in the Constitution or "necessary and proper" to the exercise of those
expressly granted. All that were not surrendered were retained in their original fulness and force. He read the Constitution, as, strange to say, Oliver Wolcott once feared that
Marshall would do, "as if it were a penal statute," and was
sometimes "embarrassed with doubts, of which his friends will
not perceive the importance." Yet, on occasion, his judgments bore the stamp of the broadest statesmanship. The
limitations upon the doctrine of the Dartmouth College case,
as expressed in the Charles River Bridge case,[1] have produced
the happiest results in freeing the States from the grasp of
monopolists, and in leaving them uncrippled in the exercise
of most important rights of sovereignty. While in the cases
of *Waring* v. *Clark*[2] and *The Genesee Chief*,[3] in which the admiralty and maritime jurisdiction of the Federal Courts is
extended above tide-water on the Mississippi and to the entire chain of the Great Lakes and the waters connected with
them, his opinions are characterized by great judicial breadth

[1] 11 Peters, 420 (1837).   [2] 5 Howard, 441 (1847).
[3] 12 Howard, 443 (1851).

of view. And in *Ableman* v. *Booth*[1] he was most emphatic in the maintenance of the supremacy of Federal law. Upon this fair record but one blot appears. The "damnéd spot" of the Dred Scott decision will not "out," and though other illustrious names must share in the infamy of that fatal blunder, yet the Chief Justice, by virtue of his eminence, must carry the blood-stain on his ermine to eternity.

Roger Brooke Taney was born in Calvert County, Maryland, on the 17th of March, 1777. His ancestors, upon both sides, were among the earliest settlers of the State, who in the time of Cromwell sought repose and liberty of conscience under the protection of Lord Baltimore's enlightened government. Their Catholic faith was inherited and faithfully kept by their renowned descendant. He was educated at Dickinson College, Carlisle, in the State of Pennsylvania, of which institution he became a student in 1792. In three years he was graduated, and began the study of the law at Annapolis, in the office of Jeremiah T. Chase, who had been appointed, but a short time before, Chief Justice of the General Court of Maryland. Upon his admission to the bar he returned to his native county, but was soon called into political life as a delegate to the General Assembly. Although scarcely twenty-three years of age, he won distinction, but declining a re-election, removed to Fredericktown, where for twenty-two years he devoted himself, with increasing success and growing reputation, to the practice of the law. He soon became employed in many important causes, and, as the Reports show, was constantly in conflict with Pinkney, Winder, Martin, Harper and Johnson. He entered every tribunal, civil and criminal, the county courts, the courts of equity, the Court of Appeals, and even Courts Martial. He was of counsel for General Wilkin-

[1] 21 Howard, 506 (1858).

son, Commander-in-chief of the United States Army, summoned before a military court upon grave and high accusations, and conducted the case to a successful issue. He incurred censure in defending a Methodist preacher for inciting slaves to insurrection, but encountered successfully both popular excitement and judicial power. In 1816 he was chosen a member of the Maryland Senate, and served for a period of five years. In 1823 he removed to Baltimore, and disputed with Wirt the sceptre of professional eminence which had fallen from the dead hand of Pinkney. He now entered upon the enlarged sphere of practice before the Supreme Court of the United States. Here he argued *Manro* v. *Almeida*,[1] an admiralty case; *Etting* v. *The Bank of the United States*,[2] involving a principle of legal ethics; *Cassel* v. *Charles Carroll of Carrollton*,[3] a claim under the original proprietary title of Maryland; *Brown* v. *Maryland*,[4] involving the question of the extent of the power to regulate foreign commerce, and *United States* v. *Gooding*,[5] an indictment for a violation of the Act forbidding the Slave Trade. In 1827 Mr. Taney, though politically opposed to the Governor and Council of Maryland, was appointed Attorney-General of the State. This office he resigned upon receiving, in June, 1831, an invitation to enter the Cabinet of President Jackson as Attorney-General of the United States. At this time he argued *McLanahan* v. *The Universal Insurance Company*,[6] a question of marine insurance; *Van Ness* v. *The Mayor of the City of Washington*,[7] and the cases of *Tiernan et al.* v. *Jackson*, *The Patapsco Insurance Co.* v. *Southgate*, and *Shepherd* v. *Taylor*.[8] His manner and

[1] 10 Wheaton, 473 (1825).

[2] 11 *Ibid.*, 59 (1826).

[3] *Ibid.*, 134 (1826).

[4] 12 *Ibid.*, 419 (1827).

[5] Wheaton, 460 (1827).

[6] 1 Peters, 170 (1828).

[7] 4 *Ibid.*, 232 (1830).

[8] 5 *Ibid.*, 580, 604, 675 (1831).

style are described as impressive, logical, clear, calm, argumentative, simple and unostentatious, addressed to the reason and not to the passions. Seven other cases were argued by him before he ascended the bench, among which was the leading case of *Barron* v. *The City of Baltimore.*[1]

As Attorney-General, Mr. Taney bore a. prominent part in the Nullification controversy, the question of the re-chartering of the United States Bank and the removal of the deposits. From the beginning he was a decided and earnest opponent of the Bank, and co-operated heartily with the President in his system of prompt and vigorous action against that institution, so much so indeed, as to call forth the protests and the censure of a powerful majority in the Senate of the United States, headed by Webster and Clay. When Mr. Duane, then Secretary of the Treasury, after refusing to remove the deposits at the dictation of the President, refused to resign his office, he was summarily removed, and Mr. Taney was invited to take his place. Although reluctant to exchange his professional position for one purely political, he felt called upon to accept what he deemed to be the post of duty, and shortly after his entry signed the famous order for the removal of the deposits from the Bank ; or, more correctly speaking, directed the collectors of revenue to cease making deposits in the Bank, leaving the amount actually on deposit to be drawn out at intervals, and in different sums, according to the course of the government disbursements. In the following December, as Secretary of the Treasury, he communicated his reasons for the removal of the deposits, but at the instance of Mr. Clay a resolution of censure upon the action of the President was adopted, as well as a declaration that the reasons assigned by the Secretary were " unsatisfactory

[1] 7 Peters, 243 (1833).

and insufficient." At the same time his nomination was rejected, and he thereupon placed his resignation in the hands of the President, and returned to Baltimore. In the following January Mr. Justice Duvall resigned his office in consequence of extreme deafness, due to the infirmities of age, and the name of Mr. Taney was sent to the Senate to supply the vacancy. It is known that Chief Justice Marshall favored his appointment, but the Senatorial opposition was so strong that it failed of confirmation; a vote of indefinite postponement being considered as equivalent to a rejection. Thus matters stood, when in the following summer Chief Justice Marshall died. The complexion of the Senate having changed in the meantime, upon the 28th of December, 1835, President Jackson sent in the name of Mr. Taney for the office of Chief Justice of the Supreme Court, and the name of Philip P. Barbour, of Virginia, for the office of Associate Justice. Mr. Clay again labored to defeat the nomination, and made a bitter assault upon Mr. Taney, but many years afterwards frankly apologized for it, and stated that he sincerely regretted the occurrence. He went even further, and called him a fit successor of Marshall. The commissions of Taney and Barbour were dated March 15, 1836.

Philip P. Barbour was of Scottish descent, his great-grandfather having immigrated to this country, and been one of the first settlers in the territory lying between the base of the Blue Ridge and the Southwest mountains, in the State of Virginia. His father, Thomas Barbour, was a man of inherited wealth and a member of the old House of Burgesses, representing the County of Orange. He was one of the Signers, in 1769, of the "Non-Importation Agreement," and was subsequently elected to the Legislature. His character was highly spoken of by Richard Henry Lee, who, in a letter to his brother, declared that he was glad that Thomas Barbour was in our State councils, for he was a truly intelligent and patriotic man. On his mother's side Mr. Barbour was related to the distinguished Judge Edmund Pendleton, who had been thought of at one time by Washington as an appointee for the Supreme Court. Philip Pendleton Barbour was born on the 25th of May, 1783, but owing to disasters which overtook his father, did not receive the liberal education which his talents and early promise would have justified. He was, however, sent to school, where he exhibited great aptitude for the acquisition of languages, and became remarkable for his mastery of Greek and Roman literature. During the early part of 1800 he studied law, but in October determined to visit Kentucky, where he began the practice of his profession. A short time after, yielding to the persuasions of friends, he returned to Virginia, and having borrowed the necessary funds, spent one session at William and Mary College. He subsequently renewed the practice of the law and applied himself unceasingly to his profession. In 1812 he was elected to the Assembly, where he continued two sessions. In 1814 he was sent to Congress and served until 1825. For many years he acted as Chairman of the Naval and Judiciary Committees, and in 1821 was chosen Speaker. So conspicuous had he become for legal knowledge, that in 1825 he was offered the professorship of Law in the University of Virginia, and was pressed by Mr. Jefferson to accept it. He refused this station, however, and was appointed a Judge of the General Court of Virginia. Two years afterwards he resigned his seat upon the bench, and was re-elected without opposition to Congress. In 1829 he served with Madison in the Convention called to amend the Constitution of his State and presided over the deliberations of the Convention in a manner which is spoken of in the highest terms.

In 1830 he accepted the position of District Judge for the Eastern District of Virginia, declining the Chancellorship and also the post of Attorney-General. He also refused nominations for a seat in the Court of Appeals, the Gubernatorial chair and the Senate of the United States. As a Federal Judge he won new distinction, and was called, in 1836, to serve in the Supreme Court of the United States. While at the Bar, he had argued before that tribunal, the celebrated case of *Cohens* v. *The State of Virginia*, involving the question of the appellate power of the Supreme Court over State tribunals. His argument, although unsuccessful, is deserving of the closest attention, inasmuch as it is characterized by great subtlety and a display of analytical power. He contended that the true construction of the Constitution limited the appellate power of the Supreme Court of the United States to a revision of the judgments of Federal Courts alone, and that although a Federal question was directly involved in the case under argument, yet inasmuch as the suit had been brought in a State court, and the defendant had not exercised his right of removal into the Federal Courts, that no question appeared upon the record of which the Supreme Court could take cognizance.

His career as an Associate Justice was brief, but his judgments sustained his reputation, and have elicited great respect. He died suddenly of heart disease on the 24th of February, 1841.

Under the Act of March 3d, 1837,[1] the number of Justices of the Supreme Court was increased to nine. Two nominations were made. William Smith, of Alabama, was commissioned upon the 8th of March, 1837, but declined the position, owing, doubtless, to his advanced years. Mr. Smith was a

[1] 5 United States Statutes at Large, Vol. II, p. 176, Chap. 34.

North Carolinian by birth, and had served as a member of Congress, and as United States Senator from South Carolina for an unexpired term, but was defeated for re-election by Robert Y. Hayne because of his opposition to the views of Mr. Calhoun.

The second nomination was that of John Catron, of Tennessee, who was commissioned upon the same day as Mr. Smith and duly accepted. He was born in Wythe County, Virginia, according to some authorities, and, according to others, in Pennsylvania, in the year 1786. He received a common school education, and in 1812 began the study of law in Kentucky, where he removed at an early age. He had taken an active part in the campaign of New Orleans under General Jackson, and in 1815 was admitted to the bar, after four years of study, in which he devoted to his work sixteen hours a day. Shortly after his admission he became State Attorney for his Circuit, and upon settling in Nashville, in the year 1818, attained high rank as a Chancery lawyer. He was chosen Judge of the Supreme Court of Tennessee in September, 1824, and served as Chief Justice in the same Court from 1830 to 1836, when he was retired under the provisions of the new Constitution of the State. He owed his appointment to his highest judicial station to the friendship of President Van Buren, who had been attracted by his great knowledge of the laws applicable to land titles, a branch of unusual importance in the portion of the Union which he represented. His power of juridical analysis was remarkable, and he sought in all cases to weigh and examine every authority cited by counsel, and accepted such only as seemed to be founded upon principle. Although himself a noted duellist, he exerted himself to the utmost to suppress the practice of duelling. He also became known for his efforts in enforcing the statutes of limitations in real estate actions. Although a

Democrat in politics, in 1860 and 1861 he vehemently opposed Secession, exerting his influence with members of Congress and others to prevent war. Owing to his Union sentiments he was driven from his native State, but, in 1862, returned to his Circuit, then the eighth, feeling that it was important that the judicial authority of the Union should be maintained. He had arranged for a special term of the Circuit Court to be held in the city of St. Louis, when he found himself penned within the rebel lines in Tennessee, and informed the District judge in Missouri that if he could effect his escape he would be present. This he accomplished, and boldly declared from the bench his approbation of all measures that had been adopted to vindicate the authority of the United States. Upon returning to Nashville, he was warned to leave the city, and, responding to his wife's entreaties and the promptings of loyalty, yielded to what he deemed to be a duty. He died in 1864, at the age of four-score years, after a life of usefulness and distinction. It was the testimony of his brethren of the Bench that, in the learning of the Common Law and of Equity Jurisprudence, and especially in its application to questions of real property, he had few equals and hardly a superior. He was distinguished by strong, practical, good sense, firmness of will and honesty of purpose. He was candid, patient and impartial.

Upon the declinature of William Smith, the office of Associate Justice was conferred upon John McKinley, of Alabama, who was commissioned in the recess April 22, 1837, and re-commissioned upon confirmation, September 25 of the same year. He was a native of Culpepper County, Virginia, where he was born upon the 1st of May, 1780. Removing to Kentucky, and subsequently to Alabama, he studied law, and became prominent at the Bar of Huntsville, where he soon acquired an influence in politics, which extended over the entire State, being chosen a member of the House of Representatives, and afterwards a member of the United States Senate, in place of Henry Chambers (deceased), in which body he served from 1826 until March 3, 1831, as a Jeffersonian Democrat. Having removed to Florence during his term, he was, on its conclusion, elected from the latter place a member of the 23rd Congress, and served continuously until 1835, when he was again sent to the Senate of the United States, from which he was transferred by President Van Buren to the Supreme Court. His death occurred in 1852. Although little known, even to the profession, he was described by Mr. Crittenden, then Attorney-General of the United States, as a candid, impartial and righteous judge, simple and unaffected in manners, bearing his honors meekly, without ostentation or presumption, shrinking from no responsibility and fearless in the performance of duty, while by Chief Justice Taney he was pronounced "a sound lawyer, faithful and assiduous in the discharge of his duties while his health was sufficient to undergo the labor. He was frank and firm in his social intercourse, as well as in the discharge of his judicial duties, and no man could be more free from guile or more honestly endeavor to fulfill the obligations which his office imposed on him."

Peter V. Daniel, of Virginia, was commissioned as Associate Justice, upon the 3d of March, 1841, upon the death of Justice Barbour. He was a native of Stafford County, Virginia, where he was born in 1785. He received from the ample means of his father the benefits of instruction by a private tutor, and was subsequently graduated from Princeton, in 1805. He read law under the direction of Edmund Randolph, the first Attorney-General of the United States, whose youngest daughter he afterwards married. In 1809 he became a member of the Legislature, a year after his admission to the Bar. He also served as a member of the Privy Council until the adoption of the new Constitution, in 1830. The office of Attorney-General of the United States, vacated by the appointment of Mr. Taney to the Treasury Department, was tendered to him by President Jackson, but he declined the post, and it was conferred upon Mr. Benjamin F. Butler, of New York. Upon the transfer of Justice Barbour from the District Judgeship to the Supreme Bench, Mr. Daniel became his successor, and upon the death of Justice Barbour succeeded to the vacancy thus created, holding the position until his death, May 31, 1860. He wielded the pen of a ready writer, was a man of cultivated literary taste, and retained through life his familiarity with the classics, quoting Latin freely in his opinions. He was resolutely opposed to all extensions of national power and jurisdiction, and with Mr. Justice Woodbury dissented from the opinion of the Court in *Waring* v. *Clark*, extending the admiralty jurisdiction above tide-water upon the Mississippi, his dissent being marked by a vigorous course of reasoning and a profound knowledge of common law decisions, by which he sought to restrict the admiralty jurisdiction. His views were marked by a certain degree of eccentricity, and do not seem to have been shared by other members of the Court. They appear with particular prominence in the Passenger Cases and the License Cases, reported by Howard. So thoroughly infused was he with the doctrine of State sovereignty in its old sense, and so determined to magnify the State, that his conception of the grant to Congress of power to regulate interstate and foreign commerce was neither large nor comprehensive. He contributed but little to the development of the law and the

J. McKinley

value of his opinions is mainly historical. The number of his dissenting opinions is remarkable, and even where he concurred in the judgment pronounced, he rarely acquiesced in the reasons assigned, preferring to state them in his own way.

Such were the Associates who surrounded Chief Justice Taney during the early part of his judicial career, and the effect of the radical change which had been made in the composition of the Bench was immediately noticeable in the first cases which came on for argument.

At the time of the death of Chief Justice Marshall three cases of unusual interest and importance were pending, involving the question of the Constitutionality of State laws. They had all been argued, and, as Judge Story intimates, although he and Marshall had been of the opinion that in each case the law criticized was unconstitutional, yet a marked difference of opinion among the Judges having arisen, the cases were assigned for re-argument. The re-argument took place before Chief Justice Taney and Mr. Justice Barbour, who appeared at the same time upon the Bench, and they, in association with Justices Thompson, McLean and Baldwin, constituted a majority of the Court whose judgment was exactly opposite in its effect to the line of precedents established during Marshall's long term of service.

The first case was that of *The Mayor of the City of New York* v. *Miln.*[1] The State of New York had, by Act of Assembly, required the master of every vessel arriving in the port of New York to report in writing respecting his passengers within twenty-four hours after arrival, and imposed a penalty upon non-performance of this duty. It was argued

---

[1] 11 Peters, 102 (1837).

that the case was governed by the decisions in *Gibbons* v. *Ogden* and *Brown* v. *The State of Maryland*, and that the statute was obnoxious to the Constitutional provision vesting in Congress the power to regulate commerce among the several States. It was held, however, by the majority of the Court, in an opinion delivered by Mr. Justice Barbour, that the statute did not amount to a regulation of commerce, but was a mere regulation of police, and was, therefore, clearly within the exercise of a power which rightfully belonged to a State. It was shown that in the first case the theatre on which the law operated was navigable water over which the power to regulate commerce extended; but in the case before the Court it was the territory of New York, over which the State had an undisputed jurisdiction for every purpose of internal regulation; besides, in the one case, the subject matter was a vessel; in the other, persons. "Persons," said the Court, "are not the subjects of commerce, and not being imported goods, the reason founded upon the construction of power given to Congress to regulate commerce, and prohibiting States from imposing a duty, does not apply."[1] Besides, there was no analogy between a tax imposed upon the sale of imported goods and the exercise of rights over persons

---

[1] This doctrine was controverted by the cases of Smith *v.* Turner and Norris *v.* City of Boston, 7 Howard, 283 (1849), in which it was determined, by a vote of five judges to four, that a State law imposing taxes upon the masters of vessels bringing passengers and immigrants into the ports of such States was contrary to the Constitution and void, the term "commerce" comprehending the intercourse of persons or passengers. The opinion of Mr. Justice Wayne is unusually interesting, and gives an insight into the inside history of the discussion in the consultation room. See also Cooley *v.* The Board of Port Wardens of Philadelphia, 12 Howard, 300 (1851), in which it is held that the grant of power to Congress does not deprive the States of the power to legislate on the subject of police and regulate pilotage fees and penalties for neglect or violation. It is interesting to note that in all these cases the opinion of the Court was far from being unanimous.

within the jurisdiction of the State. Justice Story dissented absolutely. Justice Thompson, while conceding the supremacy of an Act of Congress, contended that the State law was valid until Congress intervened by an Act with which the State law conflicted, and as no Act of Congress existed, no such conflict arose.

A second departure from the principles of Constitutional interpretation applied by Chief Justice Marshall is noticeable in the case of *Briscoe* v. *Bank of the Commonwealth of Kentucky*,[1] and the conclusion reached is in direct conflict with the case of *Craig* v. *State of Missouri*.[2] The question arose as to the meaning of the Constitutional prohibition upon the States against emitting bills of credit, and it was held, in an opinion by Justice McLean, that inasmuch as there was no limitation in the Constitution of the United States upon the power of a State to incorporate a Bank, such a power was incident to sovereignty, and inasmuch as the bills issued by the Bank were not bills of credit within the meaning of the Constitution,—that is, issued by a State, on the faith of the State, and designed to circulate as money,—the State law was a valid exercise of authority, and was therefore sustained. Justice Story again dissented, in terms of lament over the death of Marshall.

The third instance presented a striking contrast with the Dartmouth College case and Fletcher *v.* Peck in the almost equally celebrated case of *The Charles River Bridge* v. *The Warren Bridge*.[3] It is the first expression of opinion upon a Constitutional question by Chief Justice Taney, and is the first defeat sustained by Daniel Webster as counsel upon a question of Constitutional law.

[1] 11 Peters, 257 (1837).   [2] 4 Peters, 410 (1830).
[3] 11 Peters, 420 (1837).

20

As far back as 1650 there had been granted to Harvard College by the Legislature of the province of Massachusetts power to dispose of the ferry from Charlestown to Boston over the Charles River. The College received the profits from the ferry until 1785, when a Company was duly incorporated, under an Act of the Legislature, to build a bridge in place of the ferry and to receive tolls, the Company agreeing to pay to the College an annual rental which was ultimately to cease, and thereupon the bridge was to become the property of the State. The bridge was built and the rights of the College had still a considerable period to run when, in the year 1828, the Legislature incorporated another Company known as the Warren Bridge Company with power to erect a second structure over the same river between the same points in close proximity to the original bridge, with power to take tolls and ultimately to become free. The older corporation sought by injunction to restrain the exercise of the franchises of the younger company, and the decision of the State Court being in favor of the validity of the law conferring the privileges upon the defendants, the case was removed to the Supreme Court of the United States upon the ground that the State had exceeded her powers under the Constitution and had passed an act impairing the obligations of a contract. Much stress was laid in the argument upon the decisions of Chief Justice Marshall's time, and particularly the cases above referred to; but the decision of the Court sustained the sovereignty of the State in the exercise of its rights even though they might incidentally impair the value of a previous charter or contract. Chief Justice Taney based his opinion upon the broad principle that public grants were to be construed strictly, and that nothing passed by implication. Inasmuch as there was no express grant of an exclusive privilege to the plaintiffs in error, an implied contract to that effect could not be inferred. "We cannot," said he, "deal thus with the rights reserved to the States and by legal intendments and mere technical reasoning take away from them any portion of that power over their own internal police and improvement which is so necessary to their well-being and prosperity." No implied contract, he argued, could be created between the State and the Company from the very nature of the instrument in which the Legislature took the pains to use words which disavowed any intention on the part of the State to make such a contract; and in vindicating the reasons of public policy which lay at the basis of his judgment, he said:

"If this Court should establish the principles now contended for, what is to become of the numerous railroads established on the same line of travel with turnpike companies, and which have rendered the franchises of the turnpike corporations of no value? Let it once be understood that such charters carry with them these implied contracts, and give this unknown and undefined property in a line of travelling, and you will soon find the old turnpike corporations awakening from their sleep, and calling upon this Court to put down the improvements which have taken their place. The millions of property which have been invested in railroads and canals, upon lines of travel which had been before occupied by turnpike corporations, will be put in jeopardy. We shall be thrown back to the improvements of the last century, and obliged to stand still until the claims of the old turnpike corporations, shall be satisfied, and they shall consent to permit these States to avail themselves of the lights of modern science, and to partake of the benefit of those improvements which are now adding to the wealth and prosperity, and the convenience and comfort, of every other part of the civilized world."

The dissenting opinion of Mr. Justice Story, concurred in by Mr. Justice Thompson, is one of the most able and elaborate of his efforts. So despondent did he become of the fate of Federal supremacy that he wrote to Mr. Justice McLean:

"There will not I fear ever in our day be any case in which a law of a State or Act of Congress will be declared unconstitutional; for the old Constitutional doctrines are fast fading away, and a change has come over the public mind from which I augur little good." And even Chancellor Kent in a letter to Judge Story wrote: "I have lost my confidence and hopes in the Constitutional guardianship and protection of the Supreme Court."[1]

An able criticism of the decision of the majority of the Court appeared in the public prints, in which the writer, alluding to the three cases first considered, says: "In reviewing these decisions we perceive at once an altered tone and a narrower spirit, not only in Chief Justice Taney, but even in some of the old associates of Marshall, when they handle Constitutional questions. The change is so great and so ominous that a gathering gloom is cast over the future. We seem to have sunk the Constitution below the horizon, to have lost the light of the sun, and to hold on our way *per incertam lunam sub luce maligna.*"

At this distance of time it is possible to form an unprejudiced judgment of the matter, and even the most ardent advocate of Federal supremacy can scarcely regret the decision of the Court in the Bridge case. It has enabled the States to push forward the great improvements by which the surface of the earth has been subjected to the dominion of man. The principle of the Dartmouth College Case was limited in its application before it had been carried to an extreme which would have left the State governments in possession of little more than the shell of legislative power. All the essential attributes of State sovereignty would have been parcelled out without the

---

[1] Life and Letters of Story, Edited by W. W. Story, Vol. II, p. 270. See also elaborate commentary in the "New York Review," (April, 1838.) Vol. II, p. 372.

possibility of reclamation, through recklessness or something worse, among a crowd of applicants for monopolistic privileges.[1]

Cases of great variety now presented themselves, displaying in a marked manner the ability and professional training of the Court. In *United States* v. *Laub*,[2] in an action on a treasury transcript, where the defendant's vouchers had been destroyed by fire, a nice question of evidence was discussed, and the production of secondary proof permitted; in *McKinney* v. *Carroll*,[3] it was held that to give the Supreme Court of the United States jurisdiction under the 25th section of the Judiciary Act, in a case brought from the highest Court of a State, it must be apparent in the record that the State Court did decide in favor of the validity of a statute of the State, the Constitutionality of which was brought into question; but when the decision of a State Court was against the validity of a State statute, as contrary to the Constitution, a writ of error would not lie.[4] In *United States* v. *Coombs*,[5] the Court dealt with an indictment for stealing merchandise belonging to a wrecked ship, the goods being above high water mark, and held that such an act could be punished, even though done on land, because the offence tended to interfere with, obstruct and prevent commerce and navigation, which were placed by the Constitution under the protection of Congress.

---

[1] See "Constitutional Development in the United States as influenced by Chief Justice Taney," by George W. Biddle, Esq., of Philadelphia. "Constitutional History as seen in American Law," p. 133.

[2] 12 Peters, 1 (1838). See also Williams *v.* United States, 1 Howard, 290 (1843).

[3] 12 Peters, 66 (1838).

[4] Commonwealth Bank of Kentucky *v.* Griffith *et al.*, 14 Peters, 56 (1840). So also Walker *v.* Taylor *et al.* 5 Howard, 65 (1847); Commercial Bank of Cincinnati *v.* Buckingham's Executors, *Ibid.*, 317 (1847).

[5] 12 Peters, 72 (1838).

In the *Mayor, etc., of Georgetown* v. *The Alexandria Canal Co., et al.*[1] they declined to prevent, by injunction, the construction of an aqueduct across the Potomac River, and in *Garcia* v. *Lee,*[2] a case arising under a Spanish grant, held that a boundary line determined on as the true one by the political departments of the government must be also recognized as the true one by the judicial department.

A similar principle was announced in *Williams* v. *The Suffolk Insurance Company,*[3] where it was held that when the executive branch of the Government, which is charged with the foreign relations of the United States, shall, in its correspondence with a foreign nation, assume a fact in regard to the sovereignty of any country, it is conclusive on the judicial department.

A case now arose involving an interesting political question, and attracting public attention. Amos Kendall, the Postmaster General, had been directed by an Act of Congress to credit certain mail contractors with the amount of a sum of money awarded by the Solicitor of the Treasury as due to them under contracts with the Government. The Postmaster General refused to sanction the award, on the ground that the Solicitor had exceeded his authority. The mail contractors applied to the Circuit Court for a mandamus to compel the Postmaster General to pay them the award. This being granted, the cause was brought up on writ of error.[4] It was contended that the proceedings were intended to enforce the performance of an official duty and were a direct infringement on the Executive department; that the Postmaster General was alone subject to the direction and control of the President. These propositions were denied by the Court, the Chief Justice and

---

[1] 12 Peters, 91 (1838).   [2] *Ibid.*, 511 (1838).   [3] 13 Peters, 415 (1839).
[4] Kendall *v.* The United States, 12 Peters, 524 (1838).

Justices Barbour and Catron dissenting. It was held that the mandamus did not seek to direct or control the discharge of an official duty, but to enforce the performance of a ministerial act, which neither the Postmaster General nor the President had any authority to deny or control. The President was not invested with a dispensing power; such a doctrine could not be tolerated; it would clothe the President with a power to control the legislation of Congress, and paralyze the administration of justice. Such a construction of the Constitution would be novel and entirely inadmissible. In interesting contrast with this case is that of Susan Decatur, the widow of Captain Stephen Decatur, against James K. Paulding, the Secretary of the Navy,[1] in which an application for a mandamus, commanding the Secretary to pay a pension and arrearages, had been refused by the Circuit Court of the District of Columbia. In sustaining the judgment the Court, through the Chief Justice, held that as it was a matter in which the Secretary must exercise a discretion, and was not a mere ministerial act, the Court could not guide or control him in the performance of his official duties. While still later, in *Kendall* v. *Stokes*,[2] where a suit had been brought against the Postmaster General for damages in consequence of acts which the Court in its first decision had held to be official and not ministerial, the principle was asserted that a public officer acting from a sense of duty, in a matter where he was required to exercise discretion, could not be held liable to an action for an error of judgment.

So too, in *Ex parte Hennen*,[3] it was held that the Supreme Court could have no control over the appointment or removal of a clerk of the District Court, or entertain any inquiry into

[1]Decatur *v.* Paulding, 14 Peters, 497 (1840).   [3]3 Howard, 87 (1845).
[2]13 Peters, 230 (1839).

the grounds of the removal. "If the judge of the District Court be chargeable with any abuse of power the Supreme Court is not the tribunal to which he is amenable."

In all of these cases it is manifest that the Court had no disposition to encroach upon the proper jurisdiction of other departments of the government, or other tribunals.

In *McElmoyle* v. *Cohen*[1] it was held that though the judgment of a Court in one State is conclusive in another State upon the merits, yet it does not carry with it sufficient efficacy to be enforced by execution. It must be reduced to a new judgment in the new forum, and is subject to all laws relating to the remedy provided there. Hence the plea of the Statute of Limitations in an action instituted in one State on a judgment obtained in another is a plea to the remedy, and the *lex fori* must prevail.

About this time a controversy arose between the States of Rhode Island and Massachusetts[2] relative to the boundary line between them, in which Massachusetts was finally successful. Although the Court, through Mr. Justice Baldwin, sustained its jurisdiction to hear and determine a controversy between States, on the ground that the suit was brought to try a right of property in the soil and other rights properly the subject of judicial cognizance, yet the Chief Justice dissented from this view, and contended that this power does not extend to a suit brought to determine political rights, sovereignty and jurisdiction being questions outside of the pale of judicial authority, and not, therefore, within the grant of judicial power contained in the Constitution.

In 1839 the case of the *Bank of Augusta* v. *Earle*,[3] and

[1] 13 Peters, 312 (1839).
[2] The State of Rhode Island *v.* The State of Massachusetts, 12 Peters, 657 (1838); *Ibid.*, 4 Howard, 591 (1846).   [3] 13 Peters, 519 (1839).

two other cases depending upon the same principle,[1] came before the Court, presenting the sovereignty of the States in a new aspect,—in relation to their authority to create corporations, and the rights and powers of the corporations of one State to act within the territorial jurisdiction of another. It was clear that the law of comity which prevails between independent nations, and which entitles the corporations created by one sovereignty to make contracts in another and to sue in its Courts, prevailed among the States of the Union. "The States of the Union," said the Chief Justice, "are sovereign States, and the history of the past and the events which are daily occurring furnish the strongest evidence that they have conducted towards each other the laws of comity in their fullest extent." In the *Tombigbee Railroad Company* v. *Kneeland*,[2] it was held, in confirmation of this principle, that a contract made in Alabama by the agents of a corporation created by the laws of Mississippi was valid and must be sustained.

The status of a corporation was further considered in *The Commercial and Railroad Bank of Vicksburg* v. *Slocumb*,[3] where Mr. Justice Barbour, in affirming *Strawbridge* v. *Curtiss*[4] and *Bank of the United States* v. *Deveaux*,[5] held that, while a corporation aggregate was not a citizen as such, and therefore could not sue in the Courts of the United States as such, yet the Court would look beyond the mere corporate character to the individuals of whom it was composed, and if they were citizens of a different State from the party sued, they were competent to sue in the Federal Courts. But all

---

[1] Bank of the U. S. *v.* Primrose, 13 Peters, 519 (1839). Railroad Co. *v.* Earle, *Ibid.* 519 (1839).   [2] 4 Howard, 16 (1846).
[3] 14 Peters, 60 (1840). See also Irvine *v.* Lowry, *Ibid.* 293 (1840).
[4] 3 Cranch, 267 (1806).   [5] 5 Cranch, 61 (1809).

the corporators must be citizens of a different State from the party sued.

But in the case of the *Louisville, Cincinnati and Charleston R. R. Co.* v. *Letson*,[1] the important principle was established that a corporation is to be deemed an inhabitant of the State creating it, capable of being treated as a citizen for all the purposes of suing and being sued.

The doctrine was expanded from time to time[2] until the Court reached the point, which has proved so satisfactory in practice, that a naked averment that a certain company was a citizen of a State was sufficient to give jurisdiction to the Federal Courts, because the company was incorporated by a public statute of the State which the Court was bound to notice judicially.[3] And still later it was determined that a suit by or against a corporation in its corporate name must be presumed to be a suit by or against citizens of the State which created it, and no averment or evidence to the contrary is admissible for the purpose of withdrawing the suit from the Federal jurisdiction.[4]

The powers of a corporation beyond the territorial limits of the sovereignty which created it were still further considered in *Runyan* v. *The Lessee of Coster et al.*[5] A New York corporation was held to be capable of holding lands in the State of Pennsylvania subject to be divested by proceedings in due course of law, instituted by the Commonwealth alone and for its own use. Every power which a corporation exercises in another State depends for its validity upon the laws of the sov-

---

[1] 2 Howard, 497 (1844).
[2] Railroad Co. *v.* Kneeland, 4 Howard, 16 (1846).
[3] Covington Drawbridge Co. *v.* Shepherd, 20 Howard, 227 (1857).
[4] Ohio & Mississippi R. R. Co. *v.* Wheeler, 1 Black, 286 (1861).
[5] 14 Peters, 122 (1840).

ereignty in which it is exercised; and a corporation can make
no valid contract without the sanction, express or implied, of
such sovereignty unless a case should be presented in which
the right claimed should appear to be secured by the Constitution of the United States.

The pendulum was not permitted, however, to swing too
far in any one direction. An illustration of the limited
powers of the States is presented in *Suydam and Boyd* v.
Broadnax and Newton,[1] where an act of insolvency, executed
under the authority of the State of Alabama, was held to be
no bar to a recovery in an action brought in the Circuit Court
of the United States for the Alabama District, upon a contract made in New York. No State, however sovereign, could
deny the right to recover upon contracts made outside of its
own limits. Such contracts would still exist and continue to
be enforceable according to the *lex loci contractus.*

A few years later the case of *Bronson* v. *Kinzie*,[2] raised
the question of the legality of a law of the State of Illinois
passed subsequent to a mortgage contract providing that the
equitable estate of a mortgagor should not be extinguished
for twelve months after a sale under a decree of chancery
and that there should be no sale unless two-thirds of the
amount at which the property had been valued by appraisers
should be bid therefor. The law was held to be null and
void on the ground that it violated a Constitutional provision prohibiting the passage of any law impairing the obligation of a contract. From this judgment Mr. Justice Mc-
Lean dissented, drawing the somewhat subtle distinction that
the State law acted upon the remedy and not upon the contract.

This case was followed and confirmed within a year in

---

[1] 14 Peters, 67 (1840).   [2] 1 Howard, 311 (1843).

McCracken v. *Hayward.*[1]   And in two cases, decided in 1848, a State law, prohibiting banks, previously empowered by charter, from transferring bills and notes, was held to be unconstitutional, because it impaired the obligation of a contract.[2]

A singular case now arose involving the relations to each other of the different counties constituting the District of Columbia, and it was held that they did not occupy the relation borne by the States of the Union to each other. As they constitute together one territory, united under one territorial government, the residents of the county of Alexandria are not *beyond seas* in relation to the county of Washington, even though on a proper construction of the Maryland statute of limitations the words "beyond seas" are equivalent to the words *without the jurisdiction of the State.*[3]

In *The United States* v. *Morris,*[4] a question arose upon an indictment for a violation of an act prohibiting the slave trade, and the Court held that though in expounding a penal statute, it will not be extended beyond the plain meaning of its words, yet the evident intention ought not to be defeated by a forced or over-strict construction. Hence it was not necessary to constitute the offence described in the Act of Congress that there should have been an actual transportation or carrying of slaves in a vessel of the United States in which the prisoner served; it was sufficient if the vessel were engaged and under contract for the purpose.

The session of 1841 was memorable for the discussion and decision of several cases of unusual importance and magnitude. Among them was the Florida Land Claim, reported

---

[1] 2 Howard, 608 (1844).

[2] Planters' Bank of Mississippi *v.* Sharp *et al.*; Baldwin *et al. v.* Payne *et al.,* 6 Howard, 301 (1848).

[3] Bank of Alexandria *v.* Dyer, 14 Peters, 141 (1840). [4] 14 Peters, 464 (1840).

under the title of *Mitchel* v. *The United States*,[1] involving the title to the Fortress of St. Mark, the most ancient structure in America, antedating by seven years the Massacre of St. Bartholomew. Another is the case of the *Amistad*,[2] in which free negroes, who had been kidnapped in violation of the laws of Spain denouncing the slave trade as a heinous offence, were restored to freedom through the efforts of the venerable ex-President, John Quincy Adams, who, after an absence of nearly forty years from the bar, re-appeared as one of the counsel in behalf of the African appellees. The case of *Groves* v. *Slaughter*,[3] was one on the determination of which more than $3,000,000 depended, at that time a sum of much magnitude, but it is chiefly interesting as involving a discussion whether the grant of power to Congress to regulate commerce among the States vests in Congress power to regulate the traffic in slaves among the different States, and if so, whether it does not carry with it an implied prohibition on the States from making any regulations on the subject. The Constitution of Mississippi, adopted in 1832, had prohibited the introduction of slaves into that State after May 1, 1833 as merchandize or for sale. No law to enforce this constitutional provision was passed until 1837. In 1835, however, a non-resident had imported certain slaves for sale, and defence was taken to a note given by the purchaser in payment upon the ground that it was void, as in violation of the Constitutional provision. It was held that the Constitution of the State was not self-enforcing, and as the Act carrying its provisions into effect was subsequent in date to the note, that the sale was valid, and that recovery could be had. Justices Story and McKinley dis-

---

[1] 15 Peters, 52 (1841).   [2] 15 Peters, 518 (1841).
[3] 15 Peters, 449 (1841). See the able and eloquent argument of Robert J. Walker, of Mississippi, printed in the Appendix to 15th Peters.

sented.   Chief Justice Taney and Mr. Justice McLean believed that the power over slavery belonged exclusively to the States, that it was local in its character, and that the action of the State upon the subject could not be controlled by Congress either by its power to regulate commerce, or by virtue of any other power conferred by the Constitution.   Justices Story, Thompson, Wayne and McKinley were of the opinion that the provision for the regulation of commerce did not interfere with the provision of the Constitution of Mississippi.

Another phase of the same question arose in *Rowan et al.* v. *Runnels*.[1]   The Constitution of Mississippi went into operation May 1, 1833, and on the 13th of May of that year, an act was passed to give effect to its provisions.   The Court adhered to the construction of the Constitution stated in Groves *v.* Slaughter, and enforced contracts made between the days mentioned, although the Courts of Mississippi had, since that decision declared such contracts to be void.   "We can hardly be required," said the Chief Justice, "by any comity or respect for the State courts to surrender our judgment to decisions since made in the State, and declare contracts to be void which upon full consideration we have pronounced to be valid.   Undoubtedly this court will always feel itself bound to respect the decisions of State Courts, and from the time they are made will regard them as conclusive in all cases upon the construction of their own Constitutions and laws.   But we ought not to give to them a retroactive effect, and allow them to render invalid contracts entered into with citizens of other States, which in the judgment of this Court were lawfully made."

Mr. Justice Daniel dissented, holding that the construc-

----

[1] 5 Howard, 134 (1847).   These cases were again affirmed in Sims *v.* Hundley, 6 Howard, 1 (1848).

tion of a State Constitution by the State tribunals was conclusive, and it was wholly immaterial when the decision was
made.

In the case of *Martin et al.* v. *The Lessee of Waddell*,[1] a
case brought up from New Jersey, and involving immense interests, the entire proprietary right of the State under the
grant of Charles II to the Duke of York, subsequently vested
in the East Jersey Proprietors, was elaborately traced, and applied to a proprietary grant of a certain portion of the bed
of the Raritan River and Bay, the grantee claiming an exclusive right of fishing for oysters.   It was held by the
Court that the navigable waters of New Jersey had passed
to the Duke of York and to the Proprietors, but they passed
as a part of the prerogatives and rights annexed to the
political powers conferred upon the Duke, and not as a private property, to be parceled out and sold to individuals;
that the right of fishery was a part of those prerogative
rights, and that after the period of the Revolution the prerogatives and regalities which had formerly belonged to the
crown became immediately and rightfully vested in the State,
and that, therefore, any exclusive right on the part of a citizen to fish in the navigable waters of New Jersey was declared to be unfounded.

About this time the case of *Swift* v. *Tyson*[2] came before
the Court, in form merely an action upon a bill of exchange
accepted in New York, instituted by the holder, a citizen of
the State of Maine, in the Circuit Court of New York, but
containing a fruitful germ which has expanded into a system
of general commercial jurisprudence, the establishment of
which has provoked much adverse comment and discussion,

[1] 16 Peters, 367 (1842).   [2] 16 Peters, 1 (1842).

both among writers and the State judges, it being asserted by one of them, and he not the least able of our jurists, that since "the unfortunate mis-step that was made in the opinion in *Swift* v. *Tyson*, the Courts of the United States have persisted in the recognition of a mythical commercial law, and have professed to decide so-called commercial questions by it, in entire disregard of the law of the State where the question arose." [1]

The acceptance and endorsement of the bill were admitted, and the defense was rested on an allegation that the bill had been received in payment of a pre-existing debt, and that the acceptance had been given for lands which the acceptor had purchased from the drawer of the bill to which the drawer had no title, and further that the quality of the lands had been misrepresented, and the purchaser imposed upon by the fraud of the drawer. The bill accepted had been received *bona fide* and before maturity. It was held in the lower court that the later decisions of the Supreme Court of New York had established that the receipt of a note in payment of a pre-existing debt, was not such a receipt in the usual course of trade as to give the endorsee any rights on the paper beyond those against the endorser; and it was contended that the Thirty-fourth section of the Judiciary Act of 1789, which declared "that the laws of the several States, except where the Constitution, treaties or statutes of the United States shall otherwise recognize or provide, shall be regarded as rules of decision in trials at common law in the Courts of the United States, in cases where they apply," forbade the Supreme Court from departing from the view taken by the State tribunal. It was ruled by Mr. Justice Story that the

---

[1] Mr. Justice Mitchell in Forepaugh *v.* R. R. Co., 128 Penna. St., 228 (1889.)

holder was not affected by equities between the original parties; that the Thirty-fourth section of the Judiciary Act had been uniformly limited in its application to State laws strictly local; that is to say, to the positive statutes of the State, and the construction thereof adopted by the local tribunals, and to rights and titles to things having a permanent locality, such as the rights and titles to real estate, and other matters immovable and intra-territorial in their nature and character, but that it does not extend to contracts and other instruments of a commercial nature, the true interpretation and effect whereof are to be sought not in the decisions of the local tribunals, but "in the general principles and doctrines of commercial jurisprudence." This language has become the foundation of the doctrine that even in suits where the Federal jurisdiction is invoked solely on the ground of the citizenship of the parties, and not because of any distinct Federal question, the Federal courts will decide the point of law involved according to their own view of general jurisprudence, although it lead to an absolute lack of recognition of precedents in the State courts in which the controversy arose.[1] It was some time, however, before so definite a result was reached. In 1845 the Court through Mr. Justice McLean applied this doctrine to the construction of a will, and said: "The mere construction of a will by a State Court does not, as the construction of a statute of the State, constitute a rule of decision for the Courts of the United States." From this Mr. Justice McKinley dissented in a powerful opinion in which he pointed out the probable consequences of the doctrine, the contests that would ensue, and the dangers to the

---

[1] See "American Law Review," Vol. VIII., 452, "Decisions of the Federal Courts on Questions of State Law," by W. M. Meigs, of Philadelphia. See also Hare on Constitutional Law, Vol. II, 1107, 1117, and Lecture 51 *passim*.

peace and harmony of the people of the United States. In this view Chief Justice Taney concurred.[1]

The most important of all the cases considered at this time was that of *Prigg* v. *Commonwealth of Pennsylvania*,[2] which afforded a final opportunity to Judge Story of declaring a State law unconstitutional. Although the judgment of the Court was concurred in by all except Justice McLean, it is to be remarked that the Chief Justice and his associates, Thompson, Baldwin and Daniel, dissented from the reasoning and principles laid down by Story, who was supported at all points by Wayne alone.

Prigg, a citizen of Maryland, had taken a fugitive slave by force from Pennsylvania, without the certificate required by the Act of Congress of 1793, and had carried her to the State of Maryland to her owner. For this act he had been indicted under a law of the State of Pennsylvania, passed for the purpose of giving effect to the provisions of the State Constitution relative to fugitives from labor, and to prevent kidnapping, which declared that the taking and carrying away of any negro or mulatto by force or violence from the State should be deemed a felony punishable by fine and imprisonment. The act also provided a mode for the rendition of fugitive slaves by the State authorities. The fugitive slave had been brought by virtue of this law before a Pennsylvania magistrate, who refused to take jurisdiction, and Prigg had thereupon of his own will carried her off to Maryland, acting under the authority of the owner. It was held that the Pennsylvania law was unconstitutional, because the Constitution of the United States, in providing that fugitives should

---

[1] Lane *v.* Vick, 3 Howard, 464 (1845). See *contra* the earlier cases of Jackson *v.* Chew, 12 Wheaton, 153 (1827), and Henderson *et ux. v.* Griffin, 5 Peters, 151 (1831).   [2] 16 Peters, 539 (1842).

be delivered up, placed the remedy exclusively in Congress, and the States were by implication prohibited from passing any law upon the subject, whether Congress had or had not legislated upon the question. The Chief Justice believed that the Constitution contained no words prohibiting the States from passing laws to enforce the right. While in express terms forbidden to make any regulation which could impair it, there the prohibition stopped, and he saw no reason, in the absence of any express prohibition, for establishing a different rule, where, by national compact, the right of property in slaves was recognized. Justices Thompson and Daniel concurred in the judgment of reversal, because Congress by the act of 1793 had exercised its Constitutional power, and as the State law conflicted with it, it was null and void. Justice McLean, in what has been regarded as his ablest opinion, contended that the State law was valid as an exercise of police power.

We find interesting fragments of a state of society that has perished, in *Williams* v. *Ash*,[1] a solemn adjudication that the bequest of freedom to a slave is a specific legacy, and in *Rhodes* v. *Bell*[2] that the purchase of a slave in one county in the District of Columbia and sale in another entitles him to freedom, and in *Adams* v. *Roberts*[3] where an ancient manumission deed was admitted in evidence on the trial of a petition for freedom by the child of the manumitted slave. In *Jones* v. *Van Zandt*[4] the question of what facts amounted to a "harboring" of a fugitive slave, was considered, and it was held that the fugitive slave law of 1793 was constitutional and not in conflict with the Ordinance for the government of the

---

[1] 1 Howard, 1 (1843).   [2] 2 Howard, 397 (1844).   [3] 2 Howard, 487 (1844).
[4] 5 Howard, 215 (1847).

Territory Northwest of the River Ohio. The Court refused to notice "the supposed inexpediency and invalidity of all laws recognizing slavery or any right of property in man. That," said Mr. Justice Woodbury, "is a political question, settled by each State for itself; and the Federal power over it is limited and regulated by the people of the States in the Constitution itself, as one of its sacred compromises, and which we possess no authority as a judicial body to modify or over-rule."

Passing from Constitutional questions to those cases which illustrate the boundless variety of topics discussed, we find the doctrine laid down by Lord Camden examined and confirmed: that a court of equity, which is never active in relief against conscience or public convenience, has always refused its aid to stale demands, where the party has slept upon his rights for a great length of time. Nothing but conscience, good faith, and reasonable diligence can call the court into activity. Where these are wanting, the court is passive and does nothing; laches and neglect are always discountenanced; and therefore, from the beginning of equity jurisdiction there was always a limitation of suits.[1]

In *Porterfield's Executors* v. *Clark's Heirs*,[2] a question arose under the Virginia statutes establishing a land office, and the boundaries of the territory appropriated to the Cherokees, as fixed by treaties, were historically examined by Mr. Justice Catron in one of those opinions discussing Western titles by which he justified his well established reputation as a master of one of the most intricate and perplexing systems of local real estate law.

In *Vidal et al.* v. *Girard's Executors*,[3] elaborately argued

---

[1] Bowman *et al.* v. Wathen *et al.*, 1 Howard, 189 (1843).
[2] 2 Howard, 77 (1844).   [3] 2 Howard, 127 (1844).

by Webster and General Walter Jones on the one side, and
by Horace Binney and John Sergeant on the other, the law
of public charities, of superstitious uses, and of the right of a
testator to control the direction of his gift were most exhaustively considered by Mr. Justice Story in an opinion replete
with interest. Mr. Binney won the most splendid of his professional triumphs, and obtained the crown which he wore with
so much modesty.[1] The testator, Stephen Girard, whose name
has since become, through the success of Binney, a synonym for
charity, had excluded all ecclesiastics, missionaries and ministers
of every sort from holding or exercising any station or duty in
the college he sought to found, or even visiting the same; and
had limited the instruction to be given to the scholars to pure
morality, general benevolence, a love of truth, sobriety and industry. These provisions were bitterly assailed by Webster,
who declared, in terms which show how little knowledge of
the future is vouchsafed even unto the wisest: "No good can
be looked for from this college. If Girard had desired to
bring trouble, and quarrel, and struggle upon the city, he
could have done it in no more effectual way. The plan is
unblessed in design and unwise in purpose. If the court
should set it aside, and I be instrumental in contributing to
that result, it will be the crowning mercy of my professional
life." To this the Court, through the lips of Story, replied:
"The testator does not say that Christianity shall not be

---

[1] It was during the evening of the day upon which Mr. Binney closed his triumphant argument, that President Tyler offered the place made vacant in the
Supreme Court by the death of Mr. Justice Baldwin, first to Mr. Sergeant, and then
to Mr. Binney. Both declined to accept it, each alleging that he was over sixty
years of age, and had determined to accept no public office. Each requested that
the place be offered to the other, and that the fact he had declined and his reasons
for doing so be kept secret from the other. "Seven Decades of the Union," by
Henry A. Wise, p. 219.

taught in the college. But only that no ecclesiastic of any sect shall hold or exercise any station or duty in the college. Suppose, instead of this, he had said that no person but a layman shall be an instructor or officer or visitor in the college, what legal objection could have been made to such a restriction? And yet the actual prohibition is in effect the same in substance. But it is asked: why are ecclesiastics excluded, if it is not because they are the stated and appropriate preachers of Christianity? The answer may be given in the very words of the testator. 'In making this restriction,' says he, 'I do not mean to cast any reflection upon any sect or person whatsoever. But as there is such a multitude of sects and such a diversity of opinion amongst them, I desire to keep the tender minds of the orphans, who are to derive advantage from this bequest, free from the excitement which clashing doctrines and sectarian controversy are so apt to produce.' . . . Looking to the objection, therefore, in a mere juridical view, which is the only one in which we are at liberty to consider it, we are satisfied that there is nothing in the devise establishing the college, or in the regulations and restrictions contained therein, which are inconsistent with the Christian religion, or are opposed to any known policy of the State of Pennsylvania."

The Myra Clark Gaines case, which came frequently before the Court, and with varying chances of success until it ripened into a victory for the claimant, attracted an extraordinary degree of public interest, not only on account of the large amount of property involved, but because of the romantic nature of the history upon which it turned. The character of the case can be best summarized in the words of Mr. Justice Grier, when dissenting from the opinion of the majority of the Court, both as to the law and the facts: "I do not

think it necessary to vindicate my opinion by again presenting to the public view a history of the scandalous gossip
which has been buried under the dust of half a century and
which a proper feeling of delicacy should have permitted to
remain so. I therefore dismiss the case as I hope for the last
time, with the single remark that if it be the law of Louisiana that a will can be established by the dim recollections,
imaginations or inventions of anile gossips after forty-five
years to disturb the titles and possessions of *bona fide* purchasers without notice of an apparently indefeasible legal title,
haud equidem invideo, miror magis."[1]

Two cases occur in counterpart:—in one it was held
that a person in custody under a writ issued from a United
States Court could not be legally discharged from imprisonment by a State officer acting under a State insolvent law;
in the other it was held that no United States Court or
judge could issue a *habeas corpus* to bring up a prisoner who
is in the custody of a State Court for any other purpose
than to be held as a witness.[2]

In the case of *Neil Moore & Co.* v. *The State of Ohio,*[3]
the controversy arose out of the cession of that part of the
Cumberland Road lying within the limits of Ohio and the
State legislature accepting the same, and the Court, adhering
to views already expressed in the case of *Searight* v. *Stokes,*[4]
held that tolls charged upon passengers traveling in mail
coaches, but not charged against passengers traveling in other
coaches were against the contract and void, and that while

---

[1] Gaines and wife *v.* Chew, 2 Howard, 619 (1844). Patterson *v.* Gaines, 6 Howard,
550 (1848). Gaines *v.* Relf *et al.*, 12 Howard, 473 (1851). Gaines *v.* Hennen, 24
Howard, 553 (1860).

[2] Duncan *v.* Darst *et al.*, 1 Howard, 301 (1843); *Ex parte* Dorr, 3 Howard, 104
(1845).

[3] 3 Howard, 720 (1845).   [4] 3 Howard, 151 (1845).

the frequency of the departure of coaches carrying the mails was not an abuse of the privilege of the United States, yet an unnecessary division of the mail matter among a number of coaches was. The principle involved in both cases was that a State could not impose a toll on carriages employed in transporting the mail, because such a carriage must be held to be laden with the property of the United States, and a State could not tax a national agency. The exemption was not pushed, however, so as to include other property in the same vehicle, or persons traveling in it, except where they were discriminated against.

In the important case of *The State of Maryland* v. *The Baltimore & Ohio Railroad Co.*,[1] the State of Maryland had passed an act directing a large money subscription to the capital stock of the railroad company, provided "that if the Company shall not locate its road in the manner provided in the Act it should forfeit one million dollars to the use of Washington County." By a subsequent act, so much of the first act as made it the duty of the Company to construct the road upon the route prescribed, was repealed and the penalty was remitted and released. Suit was brought for the penalty, and the Supreme Court held, through the Chief Justice, that the second act of assembly did not impair the obligation of a contract, inasmuch as the effect of the first act was the imposition of a penalty by the State, which it had the right to remit, even after suit had been brought for its recovery. The scope of the law showed that it was legislation for State purposes, and a measure of State policy, which the State had a right to change at its pleasure; and neither the county nor any of its citizens had acquired private in-

3 Howard, 534 (1845).

terests which could be defended and maintained in a court of justice.

In the January Term of 1847, several celebrated cases came before the Court known as the License cases,[1] all of which arose under the much discussed clause of the Constitution vesting power in Congress to regulate commerce. The precise point involved in the first two cases was, whether a State might assume to regulate or prohibit the retail of wines and spirits, the importation of which from foreign countries had been authorized by an Act of Congress, and in the last case, whether a State might prohibit by law the sale of liquor imported from another State, there being no Act of Congress to regulate such importation. In the decision of all these cases it was unanimously determined that the laws under review were valid and Constitutional. There was much diversity of opinion, however, as to the principles upon which the cases should be decided, six judges writing nine opinions. It was fully admitted by all that if the State laws were in collision with an Act of Congress they would be unconstitutional and void. If in the Massachusetts and Rhode Island cases the law had obstructed the importation or prohibited the sale of the articles in the original cask or vessel, in the hands of the importer, it would have been void; because the importation was permitted by Congress in the exercise of its Constitional power to regulate foreign commerce; but the State laws, so the Chief Justice contended, were framed to act upon the article after it had passed the line of foreign commerce into the hands of the dealer, and had thus become a part of the general mass of the property of the State. This, he insisted, was directly within the principle as well as the lan-

---

[1] Thurlow *v.* Massachusetts, Fletcher *v.* Rhode Island, Peirce *et al. v.* New Hampshire, 5 Howard, 504 (1847).

guage of the opinion of Chief Justice Marshall in the case of *Brown* v. *Maryland.*[1]

The New Hampshire case differed from the two former in several important particulars. The law prohibited the sale, in any quantity, without license, and the sale had been made by the importer, in the original package in which the liquor had been imported from Massachusetts into New Hampshire. The case, therefore, turned, in the judgment of the Chief Justice, upon the question whether, in the absence of an Act of Congress regulating commerce between the States, all State laws on the subject were null and void. In other words, whether the mere grant of power to the General Government could be construed as an absolute prohibition to the exercise of any power over the same subject by the States. It was upon this question that a diversity of sentiment existed among the members of the Court, just as it had arisen in the case of *Prigg* v. *Commonwealth of Pennsylvania.* The view of the Chief Justice was expressed in the following language; "The controlling and supreme power over commerce with foreign nations and the several States is undoubtedly conferred upon Congress, yet, in my judgment, the State may, nevertheless, for the safety or convenience of trade, or for the protection of the health of its citizens, make regulations of commerce for its own ports and harbors, and for its own territory; and such regulations are valid, unless they come in conflict with the law of Congress."

Mr. Justice McLean contended that the State laws did not prohibit the sale of foreign spirits, but simply required a license to sell. A license to sell an article, foreign or domestic, as a merchant, or inn-keeper, or victualler, is a matter of

---

[1] 12 Wheaton, 419 (1827).

police and revenue, within the power of a State. It is strictly an internal regulation, and cannot come in conflict, saving the rights of the importer to sell, with any power possessed by Congress. To reject this view would make the excess of the drunkard a constitutional duty to encourage the importation of ardent spirits. In the New Hampshire case he held that the word "import," in a commercial sense, meant goods brought from abroad, and did not apply to the transportation of an article from one State to another. Justices Catron, Daniel, Woodbury and Grier had each his own mode of stating his reasons, though all arrived at the same result.

The interest of these cases is enhanced by the later case of *Cooley* v. *Board of Port Wardens*[1] and the recent decision of *Leisy* v. *Hardin*,[2] known as the "Original Package Case," in which the decision in *Peirce* v. *New Hampshire* was distinctly overruled, Chief Justice Fuller there holding: "The conclusion follows that, as the grant of power to regulate commerce among the States, so far as one system is required, is exclusive, the States cannot exercise that power without the assent of Congress, and, in the absence of legislation, it is left for the Courts to determine when State action does or does not amount to such exercise, or, in other words, what is or is not a regulation of such commerce."

In the case of *Cook* v. *Moffat*,[3] the question of the effect of a debtor's discharge under the insolvent laws of one State on a contract made in another State was again discussed, and decided in conformity with the decisions in *Ogden* v. *Saunders* and *Boyle* v. *Zacharie*, and it was held that the State Courts were bound to conform to the decisions of the Supreme Court of the United States declaring State laws unconstitutional.

---

[1] 12 Howard, 299 (1851).   [2] 135 U. S. Rep. 100 (1889).
      [3] 5 Howard, 295 (1847).

At this term the important admiralty case of *Waring* v. *Clarke*[1] was decided, in which the attention of the Court was called to the question for the first time whether the admiralty jurisdiction conferred by the Constitution was to be limited to what were well-recognized cases of admiralty jurisdiction in England at the time of the adoption of the Constitution, or whether that jurisdiction in a public navigable river extended beyond the ebb and flow of the tide. The collision complained of had taken place on the Mississippi River at a point where there was much doubt whether the tide ebbed and flowed. The majority of the Court, however, thought that there was sufficient proof of a tidal flow, and consequently it was not necessary to consider whether the admiralty jurisdiction extended higher. But the case is remarkable for the powerful dissenting opinions of Woodbury and Daniel, in which they pleaded for the restriction of the admiralty jurisdiction in opposition to the principles so ably contended for by Mr. Justice Wayne, and subsequently sustained by Chief Justice Taney in the case of the *Genesee Chief*, in which he asserted the bold and comprehensive doctrine that the admiralty power of the Court extended beyond the flow of the tide in all public navigable waters, and even over the great fresh water lakes.[2]

The class of cases known as the Passenger Cases[3] arose under the same Constitutional provision which had been involved in the discussion of the License Cases. The question was presented whether a law of the State of New York imposing a tax upon the masters of vessels arriving from a

[1] 5 Howard, 441 (1847).

[2] See, as to the admiralty jurisdiction on Long Island Sound, The New Jersey Steam Nav. Co. *v.* The Merchants' Bank, 6 Howard, 344 (1848).

[3] Smith *v.* Turner, Norris *v.* City of Boston, 7 Howard, 283 (1849).

foreign port, upon each steerage passenger and each cabin passenger, and upon the masters of coasting vessels for each passenger, was repugnant to the Constitution of the United States. Two points were distinctly presented: Is the power to regulate commerce exclusively vested in Congress? Is a tax upon persons a regulation of commerce? Upon both these points it was claimed upon the argument that they had been repeatedly settled by solemn judgments, notably in *Gibbons* v. *Ogden* and *Brown* v. *Maryland.* Against these, the principle of *New York* v. *Miln* was cited. The result of the deliberations of the consultation room and the judgment of the Court left both questions in an uncertainty still more perplexing than when the discussion began. Five Judges, McLean, Wayne, Catron, McKinley and Grier, declared the laws null and void, and four judges, Taney, Daniel, Nelson and Woodbury were for sustaining them; but such was the diversity and conflict of views, even among the Judges concurring in the prevailing opinion, that the reporter frankly declares that "there was no opinion of the Court as a Court."[1]

Not the least interesting feature of these cases, is the extraordinary difference in recollection between Wayne and Taney as to what had passed in the consultation-room when *New York* v. *Miln* was decided, ten years before. Each, with the most perfect sincerity and fullness of detail, states what he recalls of the discussion and of the points determined; and each, with perfect courtesy, but with characteristic firmness,

---

[1] The discussion has been settled finally by the recent decisions of the Supreme Court, which have substantially sustained the doctrine that the regulation of foreign commerce is exclusively within the control of Congress, and that no State can attempt a regulation of commerce, even though there be no Act of Congress in existence with which such a regulation could conflict. Wabash, St. Louis and Pacific R. R. Co. *v.* Illinois, 118 U. S., 557 (1886); Fargo *v.* Michigan, 121 U. S., 230 (1886).

contradicts the other and labels the statement of his opponent as a dangerous error.

The relation of the States to the Union is still further exhibited in the following cases:

The protection of citizens in the enjoyment of religious liberty was held to be entirely a matter of State concern, as the Constitution of the United States had made no provision upon the subject.[1] The Court, therefore, had no jurisdiction. Nor had it jurisdiction over a question arising out of an alleged invalidity of a statute passed by the Territory of Michigan before she became fully organized as a State.[2] Nor is a State law providing punishment for the offense of circulating counterfeit coin of the United States unconstitutional or beyond the powers of a State, even though Congress may have provided a similar punishment. The prohibitions contained in the Amendments to the Constitution were intended to be restrictions upon the Federal Government and not upon the authority of the States.[3]

In several most interesting cases it was held as to the power of eminent domain that a bridge held by an incorporated company under a charter from a State might be condemned and taken as part of a public road under the laws of that State. Although the charter was a contract, yet like all private rights, it was subject to the power of eminent domain of the State, and the Constitution of the United States could not be so construed, as to deprive the State of such a power.[4]

In *Nesmith et al.* v. *Sheldon et al.*,[5] the Court swung

---

[1] Permoli *v.* Municipality No. 1 of the City of New Orleans, 3 Howard, 589 (1845).
[2] Scott *et al.* *v.* Jones, 5 Howard, 343 (1847).
[3] Fox *v.* State of Ohio, 5 Howard, 411 (1847).
[4] West River Bridge Co. *v.* Dix *et al.* *Id.* *v.* Town of Brattleboro' *et al.*, 6 Howard, 507 (1848). [5] 7 Howard, 812 (1849).

back to the line from which it had departed in *Rowan* v. *Runnels*,[1] and declared that it was the established doctrine that the Supreme Court of the United States will adopt and follow the decisions of the State Courts in the construction of their own statutes where that construction has been settled by the decisions of their highest tribunal. And in *Nathan* v. *The State of Louisiana*,[2] they sustained the right of a State to tax its own citizens for the prosecution of any particular business or profession within the State; hence a tax imposed upon all money or exchange brokers was not void for repugnance to the Constitutional power of Congress to regulate commerce, even though foreign bills of exchange are instruments of commerce.

In *Luther* v. *Borden*,[3] a case arising out of the internal troubles and violence in the State of Rhode Island over the adoption of a Constitution in place of the Charter of Charles II—a period known in the annals of the State as "Dorr's Rebellion,"—the Court, Mr. Justice Woodbury alone dissenting, declined to take jurisdiction of what was purely a political question lying beyond the reach of judicial authority. "How can this Court," asked Webster, in argument, "invite the present Governor and the rebel to exchange places?"

"Much of the argument," said the Chief Justice, "on the part of the plaintiff turned upon political rights and political questions, upon which the Court has been urged to express an opinion. We decline doing so. The high power has been conferred upon this Court of passing judgments upon the acts of the State sovereignties and of the legislative and executive branches of the Federal Government, and of determining whether they are beyond the limits of power marked out for them respectively by the Constitution of the United States. This tribunal, therefore, should be the last to overstep the boundaries which

---

[1] 5 Howard, 134 (1847). [2] 8 Howard, 73 (1850). [3] 7 Howard, 1 (1849).

limit its own jurisdiction; and while it should always be ready to meet any question confided to it by the Constitution, it is equally its duty not to pass beyond its appropriate sphere of action, and to take care not to involve itself in discussions which properly belong to other forums."

At this point we close our view of the first half of Taney's judicial career. It is a convenient stopping-place. It enables us to cast a glance backward and mark the general results accomplished by the untiring labors of the Court. No single decision strikes the eye equal in towering majesty to those of the days of Marshall. These still remained the unapproachable bulwarks of the nation's strength; but around and about them appeared many subsidiary works, built under the direction of keen and critical intelligence, extending, supporting and maintaining their effectiveness, while at times improving their construction by reducing undue prominences or unseemly projections. , Within these, without crowding the former too closely, and without too many or too serious breaches for the purpose of room, line after line of ramparts had been thrown up around the rights of the States, within which they developed their mighty energies, nursed their resources and rounded out the full and harmonious figure of our dual system of government.

On the whole the work accomplished by Taney and his associates during the first fourteen years of his term, was quite as essential to the full realization of our welfare as a nation, and an accurate appreciation of the true character of our government as any preceding epoch in the history of the Court. It served to check excesses, to limit extravagances of doctrine, to awaken and develop new powers, to moderate tendencies, to introduce contrasts and elements which in future years could be mingled and used for the preservation of the whole, as well as for the protection of each part. The work of this period was not compactly built, however, nor uniform in design. The mind of Taney never exercised the great or predominating influence over his associates which had been characteristic of Marshall. The practice of making the Chief Justice the organ of the Court in delivering opinions was abandoned, partly, as his associates have told us, because free from vanity himself, Taney was earnestly desirous of giving them all an opportunity of expressing their views, but chiefly, as any close student of the decisions cannot fail to perceive, because upon Constitutional questions the Court lacked cohesion. McLean and Wayne were the "high-toned Federalists" of the bench, as Mr. Justice Curtis called them when first taking his place as their associate. Catron, Grier and McKinley had similar tendencies, but far less pronounced, while Woodbury and Daniel, the former a man of original and striking powers of mind, though in the main in accord with the Chief Justice, broke from him upon the development of the admiralty juris-diction. It was with Nelson that the Chief Justice most frequently concurred, and during the latter part of his career, the triumvirate which corresponded with that of Marshall, Washington and Story, was composed of Taney, Nelson and Campbell.

The Bar, during the period of which we have written, was marked by the presence of men of great professional strength. It is true that no single man exercised the potent sway over the Court or its decisions of which Pinkney or Webster could boast in the time of Marshall, but there was no departure from the general high standard of those days for learning, acuteness, thoroughness and precision, in the arguments of such exact and accomplished lawyers as Butler and Ogden, of New York, George Wood, of New Jersey, Berrien, of Georgia, and Binney and Sergeant, of Pennsylvania.

22

Pinkney's dazzling rhetoric was not much more highly colored than the burning eloquence of Choate; nor was the polished style of Wirt superior to the charm of the classic scholarship of Legaré, or the stately dignity of Seward. In the power to deal heavy blows Crittenden and Bibb, of Kentucky, might fairly vie with Chase and Stanton, of Ohio, while in the shining ranks of advocates whose union of legal learning, professional skill, logic and eloquence made them the most remarkable of all the men who appeared at that great Bar stood Reverdy Johnson, of Maryland, William M. Meredith and Jeremiah S. Black, of Pennsylvania, Caleb Cushing, of Massachusetts, Robert J. Walker, of Mississippi, and Charles O'Conor, of New York, who pressed forward to fill the gaps occasioned by the deaths of Clay, Webster and White.